D1602404

Colorado's Volunteer Infantry
in the Philippine Wars, 1898–1899

Colorado's Volunteer Infantry in the Philippine Wars, 1898–1899

Geoffrey R. Hunt

University of New Mexico Press

ALBUQUERQUE

12 11 10 09 08 07 06   1 2 3 4 5 6 7

LIBRARY OF CONGRESS CATALOGING-IN-PUBLICATION DATA

Hunt, Geoffrey, 1952–
     Colorado's volunteer infantry in the
     Philippine wars, 1898–1899 / Geoffrey R. Hunt.
          p. cm.
Includes bibliographical references and index.
ISBN-13: 978-0-8263-3700-9 (cloth : alk. paper)
ISBN-10: 0-8263-3700-7 (cloth : alk. paper)
1. Philippines—History—Philippine American War, 1899–1902—Regimental
     histories—United States.
2. Spanish-American War, 1898—Regimental histories—United States.
3. United States. Army. Colorado Infantry Regiment, 1st.—History.
4. Spanish-American War, 1898—Philippines. I. Title.
     DS683.C62H86 2006
      959.9'031—dc22

                                                            2006002332

DESIGN AND COMPOSITION: *Mina Yamashita*

For Rebecca

"Remember the *Maine*, to Hell with Spain"

—American slogan
in Spanish-American War

"Damn, Damn, Damn the Filipinos!

Cut-throat Khakiac Ladrones!

Underneath the Starry Flag,

Civilize 'em with a Krag,

And Return Us to Our Own Beloved Home."

—American marching song
in the Philippine-American War

Contents

Acknowledgments

This study is based upon my dissertation, and so I must begin by thanking my committee members at the University of Colorado-Boulder. Patricia Limerick, Ralph Mann, Fred Anderson, Lee Scamehorn, Gloria Main, and Lee Krauth all provided vital insights, through their comments and their classes and their publications, and above all by the scholarship they embody. Don Rickey Jr., Doug Scott, Jack Buschmann, John Langelier, Jerome Green, Virgil Hughes, George Monsson, Frank Harper, William Elswick, Frank Waterous, and Douglas Wilson all cheerfully shared their expertise. Virginia Steele rearranged important projects to accommodate my deadlines, and brought her keen eye to bear on photograph selection. My thanks also to Melinda McGann for her cartography.

The members of John Stewart Post Number One, Veterans of Foreign Wars, have been extremely generous in opening their collections in order to help tell the story of their founders. I researched in the historical archives at the Presidio in San Francisco, the Utah Historical Society in Salt Lake City, the United States Army Military History Research Collections in Carlisle, Pennsylvania, and the Library of Congress and National Archives in Washington, D.C. In Denver, I used materials in the Western History Collections at the Denver Public Library, the Colorado State Archives, and the Colorado Historical Society. My work was made easier by the professional staff members at each of those institutions, each of whom cheerfully shared knowledge and resources.

My parents, John and Nancy, have steadily encouraged my work. My daughter Katie has asked the kind of "so what?" questions that remind me to try to make military history intelligible and interesting to average folk. My son Aaron, Marine and historian, has challenged my conclusions and forced me to refine them. Above all, my wife, Rebecca, has made this possible. She has tolerated the intolerable, proofread the unreadable, consoled the disconsolate, and willed the unwilling, to keep me focused and moving forward, and she has given up much in the process. I trust this work will repay her faith.

Any historian must serve two masters. On the one hand, the historian owes an obligation to the reader. At the same time, the historian must be true to the past. Through their words and deeds, I have come to know a few of the men of the First Colorado, at least to a small degree, and I hope I have done them justice. In that effort, I have had a great deal of help from a great many people. I am still entirely capable of making my own mistakes, and I alone am responsible for any errors of omission or commission.

Introduction

The First Colorado Regiment enlisted in 1898 to fight Spaniards, and ended up fighting Filipinos. For months, newspaper reports and Congressional speeches had urged American intervention in the Cuban revolution against the Spanish. The destruction of the battleship *Maine* and mutual declarations of war between the United States and Spain fanned into flame the already smoldering resentment of Spain's Cuban policies. Men flocked to enlist in state volunteer regiments, among them the First Colorado Infantry. Before they could join the campaign against the Spanish in Cuba, however, Commodore George Dewey's United States Navy's Asiatic Squadron destroyed the Spanish naval squadron at Manila on 1 May 1898. Dewey lacked the infantry necessary to seize the city itself. From the western states, regular Army units and volunteer regiments assembled in San Francisco, diverted from the larger conflict in Cuba. Because of its prewar duty during labor disputes, the Colorado militia enjoyed full field equipment; Gen. Wesley Merritt of the Department of the Pacific rushed them to the Philippines.

Crossing the Pacific, they captured Wake Island. In the Philippines, state troops competed with each other and with the regulars for military distinction and press coverage. The Colorado troops pushed forward and led the assault on Manila, seizing Fort San Antonio de Abad and raising the first American flag over the capital city's defenses. With the Spanish-American War over, the Filipinos expected independence; with independence denied, tensions between the Filipinos and the Americans mounted until they flared into battle on 4 February 1899. The Coloradoans fought the *insurrectos* that first night, and went on to campaign against the Filipinos in what came to be called the Philippine Insurrection. The war to free Cubans from Spanish rule had become a war to subject Filipinos to American rule.

Gerald Linderman's landmark *The Mirror of War: American Society and the Spanish-American War* has examined the war in Cuba as an expression of late nineteenth-century American culture and politics. In the process, Linderman has detailed the links between eastern volunteer regiments and their hometowns. He observed that "regular army units . . . won the battles, but the hometown National Guard companies became the prism through which many Americans viewed and interpreted the Spanish-American War."[1] Certainly, the citizens of Colorado experienced the war vicariously, through the accounts of the men of the First Colorado. In his focus on the eastern aspects of the Spanish-American War, however, Linderman downplays the importance of volunteer regiments. In the Philippines, fighting against first the Spanish and later the Filipinos, volunteer regiments raised primarily from the western states did much of the fighting and, in fact, "won the battles." The First Colorado had a prominent role in those battles.

Richard Drinnon's *Facing West: The Metaphysics of Indian-Hating and Empire-Building* calls the process of American overseas imperialism the "obverse" of almost three hundred years of racist Indian-hating on the part of English settlers and their descendants.[2] While quite polemical, Drinnon draws powerful and at least partly persuasive connections between American attitudes toward Indians and American attitudes toward Filipinos, a connection made in a more restrained manner by Walter L. Williams in his study of Congressional treatment of Indians and Filipinos as "wards" of the United States government.[3] The attitudes of the men of the First Colorado Regiment toward the Filipinos, both before and after the outbreak of the Philippine-American War, reveal much about these Westerners' view of the world, their race, their nation, and what they came to call the "white man's burden." Surnames suggest that the First Colorado was overwhelmingly of British descent, with a sprinkling of Germans and Scandinavians. Their letters and diaries contain frequent comparisons between the Filipinos and the "coloreds," "Mexicans," and "Indians" they had observed in Colorado. Confident of their superiority to the Filipinos, the Coloradoans also expressed reservations about American actions overseas. While the commanders of the Eighth Army Corps employed Indian Wars strategies against the Filipinos, strategies in which the First Colorado participated, the way the Colorado men treated the Filipinos owed more to Civil War concepts of combat than to racism. Association with the Filipinos could lead to a grudging respect, and for some of the First Colorado, even admiration and sympathy. Reluctant participants in the Philippine-American War, the Coloradoans still regarded the fight as one for their own survival. One soldier of the First Colorado observed, "It looks to me very much . . . like our grand 'War for Down trodden Humanity' will end up in a war of conquest, and here, conquest means extermination."[4]

The First Colorado's Philippine service also points up dramatic changes in the American military. The regiment disembarked in Manila with the blue wool uniforms and black-powder Springfields of the Indian-fighting Army, obsolete material retained for reasons of economy. While the Indian-fighting regular Army had learned and adopted modern small-squad infantry tactics, especially in the Apache campaigns, the militia was led by Civil War veterans and still used the Civil War tactics of the company front and the bayonet charge. Effective enough against strikers, such tactics and equipment would not succeed in the Philippines. Perry Jamieson has examined the process by which the U.S. Army modernized its weapons and tactics in *Crossing the Deadly Ground: United States Army Tactics, 1865–1899*; Graham Cosmas has done the same for Army structure and organization in *An Army for Empire: The United States Army in the Spanish-American War*.[5] Whatever the regular army was doing, the state militias had to a great degree followed their own courses in the years after the Civil War. The First Colorado mimicked Civil War regiments in its prewar training, its recruitment methods, its connections to Colorado communities and to the state as a whole, and in its command structure. Faced with the realities of modern warfare, the First Colorado quickly modernized, but on its own terms, retaining those aspects of the Civil War model that suited them and adopting such components of regular army doctrine as seemed useful. One year to the day after landing, the militia re-embarked in khaki, carrying "smokeless powder" Krag-Jörgensen magazine rifles, and the memories of a conflict that had devolved from trench warfare to guerrilla tactics. In a symbolic sense, the First Colorado Regiment enlisted in the nineteenth century and returned home in the twentieth.

Fred Anderson has demonstrated in *A People's Army: Massachusetts Soldiers and Society in the Seven Years' War*, that as long ago as 1755, American volunteer militiamen viewed their enlistment as being for a specific campaign, and bitterly resented any service beyond the end of that campaign.[6] The Colorado troops felt they had enlisted for a specific campaign and purpose: to defeat the Spanish. With that task accomplished, they chafed in their role as occupying conquerors. They served one year fighting an ugly Asian war that steadily declined in popularity back home, a war modern Americans have largely forgotten. Their physical and emotional separation from Colorado and the continental United States had heightened their sense of identity. A self-selected community of men, the regiment had built strong bonds of friendship and mutual obligation, almost equaling in intensity the family ties they had left behind. Upon their return home, the First Colorado's members sought to perpetuate those ties, and that separate male sphere, by forming veterans' organizations that combined aspects of fraternal orders with the Grand Army of the Republic. That community of veterans slowly dwindled until the last man died, but their effort lives on in the Veterans of Foreign Wars.

As historians and political scientists propose and examine overall models of imperialism, or modernization, or conquest, the actual protagonists can get lost. No scholar has taken a specific western regiment and examined its experience in detail within the broader framework of the Philippine Wars. The First Colorado Infantry, U.S.V., represents an ideal lens through which to examine the expectations and experiences of citizen soldiers in America's quest for empire. The First Colorado stormed Manila, and then fought in the first seven months of the Philippine-American War; the men of the regiment were involved in the great events of the Philippine campaigns and loudly expressed their opinions on them. A second advantage of examining the First Colorado is the wealth of information available on the regiment.

As states sent their volunteer regiments off to war, newspapers in large cities assigned correspondents to accompany them. Small-town newspapers instead often commissioned a member of the regiment to serve as a reporter. Recognizing the degree to which hometown political connections could be brought to bear on the Army's conduct of the war, in the summer of 1898 Secretary of War Russell Alger prohibited military personnel from writing for publication.[7] Alger could prohibit, but not prevent. Correspondents might cast their reports as letters home, which relatives would then share with the newspapers. The Colorado men simply ignored Alger's order. Two of the main Denver dailies had former employees, professional reporters before the war, who enlisted in the ranks of the First Colorado. Arthur C. Johnson wrote for the *Rocky Mountain News*, and Harry McCauley sent reports to the *Denver Times*. Their vivid accounts provided broader coverage than usually found in the standard regimental histories. To be sure, one of those reporters, Arthur C. Johnson, did produce an example of the "regimental history" genre, in his *Official History of the Operations of the First Colorado Infantry, U.S.V. in the Campaigning in the Philippine Islands*, included in Colorado editions of Karl Irving Faust's more widely published *Campaigning in the Philippines*.[8] Walter W. Weber, in *The First Colorado Infantry, U.S.V.: Spanish War, 1898/Philippine Insurrection, 1899*, wrote another regimental history, with details of battles but little information on the men themselves.[9]

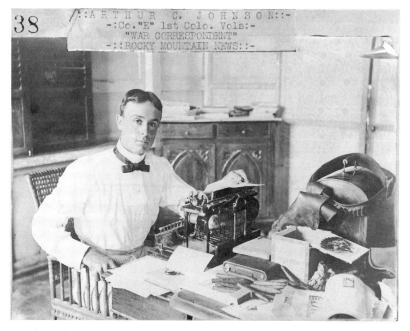

1. Arthur Johnson with the tools of the trade. *Photo courtesy of John Stewart Post Number One, Veterans of Foreign Wars.*

The newspaper accounts of Johnson and McCauley, while rich in detail, represent a tricky resource for the historian. The two men were reporters of events, often eyewitness reporters. At the same time, their access to information was limited, for they were serving enlisted men with military duties of their own. They were also players in the very events they recorded. Despite their enlisted status, Johnson and McCauley were allowed a certain amount of access to regimental headquarters, where the officers clearly understood the power of the press. At the same time, publication of accounts critical of the regiment's officers would jeopardize that access, and so the correspondents did not enjoy a free rein in their reporting. And, they knew that every word would be avidly perused by both the readers back in Colorado and, eventually, the reporters' fellows in the ranks. The men of the regiment expected to return home and wanted to comport themselves honorably so that they would be welcomed as heroes. They expected "their" reporters to reflect that image. In that light, the accounts of Johnson and McCauley take on layered meanings, and what they chose to say about the experience of the First Colorado can be revealing on multiple levels. In 1898 and 1899, state residents did not regard the federal government as a significant source of information. The Army did not control news coverage, and hometown newspapers therefore provided local citizens with a more detailed—what Linderman calls "intimate"—experience of the war than would be true of twentieth-century conflicts.[10] The newspaper accounts are a rich source, but one to be mined carefully.

Diaries offer another source of personal information about the regiment. Corporal Roy Harris began a "diary" in San Francisco, a sort of Victorian day-scheduler. Its pocket format prevented him from writing extended entries, but the corporal's precise notations yield important details about daily life. One always suspects that extensive diaries are in fact meant to be read by someone other than the author, which flavors the diary's credibility. The Harris diary appears to have been intended to be read by Harris alone, perhaps as a guide to later memoirs. Unfortunately, like modern day-schedulers, his diary ends on the last day of the year, and so the events of 1899 are missing.

In 1968 and 1969, Don Rickey Jr. participated in a U.S. Army project to send questionnaires to Spanish-American War and Philippine-American War veterans. Those questionnaires contain useful, but usually very brief, bits of information. In the process of administering the questionnaires, however, Rickey also solicited any additional information the veterans might have, for deposit in the U.S. Army Military History Research Collection at Carlisle Barracks, Pennsylvania. Two brothers, originally from Wauneeta, Nebraska, enlisted together in the First Colorado. Arthur and Guy Sims served average terms with the regiment, attracting no special attention from their officers, but after the war each prepared extensive accounts of that service. Arthur cast his in the form of a 162-page typescript autobiographical novel. While the plot is fictional, the novel supplies details of soldier life and information on soldier attitudes. Guy's narrative, also autobiographical, is intensely personal and frequently vitriolic, and like Arthur's manuscript full of information. Neither account is unbiased, and both were intended for public use; within those limitations, they remain the best of the First Colorado memoirs.

From Philadelphia, civilian author Henry F. Keenan compiled a quirky "history" of the Spanish-American War. *The Conflict with Spain: A History of the War*, while almost useless as a history, contains important accounts of the First Colorado's passage to the Philippines on the *China*, and of life in camp outside Manila. Although Keenan only cites an "anonymous Western volunteer" for those accounts, internal evidence establishes the regiment in question as the First Colorado. Various archives contain examples of public and private correspondence from other members of the First Colorado, ranging from Gen. Irving Hale's papers down to the letters of individual privates. Although these various individual stories provide illuminating insights into the viewpoints and experiences of some of the men of the regiment, the majority of those who served remain mute. At the same time, it is important to remember that individuals can embody mainstream opinions and attitudes. From all of these sources, and by perusing muster rolls and other official records, it is possible to go beyond simple accounts of combat exploits to build a window into the world of the citizen soldiers at the sharp edge of empire. Unfortunately, no Filipino accounts currently available mention the First Colorado; such accounts would add greatly to the understanding of how the Coloradoans interacted with the people of the Philippines.

The Philippines are a long way from Colorado, and the circumstances through which Colorado militiamen found themselves fighting in a land across the Pacific Ocean started in Havana, Cuba. The USS *Maine* exploded and sank in Havana Bay on 15 February 1898, killing 266 of her 354 crew members. The blast that rent the night also rent relations between Spain and the United States, relations already strained by

Spanish measures to suppress the Cuban insurrection. The Panic of 1893 had devastated America's economy, and also Cuba's; Cuba grew and exported sugar, and low sugar prices in America meant low wages in Cuba. By February of 1895, economic crisis turned into political and military upheaval when rebel Gen. Máximo Gómez y Báez launched a new revolution against Spanish rule.[11] The insurrectos conducted a campaign of guerrilla warfare, burning sugar fields and attacking isolated Spanish sentries. Since American companies had almost $50 million invested in those fields, the United States took an immediate interest in the conflict. Spain sent Gen. Valeriano Weyler to crush the rebellion, which he attempted to do through a policy he called *reconcentrado*, the herding of civilians into grim "reconcentration camps" to deny the rebels support. The reconcentrated populations suffered and died, the rebellion blazed on, and the United States suggested reforms. American "yellow press" newspaper publishers Joseph Pulitzer and William Randolph Hearst vied with each other to bring their readers the latest details of "Butcher" Weyler's atrocities. Although Spain did recall Weyler and promise modest reforms, riots in Havana in January of 1898 led the United States to send the *Maine* "to protect American citizens."[12] Surely, she also served to demonstrate American insistence that Spain solve her rebellion, and soon.

It did not matter that the *Maine* had no clear mission in a foreign harbor. After the explosion, it did not matter that the Spanish launched rescue efforts and saved those officers and men who did survive. And after 21 March 1898, when a U.S. Navy Court of Inquiry concluded that the *Maine* had been destroyed by an underwater mine, it did not matter that the only party who stood to gain by provoking a war between Spain and America, the insurrectos, lacked the technology to build and employ such a device.[13] None of this mattered. Americans blamed Spanish perfidy for the *Maine's* destruction, and the cry went up across the land, "Remember the *Maine*, to Hell with Spain!"

Diplomatic bungling, belligerent politicians on both sides of the Atlantic, and rebel intransigence all drove the two nations toward war.

If war came, the United States anticipated invading Cuba, and that posed a problem, for in 1898, the United States Army numbered a grand total of 28,000 men, most of them scattered around the American West.[14] The Army began moving its regulars east in mid-April, as relations between Spain and the United States continued to deteriorate. In Denver, Colorado, the Seventh Infantry and a small detachment of the Second Cavalry were stationed at Fort Logan, just south of town.[15] On the evening of 16 April 1898, the Denver Club held a banquet for the infantry and cavalry officers, as the regulars prepared to move out.[16] On 20 April 1898, Congress recognized Cuban independence and authorized American force to ensure it. While short of a declaration of war, it was not far short.[17] Denver gave "her" regulars a fine send-off. In the early afternoon, the men of the National Guard assembled at their armories, and the Civil War veterans in the Grand Army of the Republic met at the Brown Palace hotel. Both bodies, along with a crowd of citizens, marched down to the train depot to meet the Seventh Infantry.[18] As the regulars boarded their trains, the National Guard's band played "Hot Time in the Old Town Tonight," "Dixie," and, finally, "Auld Lang Syne."[19] The Seventh Infantry steamed out to the Army's assembly point at Chickamauga, Georgia, and then on to Cuba to battle the Spanish at El Caney and San Juan Hill.[20]

The regular army was too small to simultaneously invade Cuba and station troops around the United States. On 23 April 1898, President William McKinley called for 125,000 volunteers, to serve for two years or until the war was over, their numbers to be drawn from each state and the District of Columbia in proportion to their percentage of the total population. Late that day, Colorado received word that her quota would be 1,324 men. Colorado's National Guard, consisting of two understrength infantry regiments, two troops of cavalry, an artillery battery, and assorted small support units, numbered 1,300 men, and so it seemed likely that all who wanted to fight against the Spanish would have a chance. On the other hand, men would have to pass rigorous physical examinations, and Colorado Adj. Gen. Cassius Moses estimated that perhaps only 1,200 would actually be found fit enough to serve.[21] Clearly, the militia would have to enlist additional recruits in order to meet its quota. That did not seem like it would pose a problem, however, for on 24 April 1898, Spain declared war on the United States, a favor the United States returned the following day, and patriotic fervor brought men flocking to the ranks.[22]

As the United States gathered its troops, both volunteer and regular, it also had to guard against Spanish attack. Spain lacked either the military power or the desire to invade the United States itself, but Spanish fleets theoretically could appear off of America's shores and threaten her coastal cities with bombardment. The United States Navy therefore set out to find and destroy the ships of the Spanish navy. In the Atlantic, a Spanish fleet commanded by *Almirante* Pascual Cervera y Topete left the Cape Verde Islands on 29 April 1898, while the Americans tried to track it. On the other side of the world, the Spanish Pacific Squadron lay anchored in Manila Bay. Two days after the declaration of war, the United States Navy's Asiatic Squadron, commanded by Commodore George Dewey, sailed from Hong Kong for the Philippines.[23] On 1 May 1898, the American flotilla opened fire on the anchored Spanish ships, sinking every one of them by noon.[24] On the following day, Dewey's sailors and marines destroyed ammunition magazines around the Spanish naval yard at Cavite, around the bay south of Manila, and on 3 May 1898, they occupied Cavite.[25] Unable to reach an accommodation with the Spanish regarding joint use of the underwater telegraph cable, Dewey cut the line. That decision made military sense, but also would lead to far-reaching consequences; cut off from their respective capitals, the Americans and Spanish in the Philippines would continue fighting after the armistice ending the war.[26] For the moment, without additional ground forces, the Americans could go no further. Dewey was out of coal, and with the United States and Spain at war, the fleet could not leave, for under the Law of War, belligerents could only enter neutral ports for short periods of one or two days, or else risk internment. Also, with German and British ships in Manila Bay, Dewey was reluctant to leave a power vacuum in a port his country might wish to retain. And so, the American fleet waited at anchor off Cavite.

The Spanish still controlled Manila. Its capture by the Americans would give the United States a bargaining chip to help enforce its will in Cuba. It might even offer a port facility for the Asiatic Squadron. President William McKinley determined to reinforce Dewey's fleet with sufficient ground forces to take Manila.[27] But while the Spanish in Manila awaited the arrival of more Americans, they had troubles of their own, in the form of a Filipino rebellion. Spain had claimed the Philippine Islands since the sixteenth century, but Spanish influence was concentrated on the port of Manila. With over 7,000 islands and 7 million Filipinos in the archipelago, it was impossible for the Spanish to exert real control over the vast bulk of the people.[28] On the other hand, the Filipinos were divided into numerous tribes, with different languages and traditions, and with no tradition of unity they had presented no concerted resistance to the coming of the Europeans. Before the Spanish, the largest form of political organization had been the village, actually an extended family. Catholic theology, with the father and mother and son, fit well with traditional beliefs and reinforced the existing network of blood covenants between tribes. Filipino society was based on actual and ritual kinship ties, with the ritual relatives being called *compadres*. The *compadrazgo* system was a web of personal connections and obligations that bound individual Filipinos to others.[29] Such webs of relationships were headed locally by Filipino *principales*, who accepted Spanish hegemony in return for Spanish confirmation of their local authority. The principales dominated the countryside, and the Spanish dominated the few towns.

In the Spanish hierarchy in the Philippines, natives of Spain, called *peninsulares*, held all the highest secular and religious offices. Below them on the social ladder were the *criollos*, people of Spanish descent but born in the islands. Next came the *mestizos*, of mixed European and Filipino ancestry, followed by Chinese or people of Chinese-Filipino descent.

The Chinese were the artisans and merchants of the towns, and many married Filipinas and became Christians. The Filipinos themselves were at the bottom of the Spanish list, and across the entire scale, money and color determined one's status.[30] This rigid caste system matched that of traditional Filipino society, and so Spain's rule was relatively tranquil until the Philippines developed an export economy late in the eighteenth century. Peninsulares dominated trade in hemp, sugar, and tobacco, and vied with the principales over control of the land, a competition that led to increasing tension.[31]

Late in the nineteenth century, the sugar market boomed, and the principales converted more and more land to sugar production. Reliance on cash crops reduced the amount of acreage devoted to growing food, carrying with it the dangers of increased reliance on world markets and foodstuffs imported at a higher cost than those formerly grown in the Philippines. The principales and Spanish prospered, while most Filipinos suffered.[32] *Ilustrados*, educated middle-class and wealthy Filipinos without a secure place in the society, began to agitate for expanded access to economic opportunity. They sought the right to assume official positions, to curb the power of Spanish religious orders, and to exclude the Chinese, but as "elite conservatives" they were trying to gain entry to Spanish privilege for themselves, not for the mass of Filipino peasants. Despite the Chinese-exclusion plank of the ilustrados, the children of rich Chinese mestizo families often embraced Filipino nationalism to counter Spanish rule. One such Chinese mestizo was a Cavite Province principal, Emilio Aguinaldo y Famy.[33]

In 1892, Andrés Bonifacio founded the "Highest and Most Honorable Society of the Sons of the Country," or Katipunan society, in Manila. Bonifacio's revolutionary movement appealed to the Tagalog people around Manila, but other Filipino tribes perceived his movement as a threat and allied with the Spanish against him. Betrayed in August of 1896, Bonifacio fled Manila and issued the "*Grito de Balintawak*," the declaration that marked the beginning of the Filipinos' revolt against the Spanish. The Katipunan forces were based on village militias, and because those militias insisted on defending their towns, the Spanish could engage and defeat them. As the Katipunan survivors took to the hills, Bonifacio's control of the loose movement collapsed, and he eventually was executed in the spring of 1897 by the troops of one of his rivals, Emilio Aguinaldo.[34]

The Spanish continued to pursue the Katipunan leadership through the summer. On 6 September 1897, Aguinaldo switched tactics, and from his hideout in the Bulacan Mountains, decreed that henceforth the Katipunan would emulate the Cuban insurrectos by conducting a guerrilla campaign against the Spanish. He amplified his decision with an 11 November 1897 order, "Regulations for the Organization of Sandahatan Forces." *Sandahatans* were village militias, commanded by officers appointed by village councils. This system linked the Katipunan military to the system of principales, and provided an automatic allegiance and support system for the peasants who filled the ranks. At the same time, the function of the sandahatans was to stage guerrilla assaults against the Spanish, not to occupy a town; if pressed, they were to hide their weapons and blend into the civilian population. Rather than continue to pursue Aguinaldo's rebels, the Spanish bought him off, in the Pact of Biac-na-Bato. In December of 1897, Aguinaldo and some of his fellow rebels sailed for Hong Kong with 400,000 pesos and Spanish promises for reform.[35]

By treating with Aguinaldo, the Spanish had confirmed his leadership of the revolution. Even with Aguinaldo in exile, troubles continued. Seeking to strengthen his hand against the Spanish, Dewey retrieved Aguinaldo from Hong Kong on 12 May 1898. Aguinaldo's reintroduction to his native land had unintended consequences. The Katipunan revolution spread, Spain's Filipino allies deserted her, and soon Spanish authority was reduced to Manila and its environs.[36] Manila itself contained perhaps 350,000 people of all races and nationalities; of that number, about 10,000 were Spanish.[37] There was a substantial international business community of Europeans and Chinese, and even a few Americans. One American had imported a coal-fired generating plant from Cleveland, and equipped Manila with electric arc street lamps.[38] After operating the Astor House in Hong Kong, an American named Johnson had come to Manila as a cinematographer, and ended up as Aguinaldo's Chief of Ordnance.[39] The vast majority of Manila's population, however, consisted of native Filipinos. "Old Manila" was surrounded by sturdy masonry walls; most of the buildings were stone. Large portions of the city, including most of the businesses, lay outside the walls in "New Manila," built of wood.[40] From a line of trenches and wooden blockhouses outside the walls, Spanish Gen. Fermin Jaudenes defended Manila's occupants with a force of 13,000 Spanish troops.[41]

Against him, Emilio Aguinaldo's rebel government arrayed 30,000 insurrecto soldiers, commanded by Gen. Antonio Luna. The Filipino forces threw up fourteen miles of trenches north, east, and south of Manila; Manila Bay lay to the west of the city. Despite their numbers, the insurrectos lacked the strength to actually take Manila by storm.[42] The Spanish lacked the strength to drive them away. For his part, Commodore Dewey regarded Aguinaldo as a natural ally. He had brought the Filipino patriot back to the Philippines, and from the captured Spanish arsenal at Cavite, Dewey distributed 5,000 modern Mauser rifles, along with ammunition, to Aguinaldo's forces.[43] At the same time, Dewey had no instructions from Washington regarding President McKinley's intentions in the Philippines, and so he declined to commit himself or the United States to any formal alliance. On the other hand, he did not object when, on 24 May 1898, Aguinaldo claimed dictatorial power over the islands. Although Dewey received word on 26 May from Navy Secretary John D. Long, directing him to avoid any alliance with the Katipunan, his silence on 12 June, when Aguinaldo proclaimed Philippine independence, and on 24 June, when the Filipino leader declared himself president, all seemed to Aguinaldo to imply assent.[44] The situation, at once confused and confusing, only got more so when the first western volunteer regiments of the American reinforcements arrived on 30 June 1898.

CHAPTER ONE

Remember the *Maine*

Twenty thousand Denver citizens turned out on 17 April 1898 for the Colorado National Guard's drill in City Park. War fervor was at a pitch, and the city's five militia companies were center stage. The guardsmen marched and wheeled in a series of Civil War–style maneuvers until the infantry formed a skirmish line, and with bayonets fixed, charged while the crowd cheered. Gettysburg echoed in the huzzahs of the citizenry. The *Rocky Mountain News* reported that "no sight could have been prettier," and concluded "the wheels were made in perfect style." The band played Civil War tunes, and at close of day the crowd gathered around the mortar and two great cannons at the City Park Pavilion, while grizzled members of the Grand Army of the Republic gravely expounded on the power of the antique weapons.[1] From years of service between 1861 and 1865, those veterans were all-too-familiar with the massed volleys and skirmish formations of the militiamen. In the intervening years, however, new weapons and new enemies had dictated new tactics. The methods that had shattered Pickett's Charge, while sufficient on occasion to overawe strikers or deputized thugs, would ill serve Colorado's sons against Spaniards armed with Maxim machine guns and Mauser rifles.

At the end of the Civil War, about three million Americans were intimately acquainted with the linear tactics imposed by the muzzle-loading musket.[2] A trained infantryman could load, aim, and fire his musket three times a minute, if standing. Kneeling, or lying down, or crouched behind some kind of cover, he was lucky to fire once a minute. In order to direct both the firing and the movement of the men—what the military today calls "command-and-control"—the drill manuals of the eighteenth and early nineteenth centuries emphasized a constant light elbow-to-elbow touch, with the men standing side-by-side in a rank. By the Civil War, the standard drill called for the men to march to a battlefield in a "column of fours," i.e., in long lines moving down a road four abreast, and then to rapidly deploy into two ranks facing the enemy. Thus, if a company contained eighty privates and corporals, the front and rear ranks would hold forty men each.

From a company "front," or battle formation, the entire company could fire as one, in a single volley, with the rear rank firing through the spaces between the men in front. In addition, the company could fire straight forward, or at oblique angles to the right or left. In order to fire directly right or left, however, the entire company had to "wheel" to face the threat, turning like a gate on a hinge, a time-consuming maneuver that left the unit vulnerable to a flanking attack by the enemy.

While Civil War soldiers usually fought in a regimental front, shoulder-to-shoulder, commanders sometimes deployed "skirmishers" forward to probe for or detect the enemy. In the skirmish drill, a company could move forward and, extending out in a single rank, with five paces between each man, cover an entire regimental front. With single-shot weapons, those skirmishers were extremely vulnerable, and so they relied upon each other, and were organized into groups of four, called "comrades at arms." Ordinarily, the four men stood together in ranks, two front rank men and the two men behind them. When ordered forward as skirmishers, they marched out as a formation of fours, and then, on order, deployed out into a single rank, on line with all the other "comrades at arms." Two men would fire, and then reload; when they were ready, the other two men fired, and so half of the skirmish line was loaded at any given time. As skirmishers, they could take shelter behind any available cover, or lie down if there was none. Hard-pressed, they could "rally by fours," reassembling their formation of four comrades-at-arms, and then fall back on the main body. Of all Civil War tactics, the skirmish drill offered the individual soldier the most flexibility.

Perry Jamieson, in his book *Crossing the Deadly Ground: United States Army Tactics, 1865–1899,* has examined the army's slow modernization of tactics after the Civil War. The Indian Wars in the American West provided ample proving ground. U.S. Army commanders emphasized offensive operations. They quickly realized the futility of defending every post, town, and mile of railroad in the vast West. Aggressive generals like Phil Sheridan and William Sherman, convinced in the Civil War's Georgia and Shenandoah Valley campaigns of the necessity for total war, carried that approach to the Indians of the plains.[3] Strategically, they employed multiple converging columns of infantry and cavalry, usually in a summer campaign, to try to encircle and capture a "hostile" band. The most famous, and for the Army, most disastrous example of this policy is surely the Custer-Crook-Terry-Gibbon Powder River Expedition of 1876.[4] Almost as famous is the 1877 campaign against the Nez Percés led by Looking Glass and Joseph, in which Col. Nelson Miles interposed his command between the fleeing Indians and the Canadian border when they were only forty miles from safety.[5]

On the other hand, Civil War tactics did not lend themselves to the Indian Wars. Men standing in massed ranks could rarely identify a target at which to aim, and their opponents most often pursued a policy of *guerrilla* warfare, using ambush and hit-and-run raids. To defend against ambush, the infantry on the march began to deploy advanced guards, flankers, and rear guards. In combat, both cavalry and infantry usually used the skirmish line, as at the Battle of the Rosebud in 1876.[6] Gen. John Gibbon believed that the very nature of western Indian fights moved the army from Civil War formations to a system of open-order fighting. Writing in *United Service* in 1879, he concluded that "the peculiar drill of men in masses, and the 'elbow touch' of the regular soldier, admirable as they are in ordinary warfare, are utterly thrown away in contests with the Indian."[7]

Adoption by European armies of repeating rifles, as well as the exacting classes conducted by such schoolmasters as Sitting Bull and

Geronimo, both suggested the adoption of more open formations. A line officer, writing in an 1886 *Army Navy Journal*, explained that in an era of breech-loading infantry rifles, Gatling guns, and rapid-firing artillery, troops in traditional double ranks were

> simply food for gunpowder. The single rank formation is now and will be the only one used in battle, unless, indeed, the line shall become still more attenuated by the introduction of an open order system.[8]

Historians generally use the Wounded Knee fight of 1890 to close their consideration of the Indian Wars. But on New Year's Day of 1891, it was not at all clear to the troopers of the Seventh Cavalry, tumbling the Indian dead into a mass grave, that their Indian-fighting days were done.[9] Between Appomattox and Wounded Knee, an entire generation of Army commanders, first blooded in the Civil War or even before, had campaigned against the Indians in the West for a quarter of a century. In that long and frustrating service, they had faced new enemies, and utilized both new weapons and tactics. They had enjoyed ample time to reflect on what worked, and what did not. The Army's experience in the Indian Wars would directly relate to its strategy and tactics in the Philippine-American War. Walter Williams has pointed out that, of the thirty American generals who served in the Philippines between 1898 and 1902, twenty-six, or 87 percent, had fought Indians in the West. Of the remaining four, three were westerners and the other had "some experience" in the West.[10] What the Army knew about fighting Indians was what it would "know" about fighting Filipinos. In 1891, the Army printed a new family of manuals, one for each branch of its combat arms.[11] Generally referred to as the "Leavenworth Board Manuals," they still contained drill instructions. They contained as well, the first actual tactics, as opposed to drill, manuals ever adopted by the United States Army. The *Infantry Drill Regulations, United States Army* emphasized more flexible use of a regiment in combat, and that by necessity required more initiative from both individual company captains and majors commanding a battalion formed from several companies. The new manuals specifically incorporated loose-order tactics, based upon a "squad" of two "fours," consisting of seven privates and a corporal. Inevitably, such a system therefore required more initiative on the part of its noncommissioned officers, as well.[12]

The lowly corporal gained unprecedented authority in the 1891 tactics. The new manual specifically called for squads to attack in single-rank open- or loose-order formation, with squads leap-frogging forward in short rushes from one point of cover to another. As one squad advanced, another would provide covering fire from its halted position.[13] According to the manual, the captain still directed the overall movement of the company and, in theory, ordered the number of volleys each squad fired at each halt.[14] At the same time, extended order single rank tactics spread the men over a very large front. In an era before the field radio, the officers experienced serious problems of command-and-control. Even when captains entered the lines with their men, and with the two lieutenants directing the platoons, in combat the officers could not oversee all of their troops, especially as the squads leap-frogged. Not until the Second World War would battlefield communications allow fuller exploitation of the open order. It is worth noting that both the United States Army and the Marines still use the 1891 tactics in a modified form, called "fire and maneuver," in which squads or "fire teams" cover each other's advance by "laying down a base of fire."

As the United States Army adopted, tested, and trained in its new tactical system, what of the National Guard? The industrial unrest of the last quarter of the nineteenth century caused considerable alarm among wealthy and middle-class Americans. The rise and fall of the Paris Commune in 1871, in which the French Army killed 20,000 defiant Parisians, seemed a portent of anarchy.[15] With that foreign example still fresh in American minds, the "Great Upheaval" of the 1877 Railroad Strike seemed like the nightmare of class warfare realized.[16] From Martinsburg, West Virginia, the strike spread first to Baltimore, then to Pittsburgh, and then on as far as Chicago, Omaha, and even San Francisco. After state militias proved unable or unwilling to suppress the strikers, federal troops finally crushed the nineteenth century's "most violent nationwide industrial strike." The conflict had paralyzed transportation, and with over 100 lives lost, the Railroad Strike seemed to "men of property" less like a labor movement than a revolution.[17]

The "Great Upheaval" revitalized the nation's state militias, now reincarnated as strike-suppression forces. By the 1890s, thirty-eight states called their militia forces the "National Guard." The term is confusing, for the militias in no way approximated the modern National Guard. Under the existing laws, there was no clear way to incorporate the militias into any national war effort. Generally, the militiamen and state officials assumed that, under the United States Constitution, the President could mobilize the state forces for any of three reasons: to suppress insurrection, enforce federal law, or repel foreign invasion.[18] Strikebreaking fell under the first two categories. In towns and cities all across the nation, particularly in communities dominated by large industries with restive workers, fortified armories rose up, in the words of Jeremy Brecher, "to protect America, not against invasion from abroad, but against popular revolt at home."[19] Even in the instance of a hypothetical foreign invasion, however, there was no mechanism for "call-up," and it was not at all clear whether or not the President could order the state troops to serve outside the United States.[20]

Colorado's militia, organized "to suppress insurrection" like its peers in other states, actually performed a variety of different missions in the years before the Spanish-American War. In the crisis caused by the economic depression of the Panic of 1893, the militia established and administered "Camp Relief" in Denver, a tent colony to house and feed desperate unemployed miners. In the 1894 "City Hall War," the governor called up the militia to enforce his ouster of corrupt Denver politicians.

During labor unrest in the Cripple Creek district in 1894, the guardsmen actually protected miners from a mob of deputized thugs in the employ of the mine owners, and when Cripple Creek burned in 1896, the guard housed the homeless and guarded against looters. Only in the Leadville strike of 1896–1897 did the militia perform the duty expected by the mine owners, that of cowing strikers and protecting mine property and "scab" workers imported to break the strike.[21]

On the eve of war, most state militia units were poorly trained, and even those that drilled often frequently used only the old Civil War linear tactics. In 1897, fewer than 50 percent of the states regularly instructed their officers, and even fewer ran promotion tests.[22] Given its frequent service, it is perhaps understandable that Colorado's militia trained diligently. In 1889, the legislature appropriated funds for an annual "Camp of Instruction." On 4 September, the militiamen set up "Camp Cooper" near the Army's Fort Logan, seven miles south of Denver. There, in the first of what became annual exercises, they practiced camp life and marksmanship for a week; they do not seem to have conducted any tactical maneuvers.[23]

State militia officers had access, if they so desired, to the army training manuals. In 1879, with the approval of General Sherman, young regular army officers set up the Military Service Institution of the United States. Open to both regular and militia officers and run by the Commanding General of the Army, this voluntary society ran a sort of correspondence course, which studied and debated strategic and tactical issues.[24] And even before the 1891 tactics manual went to press, the *Army and Navy Register* published the new guidebook in twelve issues through the fall of 1890. Besides the Government Printing Office's press run, New York's D. Appleton and Company produced four editions of the 1891 manual, in 1891, 1892, 1893, and 1895, before the outbreak of the war with Spain.[25] So, militia officers, Colorado's included, had no excuse for ignorance of the new system of tactics.

Against strikers, the old Civil War linear volley, followed by a steady advance at "charge bayonets," would usually clear a street. The new tactical warfare manual was written for a conflict with Indians or a European enemy, not for street fighting against armed workers. The 1894 City Hall War demonstrates how militia commanders had to adjust their practices in the course of actual operations in the field. In 1894, the Governor of Colorado appointed, and could fire, the members of the Denver Fire and Police Board. Populist Governor Davis H. Waite ousted Board President Jackson Orr (a Populist) and board member D. J. Sweeney (a Democrat), accusing them of extending police protection to various gambling establishments.[26] On the morning of 15 March, Denver police officers gathered guns, ammunition, and explosives from stores around town.[27] The Denver Police, Arapahoe County Deputy Sheriffs, and "Special Police" officers incorporating members of Denver's gambling interests, then turned City Hall into a fortified barracks.[28] In response, Governor Waite issued a flurry of commands to the Colorado National Guard. Special Order No. 242 ordered Col. A. W. Hogle to assemble the Denver companies (B, E, and K) of the First Regiment. Other special orders called up the Chaffee Light Artillery and the Signal Corps, and placed the entire command under the Colorado Adjutant General, Brig. Gen. T. J. Tarsney. The troops dutifully assembled at their armory at 1:00 P.M., and at 2:00 P.M. began their march on City Hall.[29]

The guardsmen marched down Denver's streets in a company front formation, spanning the street in two ranks, shoulder-to-shoulder. One block from City Hall, the infantry deployed into a single loose-order rank, with the space of one man between each soldier. Behind and flanking the infantry, the artillery set up two Gatling guns and two twelve-pounder napoleon cannons. The militia's situation was not enviable. Armed toughs allied to the police-gambling combine swarmed the upper floors and roofs of the buildings overlooking the guard.[30] A crowd of onlookers, including many women and children, swirled around the troops and blocked the space between their position and City Hall. When the guardsmen, with fixed bayonets, prepared to clear the crowd away, a file of police under Sergeant Barr interposed themselves between the citizens and the militia. The militia halted, and the police moved the crowd back.[31] But, if hostilities were to break out, it was clear that not only would civilians be harmed, but also that the guardsmen's position, due to the hostile gunmen overhead, quickly might become untenable. The simple tactics of a line of armed soldiers, sufficient to guard a mine against strikers, would not suffice in an urban setting against determined opponents.

After surveying the situation, the National Guard's officers decided that, if ordered to assault City Hall, they first would withdraw their force to the west bank of Cherry Creek, posting the infantry to keep the crowd from crossing the watercourse. From the far side of the creek, the artillery then could safely shell City Hall into submission or ruin. Fortunately for all concerned, a spirit of compromise (and the threat of federal troops arriving from Fort Logan) prevailed, and the "City Hall War" ended without a shot fired.[32] The affair does demonstrate, however, the guard's ability to modify their traditional tactics to meet new requirements in the field.

The Colorado militia officers had the opportunity, if they chose to take advantage of it, to observe the 1891 tactics in action at nearby Fort Logan, home to the Seventh United States Infantry. The regulars routinely drilled in the new tactical formations. A photograph, dated to the late 1890s by the uniforms of the men, shows Company B of the Seventh Infantry marching at Fort Logan in the 1891 column-of-fours formation.[33] And in August of 1897, the First Colorado held a one-week Camp of Instruction in conjunction with the Seventh Infantry, on the grounds of the Broadmoor Hotel in Colorado Springs. All eight companies of the militia were there, each with at least 60 percent of its complement in attendance. "The guardsmen benefited immensely from the week's instruction and the association with the regular infantrymen."[34] The regiment's commanding officer, Col. Thomas W. M. Draper, handled all social and financial affairs, but the First Colorado's new Lt. Col. Irving Hale was in charge of training. On one day, the regulars captured a wagon train convoyed by national guardsmen commanded by Hale, but on the next, the militiamen successfully stormed a position the Seventh Infantry had been ordered to hold "at all hazards."[35] Despite such camps, the Colorado militia lacked the most basic training facilities, and did not even have a rifle range on which to practice marksmanship.[36]

In peacetime, such drills were in large part social events. As war loomed, however, they took on a much more earnest tone. Notifying the public of the 17 April 1898 City Park drill, the *Rocky Mountain News* explained, "as the time for war seems to be drawing near the National Guards in Colorado are growing zealous in their desire to become proficient soldiers."[37] At 11:00 A.M. on Sunday, 17 April, five companies of the First Colorado Infantry marched into the park from their armory at Twenty-sixth and Curtis Streets. Under the watchful eye of Brig. Gen. Irving Hale and his staff, they went through their paces.[38] Governor Alva Adams had appointed Hale, an 1884 West Point graduate, lieutenant colonel of the First Colorado in May of 1897, and colonel on 23 October 1897. After only a month, however, Hale became brigadier general and commander of the First Brigade of the Colorado National Guard, upon the sudden death of his predecessor, Brig. Gen. E. J. Brooks, on 20 November.[39]

The officers ran their men through a series of battalion maneuvers. Performing the old Civil War–style "wheels," in which a line of men pivoted like a gate on a hinge, they "swung about the field" and "swung corners." Then they formed a skirmish line and charged with fixed bayonets. At the halt, they pantomimed the routine for loading and firing although, to conserve ammunition, at the command "fire" the only sound was "clicking hammers" as the men pulled their rifle's triggers without having loaded a cartridge. Ordnance sergeants must have winced at this abuse of fragile firing pins. The troops broke for lunch, drilled again, and then marched in a formal dress review. After the review, the officers inspected the men's weapons, and then the day ended with "closed line drilling."

Part of the purpose of the drill was recruitment, and young men in the crowd, swept up in the martial spirit, expressed their intent to join the guardsmen.[40] While these evolutions thrilled the crowd, they did little to prepare the First Colorado for modern combat. Perhaps the only realistic drill of the day was carried out by the hospital corps, who rushed onto the field with litters and retrieved a volunteer "casualty." The "wounded" guardsman expected real medicinal whiskey in the flask proffered by the steward; finding only air, he vowed never to volunteer as a victim again. General Hale recognized the limited utility of the day's drill, and at close of day issued his General Orders No. 4.

I. Beginning Monday, April 18, 1898, all troops will drill nightly until further orders.

II. Drills will be held out of doors as far as practicable, and will be principally devoted, in the infantry and cavalry, to guard duty, extended order, firings, advance and rear guard, and in the artillery to guard duty and service of the guns.

III. Commanding officers will make a special effort to secure full attendance, sending verbal or written notice of this order to each member, and stating on report of drill the reason for each individual absence.

IV. Schools of instruction will be discontinued while this order is in effect.[41]

Part two of those orders emphasized practice in modern tactics, and part four specifically suspended any instruction in the old close-order drill. And so, for the next week, the peacetime militia of strikebreakers finally turned its energies toward preparing for war. Each night, after a day's work at their regular, individual jobs, the men of the First Colorado assembled and trained, emphasizing the 1891 tactics manual.

The week's effort produced significant improvement. And, in that week, the urgency of the drill was driven home to both the citizens of the state and the militiamen, first when the Seventh Infantry regulars from Fort Logan entrained for the southeast on 20 April, and then again on the following day when Spain expelled the American ambassador.[42] On

23 April 1898, President William McKinley called for 125,000 volunteers to serve for two years, drawn from each state and the District of Columbia in proportion to the total population.[43]

The next day, Sunday, 24 April 1898, the First Colorado soldiers demonstrated their new proficiency. Hale detailed one company, and the Gatling guns, to hold a position on Brickyards Hill, just north of City Park. The defenders quickly improvised fighting positions in the furrows excavated by the operations of the brick works. Against them, Hale sent four companies of infantry up from City Park, supported from the rear by two twelve-pounder Napoleon guns. The attackers advanced by squads, alternately rushing forward and then throwing themselves flat while another squad "fired" to cover them. Then the prostrate men rose, "fired" from one knee to cover the other squad's advance, and then themselves rushed on again. Two hundred yards behind, the main support body followed. As the assault moved up the hill, the infantry defenders fell back, while the Gatling guns galloped off toward the rear at oblique angles, then wheeled and "fired" on the attacking infantry from its flanks. Bringing the squads together, the attackers moved forward in alternating platoons, rushing, dropping, and firing. When they got close enough, they stormed Brickyards Hill in a frontal bayonet charge. After the tactical exercise, the guardsmen finished the day's practice with skirmish drill, in both close and extended order.[44] Against Spanish barbed wire and Maxim machine guns, such tactics still were likely to result in high American casualties, but the simple bayonet charge of the previous Sunday would have meant annihilation. The next day, 25 April 1898, Congress formally declared war on Spain.[45] Colorado immediately began to gather in its National Guard units from around the state, bringing them together in Denver. First, the state had to determine which of its various units the Army wanted.

Militia companies were based in individual communities, with strong local identities. The Colorado militia's frequent service in the mining camps had forced the individual companies to evolve from mere "marching and chowder societies" to true components of a larger military force. The cost and composition of that force proved of recurring interest to the statehouse. In the decade before the Spanish-American War, the legislature tinkered with the militia's structure, alternately forming it into one regiment with two battalions, or elevating each battalion to regimental status. In truth, the state didn't have enough companies to constitute two full regiments, and one regiment required fewer officers (and so less pay) than two. That was precisely the problem with a single regiment, however, since communities valued the prestige of having local citizens with high rank, and having two regiments doubled the number of colonels, lieutenant colonels, and majors. On 2 April 1889, for reasons of economy Colorado reorganized its militia, compressing it from two partial regiments into one twelve-company regiment. The old First Regiment, drawn from Denver, Boulder, Colorado Springs, Central City, and Aspen, became the First Battalion, with six companies. The original Second Regiment, recruited in Pueblo, Canyon City, Lake City, Ouray, Alamosa, Leadville, and Monte Vista, became the Second Battalion, also with six companies. At the same time, the state reduced its cavalry squadron to two troops, with Troop A attached to the First Battalion and Troop D attached to the Second.[46] That organizational division, between northern and southern Colorado, reflected very real rivalry between sections of the state.

On 15 April 1893, bowing to political pressure, the legislature changed its mind, and turned the two battalions back into "regiments," at least on paper, and forming a brigade of two regiments of infantry, two troops of cavalry, one light battery of artillery, and a signal corps company. The statehouse authorized a maximum of 151 officers and 2,694 enlisted men. Theoretically, each infantry regiment was to be organized into three battalions, but with the First Colorado containing only six companies, and the Second Colorado seven, such a plan made little sense. By June of 1893, when the effects of the Panic of 1893 hit Colorado, the reorganization was complete.[47]

In a crisis, the legislature could augment the militia by funding and recruiting new companies. As of 21 September 1896, just before being called to duty during the Leadville Strike, the First Colorado consisted of seven companies, drawn from Denver, Longmont, Boulder, and Greeley. The Second Colorado's eight companies came from Pueblo, Lake City, Monte Vista, Colorado Springs, Cripple Creek, and Leadville. During the strike, the militia recruited five more companies and mustered them into state service at Leadville, with one company going into the First and the other four into the Second Colorado. All five of the new companies disbanded after the strike was over.[48]

As part of a national reorganization, the state militia became the National Guard of Colorado in 1897, by an act of the General Assembly. The governor served as the commander-in-chief, except when the guard was called into federal service. He appointed an adjutant general, to serve as chief of staff, an assistant adjutant general, an inspector general, a surgeon general, a military secretary, and two or more aides-de-camp.[49] In that year, the National Guards of the United States totaled 114,000 men and officers, including 4,800 cavalry, 5,900 field and coastal artillerymen, 100,000 infantry, and assorted supply and service units. Five states maintained divisions, twenty-five states (Colorado included) supported brigades, and the rest had only regiments. There were very few support units, and Colorado was unusual in having a hospital corps.[50] Mine owners valued the Colorado militia as a strike-suppressing force, but the guard also protected strikers in 1894, and fed and sheltered miners in 1893 and 1896. Given the Colorado militia's varied duties, it enjoyed broad support among the people of the state. Colorado relied heavily on its guard, ensured that it was fully equipped for field duty, and was proud of it.

In fact, most states valued their National Guards, and governors proved reluctant to surrender them to federal control, even with a Spanish war in the offing. On 16 April 1898, after several days in conference with state militia officers, Secretary of War Russell Alger recommended, and President McKinley agreed, that the state units would keep their individual identities, much as in the Civil War, and that the United States government would issue special commissions to the state officers.[51] Each volunteer regiment would consist of twelve companies, with each company containing, on paper, eighty-four privates, nine corporals and sergeants, two lieutenants, and a captain. At the head of each regiment, states could appoint a colonel, lieutenant colonel, two majors, an adjutant, quartermaster, chaplain, sergeant-major, and a quartermaster-sergeant. Colorado, in addition, had two surgeons and their assistants, to make up its hospital corps.[52]

In apportioning the call for volunteers, Colorado's population warranted its supplying one regiment of infantry. On 25 April 1898, Secretary of War Alger cabled Colorado Governor Alva Adams to request one infantry regiment and one light battery of artillery. The infantry regiment was to consist of twelve companies of 1,176 men, augmented by a band, hospital corps, and officers to a total of 1,212. The battery would add another 175 men, for a total of 1,387.[53] The secretary also stated, "It is the wish of the president that the regiment of the National Guard and the state militia shall be used as far as their number will permit for the reason that they are armed, equipped, and drilled."[54] Enlisting members of the militia, already trained and outfitted, made more sense than starting from scratch with civilians drawn from the streets.

The battery was elated, but the cavalry troopers despaired. On 26 April 1898, Capt. W. G. Wheeler of B Troop announced that his men were prepared to enlist as infantry, or to volunteer for Col. Leonard Woods's proposed regiment of cowboys rumored to be forming back east.[55] Positions reversed the next day, however, when news arrived at noon that the artillery would not be needed, and that the cavalry would go instead. In response, the officers of the state's Chaffee Light Artillery petitioned Colorado's Senator Edward O. Wolcott and Representative John F. Shafroth to have the artillery called up as well, but it was not to be.[56]

While the cavalry and artillery vied for the right to go, the state's infantry had to consider how to create one regiment out of two. On paper, at least, the state had sixteen infantry companies, divided between the First and Second Regiments. The new regiment would contain only twelve companies.[57] On the other hand, not all National Guard companies were up to strength, so every guardsman who wanted to fight the Spanish could probably find a place, although perhaps not in his original company. That the prewar militiamen would be interested in going to war was not at all assured. In Danbury, Connecticut, the National Guard refused to volunteer for the Spanish War. Temporary duty against striking workers was one thing, service overseas against armed Spanish soldiers was quite another. Some 1,500 angry factory workers staged an "indignation meeting" and volunteered in the militiamen's stead. They demanded the National Guard's uniforms, since the militia would not be needing them, at which point the guardsmen volunteered to a man.[58] America had not fought a foreign war since 1847, and now the nation was entering its first overseas war; the idea took some getting used to.

As Colorado's National Guard took stock, twenty men requested or received discharges at the outbreak of the war.[59] At the same time, each company began enlisting new recruits, to bring its numbers up to the authorized level. The five Denver companies of the First Regiment held their well-publicized drill in Denver's City Park on 17 April 1898, partly to demonstrate their skill and partly to recruit volunteers from among the crowd of 20,000 onlookers.[60] And from the farms and the towns, men enlisted. At first, that could be a pretty informal process.

Arthur Sims was working at the Manhattan Dairy when news came of the *Maine*. Sure that war was coming, he decided to join the National Guard in April. The streetcar line ran right past the dairy, and Sims could ride into town for five cents. Learning that Company K drilled one night a week, Sims showed up at the armory at Curtis and Twenty-sixth Streets to enlist. He entered the main doors into a deserted assembly hall. In a side room, he saw uniformed men singing "Sweet Rosie O'Grady" and waltzing to their own music. Clearly, they were assembling for a weekly "drill," but not actually doing any training, at least when Sims arrived. He asked for Capt. William Cornell and expressed his desire to join up. The officer took a blank form from his desk, filled it out, Sims signed it, and then Captain Cornell said "Attention." The dancers came to attention while the captain administered the oath. Then the officer ordered, "Sergeant . . . , teach him the facings."[61] In that casual manner, Arthur Sims entered the service and received his first basic training. Other men brought more military experience. Ralph Lister had been a member of the cadet corps at West Denver High School, and made Captain of Cadets in 1897, the year he graduated. His military bearing and modest training counted for a great deal in the expanding militia, and he entered the First Colorado as a second lieutenant.[62]

Provided a man was in good health, he could usually enlist, but membership was not open to all. A group of black residents of Manitou met on 26 April 1898 and declared,

> Whereas, we Afro-American citizens, deeming that we are citizens in every sense of the word, and believing that every American citizen should defend his country with his life, therefore be it Resolved: That we organize a company of one hundred men immediately.[63]

The patriotic assembly broke up with the determination to work with Colorado Springs and Colorado City to assemble the required number. In like vein, 150 "colored citizens" of Denver met on 27 April at Shorter A.M.E. Church in a meeting chaired by Rev. Oscar J. M. Scott. After patriotic speeches and a "stirring address," they

> Resolved, While we deplore the absence of a colored company in our state militia organization, we are nevertheless patriotic, and tender our services to the governor of the state of Colorado as volunteers; therefore be it further Resolved that we commend W. J. Baker in his effort to organize a colored company in the county of Arapahoe.[64]

Only four years before, during the Cripple Creek labor unrest of 1894, at the behest of the mine operators the sheriff recruited over 1,000 "special deputies" from urban bars. The National Guard intervened on the side of miners and townspeople to protect them from the sheriff's gang. As proof of the dangerous nature of the threat, National Guard Adj. Gen. Thomas J. Tarsney cited the sheriff's "colored deputies."[65] The militia was not going to be enlisting any black recruits. Still, at least two black Coloradoans did go with the regiment, hired by officers as servants.[66] Col. Irving Hale's orderly was George Hopkins, a "genuinely black Southern negro" who ended up directing the kitchen at the regimental headquarters.[67] Blacks as civilian servants might be permissible, blacks as enlisted representatives of official authority were not.

The Colorado militiamen displayed their prejudice against other minorities as well. They referred to the Chinese as "Chinks," or at best, "Chinamen."[68] In August of 1897, the National Guard held a "Camp of Instruction," a sort of boot camp, at the Broadmoor Hotel in Colorado Springs. When they opened what they called "Camp Adams" to the public, one of the visitors was "John Chinaman." The guardsmen grabbed the protesting Chinese, threw him on a blanket, and then, with a group of men holding the edges of the blanket, began tossing him ever higher in the air. The regiment's colonel finally rescued the victim, and he hurriedly left camp to the laughter of the troops.[69]

As the militia prepared to go to war with Spain, one might expect that they would take advantage of Colorado's large Hispanic population to enlist some native Spanish-speakers. No Hispanic surnames appear in either the prewar or wartime militia muster rolls. Indeed, there was some question as to whether the guard would enlist Roman Catholics. Father T. H. Malone telegraphed Secretary of War Alger on 28 April 1898, reporting that militia officers at Cripple Creek were refusing to enlist Catholics. According to the priest, "the Catholics of the state ask your protection from this insult."[70] In fact, Catholics did enlist to fight the Spanish. Volunteers from the Knights of St. John, a Catholic fraternal order organized into local "commanderies," asked to be accepted into the guard as a unit, and were not accepted on those terms. Nonetheless, several members of the Knights' Marquette Commandery enlisted as individuals with no difficulty.[71]

The idea of self-selected groups enlisting as a body harked back to Civil War practice. On 15 May 1898, a newspaper article called for Swedish-Americans to form a company.[72] The militia, however, was incorporating new recruits into the existing companies, and the only unique identity of any of the units revolved around their home town. That identity was very strong, and the various communities sent "their boys" off to the assembly point in Denver with enormous pride. As Boulder's Company H prepared to travel to Denver on 28 April 1898, the Grand Army of the Republic and the Women's Relief Corps, groups formed to commemorate the Civil War, gave the troops a reception in the Masonic Temple. The Knights of Pythias band played, and the ladies of the Women's Relief Corps gave Company H a beautiful flag. While the men boarded the special cars, thousands of Boulder citizens gathered at the depot to wave them off.[73] In Greeley, businessmen threw a banquet, with 250 guests, for Company D at the armory before the soldiers left.[74] In Cripple Creek, the Grand Army of the Republic marched alongside Company G as they set out; Lake City held a dance in the armory for their company.[75] Students of Colorado College in Colorado Springs took up a subscription, and in a 25 April ceremony at North Park, gave the four companies from their area a "beautiful flag."[76]

Denver's companies simply assembled at their armory. Guy Sims, still a civilian, went down to watch his older brother Arthur leave. Men rushed in and changed from civilian clothes into their uniforms, and then gathered their weapons and equipment. The companies lined up around the walls of the assembly room, and waited for orders. Finally, they began to sing a popular tune of the day, "Banks of the Wabash." Guy Sims had not liked the song before, "but when the whole Battalion sang it in chorus, it was thrilling."[77] Called to attention, at the command

"Right forward, Fours Right" they marched by squads around the room and out into the rain, on their way to meet the other companies coming in from out of town.[78] As the home team, they received no elaborate send off, since they were only marching out to camp at City Park; Denver's farewell would come when the troops finally left the state.

When Company H arrived at the depot in Denver on the afternoon of 28 April 1898, they marched in a column to the Curtis Street Armory, where they supplied themselves with "the further equipment with tin plates, cups, knapsacks and blankets," and then marched on to "Camp Adams." There, they pitched their tents and ate their supper.[79] Camp Adams, named for Governor Alva Adams, was the designated assembly point for the entire National Guard. Immediately to the north of City Park lay the city's brickyards; straight east across Colorado Boulevard from the brickyards, in a cactus patch at the northeast corner of East Twenty-Sixth and Colorado, Camp Adams occupied a tract 600 feet wide and a mile long.[80] Pvt. Arthur Baker recalled,

> Camp Adams was, upon our arrival, in its infancy. A few of the companies had arrived and "staked their claims," but many were yet to come. All through the night, troops continued to arrive, pitch tents and settle down and when the morning of the twenty-ninth broke, bright and clear, Camp Adams was a reality.[81]

Still unclear as to the eventual organization of the Colorado contingent that would actually go to war, the military commanders laid out the camp with three smaller encampments within it: a camp for the First Infantry, a camp for the Second Infantry, and a camp for the battery and the cavalry.[82]

Almost immediately, they changed their minds, for the National Guard had finally decided on a plan for consolidating the state's two infantry regiments into one. The first, and politically most volatile, decision regarded the field commanders. Early estimates had predicted that Brig. Gen. Irving Hale, commander of the First (and only) Brigade of the Colorado National Guard, would assume command of the consolidated regiment. Hale had first arrived in Colorado at the age of four, after a forty-day wagon journey from St. Louis to Central City. His father, Dr. H. M. Hale, was the University of Colorado's first president, and his tutoring supplied Irving Hale's entire education until 1873, when young Hale enrolled in East Denver High School. He graduated in 1877, East Denver High's first honors graduate. After a year of hiking and trapping in the Rockies, Irving Hale had operated a freight line between Central City and Grand Lake until 1880, when he was admitted to West Point. He graduated in 1884 with a final examination score of 2,074 out of a possible 2,075; he had forgotten to cross a "t."[83]

The Army sent him through a post-graduate course in "torpedoes" (the current term for electrically controlled harbor defense anti-shipping mines) and civil and military engineering, after which he became a lieutenant and instructor in the torpedo service. An avid hunter and marksman, he represented the Battalion of Engineers in the Army's national rifle competition at Fort Niagara in 1888, where he won the division gold medal for the best four days' score. After a term as instructor at West Point, Hale resigned his commission in order to lay out Denver's first electric streetcar line. He then became General Manager of the Rocky Mountain Division of Edison General Electric Company, later called simply General Electric.[84]

Hale had served in the state's First Regiment as lieutenant colonel and colonel, until his unexpected elevation to brigadier general in November 1897 upon the death of his predecessor.[85] While the obvious candidate to lead the regiment, Hale was from Denver, and originally part of the First Regiment. The position of lieutenant-colonel, or second-in-command, could go either to Henry McCoy of Pueblo, colonel of the Second Regiment, or to Colorado Adj. Gen. Cassius Moses, the National Guard's top administrative officer through which the governor directed all orders.

Moses, like Hale, was from Denver. Since the First Regiment drew from the northern part of the state, and the Second Regiment's units came from the south, it was important to balance the appointments. By 28 April 1898, Governor Adams had selected Hale as colonel, McCoy as lieutenant colonel, and Moses as one of two majors. After Hale's promotion to general, Lt. Col. Charles Anderson had been acting commander of the First Regiment. With an eye to treating each of his two prewar regiments equally, Adams promoted Anderson to colonel and commander of the First Regiment on 28 April 1898, and then promptly made him the second major in the new combined unit.[86] Politically, the governor could have done little else, but these arrangements gave three of the top four positions in the new regiment to Denver men, and Pueblo felt slighted.[87] Former Adjutant General, now Major, Cassius Moses also felt slighted, since he now ranked below his former subordinate McCoy, but he swallowed his disappointment and made the best of it. Those political maneuverings, however, were nothing compared to consolidating the companies into twelve.

Arthur Baker diplomatically described the process.

> During this time the officers were engaged in the not altogether pleasant task of merging two Regiments into one. In order to accomplish this many officers had to be dispensed with and in most cases, it was a case of survival of the fittest, which resulted in the formation of a single Regiment with such officers and instructors as would make the Colorado Volunteers equal to any in the service.[88]

The consolidation was not as neat as Baker would have his readers believe. Between them the two prewar regiments had fifteen companies, some of which were seriously understrength. The regimental officers folded the companies together into twelve new companies, lettered "A" through "M." (In the United States military, there is no Company

J, due to potential confusion with "I.") In most cases, they managed to retain the letter designations of the prewar companies in their new incarnations, so that, for instance, Company C of the Second Regiment became Company C of the First Colorado Volunteers. But, in the process, five smaller companies lost their individual identities through merger.[89] Fifteen prewar companies required fifteen captains and thirty lieutenants; twelve wartime companies required only twelve captains and twenty-four lieutenants. A selection board thinned the ranks. Some officers accepted demotion gracefully, even when they ended up as sergeants; others did not. Most men were fiercely loyal to "their" hometown officers, and resented any implication that they were not as good as any other company's commanders. On 28 April 1898, the members of Company G of Cripple Creek unanimously expressed their confidence in Capt. David Howard and "denounced attacks on him as malicious falsehoods."[90] They need not have worried, for he passed his examination by the board. Two companies from the First Regiment, A of Denver and C of Longmont, refused to join the new regiment, feeling that their officers had been treated badly. Some of the individual soldiers from those companies did, however, choose to enlist.[91] One officer, Lt. Neil C. Sullivan of Company C, joined Boulder's Company H as a private and almost immediately was promoted to sergeant.[92]

As finally assembled, Companies A and C hailed from Pueblo, and B, E, I, and K from Denver. Greeley supplied Company D, F and L came from Leadville and Lake City, G from Cripple Creek, H from Boulder, and M from Colorado Springs.[93] Replacements were sent wherever they were needed, but this represented the original source of the companies.[94] The hometowns maintained their special allegiance to their own companies through the war. Companies were assigned randomly to the three battalions, and so the officers made up bits of doggerel incorporating the company letters as a mnemonic device. "Iberian Kites Come Down" reminded the men that Lt. Col. Henry McCoy's First Battalion contained Companies C, D, I, and K. "All Greenies Eat Fast"

Table 1: **Colorado National Guard Reorganization**

Community	Pre-War Company	Pre-War Regiment	1st Colorado
Denver	Band	1st Infantry	Band
Pueblo	B	2nd Infantry	A
Denver	B	1st Infantry	B
Pueblo	C	2nd Infantry	C
Greeley	D	1st Infantry	D
Denver	E	1st Infantry	E
Leadville	F	2nd Infantry	F
Cripple Creek	G	2nd Infantry	G
Boulder	H	1st Infantry	H
Denver	F	1st Infantry	I
Denver	K	1st Infantry	K
Leadville	E	2nd Infantry	L
Colo. Springs	H	2nd Infantry	M
Lake City	A	2nd Infantry	F and L

referred to Companies A, E, F, and G in Maj. Cassius Moses's Second Battalion, and "Last Battalion Moves Hastily" placed Companies B, H, L, and M under Maj. Charles Anderson in the Third Battalion.[95] With the companies of the new First Colorado Infantry finally sorted out, the officers restructured Camp Adams from a two-regiment camp into a camp of three battalions of four companies each. On the morning of 29 April 1898, the men arose to the bad news, and undid all their work of the night before. Each battalion was issued twenty-four Sibley tents—Army tipi-style tents holding sixteen men each, sleeping feet to the center like spokes on a wheel. The men set up the big shelters and improved the camp through the day, until the commissary issued candles. As night fell, they chatted in their quarters, introducing themselves and speculating about the next day. "Lights Out" came at 10:00 P.M.[96]

In his study of volunteer soldiers in the Seven Years' War, Fred Anderson found that "at the rendezvous point the provincials met the other members of their regiments and began, perhaps for the first time in their lives, to create a community that was defined by common purpose rather than by geographical accident."[97] Even in 1898, some of the First Colorado recruits had never before ventured far from home, and in the camaraderie of the ranks they found an exhilarating fellowship and a sense of accomplishment lacking in their civilian lives. That pride came from constant drill, desperately needed as recruits continued to enlist. Immediately, on General Hale's insistence, the men resumed training.[98] Daily life at Camp Adams revolved around drill. Each morning started with Guard Mount, followed by Squad Drill and Company Drill until noon. After dinner, the men turned to Battalion Drill and Regimental Drill, ending with a dress parade and, sometimes, a review by the governor.[99] In that shared experience and slowly growing competence, the men came to think of themselves as fellows.

The men at Camp Adams reacted enthusiastically to the news of Dewey's victory, but quickly began to hear rumors that, instead of being sent east to fight in Cuba, they instead might travel to Manila. If anything, their officers redoubled their efforts to turn the First Colorado into an effective regiment. Maj. Clayton Parkhill, regimental surgeon, organized a general round of physical examinations on 3 May 1898; many of the men failed.[100] The regiment continued to enlist new recruits to make up the shortfall.

The First Colorado mustered into federal service on 8 May 1898. That required their discharge from the National Guard of Colorado and subsequent enlistment into the First Colorado Infantry, United States Volunteers.[101] Their enlistments were backdated to 1 May 1898. For the prewar members of the National Guard, their lines in the muster rolls end with a rubber stamp, "Honorably discharged G[eneral] O[rder] No

72. A[djutant] G[eneral's] O[ffice], June 13 1898. M[ustered] I[nto] Colo Vols., U.S.A[rmy], May 1, 1898 accnt. Spanish-American War."[102] Guy Sims believed that the backdating was to give Colonel Hale seniority over other volunteer colonels, but the state had another motive.[103] When state officials mobilized the National Guard on 28 April 1898, they estimated that the Camp Adams encampment would cost about $27,500. Of that amount, $555 was covered by the military poll tax, and the rest would have to be covered by certificates of indebtedness, purchased by Colorado citizens.[104] When the National Guard deployed to police the Leadville strike in 1896 and 1897, the state had paid for the campaign with $100,000 in such certificates. For the war with Spain, William Cooke Daniels pledged the Daniels and Fisher Company to issue clothing and equipment to the troops at cost, with the state to pay when it could, and private citizens also had offered interest-free loans. The governor declined the offers, and instead decided to rely on the certificates of indebtedness.[105] The state also learned on 28 April that the United States government would repay the states for their expenses.[106]

Backdating the men's enlistments shifted eight days of payroll from the state to the federal government, and reduced the amount that the state would be obligated to pay each man as he discharged from the National Guard. On Sunday, 8 May 1898, the new regiment mustered into federal service, with Capt. E. F. Willcox, Sixth United States Cavalry, serving as the mustering officer. Since it was a sort of "field day," the public was there to watch as the troops marched, one company at a time, to take the oath.[107] As each man signed, Governor Adams handed him four silver dollars, fresh from the mint, as his pay for state service.[108] One private noted sarcastically,

How happy we were! How we blessed the kind Providence which had made each of us the proud possessor of four silver dollars. True it was, some greedy ones thought they should have received state pay for all the time they served under the state and that

Gov. Adams should have exercised his principles of economy
where fewer people and larger salaries were concerned, but each
of us had received four dollars.[109]

At the time of muster, the First Colorado had 46 officers and 970 enlisted
men. The regiment recruited additional men in San Francisco and
Hawaii, on the way to the Philippines, and in June, after the regiment had
left for the war, recruiting officers sent on another 166 men. Another 110
replacements reached the Philippines in late November. All told, a total
of 1,364 men served in the First Colorado Infantry during the Spanish-
American War and the Philippine-American War.[110] One result was that,
once the follow-on recruits had arrived in the Philippines, each company
had 97 men, almost a full complement. And, the regiment's recruiting
officers had carefully screened out any men in poor health. Unable to
pass the physical, for instance, Coloradoan Damon Runyan chose to
enlist in the Tenth Minnesota, and served in the Philippines with that
unit instead. The combination of companies nearly at their authorized
strength, containing men in good physical condition, meant that the First
Colorado remained an effective fighting force through its service. After
a month and a half of fighting the Filipinos, for example, on 18 March
1899 the minimum number of men fit for duty in any First Colorado
company was sixty. On the same date the First Nebraska Infantry, with
only eighty men per company at muster, had some companies with only
thirty men able to serve.[111]

The muster records indicate some vital statistics about the men,
although many of the records are incomplete. Regimental Adjutant
Alexander Brooks, for instance, who enrolled many of the replacement
recruits, was notoriously lax about filling in all the blanks on the enlistment forms. Despite such lapses, the muster rolls reveal a profile of the
regiment. Ages at time of muster are available for 1,284 men. The youngest
was 17, the oldest 52, but that range obscures the youth of the regiment.
The mean age of the regiment was 25 years, 7 months, and the median age

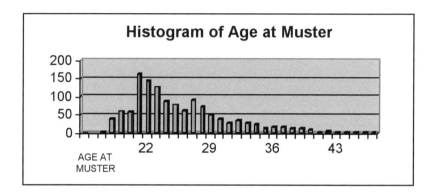

was 24. The men's ages do not lend themselves to an analysis by mode, but fully 33 percent of the regiment was aged 21 through 23, inclusive. The First Colorado was relatively young, comparable to the mean age of 26 for the American military in World War II. On the other hand, the mean for Americans in Vietnam was 19, and by that yardstick, the Coloradoans were ancient.

Only 12 percent of the recruits were foreign-born. Although primarily drawn from Europe, they also included natives of India, Chile, and Argentina. Canada supplied 28 men, as did the Scandinavian countries. The British Isles (including Ireland) furnished 47 recruits, and 34 Germans enlisted. The other 88 percent of the regiment were born in the United States. Of the 1,141 men for whom birthplace is known, 10 percent were born in Colorado. Almost as many came from Iowa. The single largest contingent of men hailed from Illinois, 11 percent of the total, and 8 percent came from Missouri.

The men of the regiment listed a great range of employment at the time of muster, or at least 1,282 of them did. Such colorful job descriptions as "elevator pilot" and "cow puncher" vie with "magician" for the most whimsical. The days preceding the mustering-in ceremony were marked with steady downpours, which may have inspired Pvt. Otis Glass to list his position as "rain inspector." With Colorado's mines still recovering from the Panic of 1893, miners could easily look to the military for a source of regular employment. Eighteen percent of the regiment came from some aspect of mining. Another 8 percent were involved in agriculture, most as farmers. Nineteen percent were employed in industrial work, ranging from iron moulders to masons. Another 9 percent worked in service and retail jobs, as butchers and bakers and elevator pilots. Thirteen percent were bookkeepers and clerks. Twenty-five of the men worked for either a railroad or a streetcar line. Ten percent of the men simply listed "laborer" under employment. Seventy, 5 percent of the total, left their studies to enlist. Only 6 percent were professionals, with skills ranging from civil engineers to the bar. They brought diverse skills to the regiment, most of which did not apply to fighting, but many of which would nonetheless prove useful in the Philippines.[112]

As late as 7 May 1898, Secretary of War Alger wired Governor Adams and advised that the First Colorado would move to Camp George H. Thomas at Chickamauga, Georgia, as soon as the regiment was fully equipped. At the muster, it still seemed that the First Colorado would fight in Cuba. On 13 May, however, the War Department ordered the First to move to San Francisco, and from there to the Philippine Islands.[113] The two cavalry troops, on the other hand, were detailed to report to Col. Jay L. Torrey at Fort D. A. Russell, Wyoming. "Torrey's Rough Riders," as his Second Volunteer Cavalry Regiment was known, contained troops from Wyoming, Nevada, Utah, Idaho, and Colorado, and Colonel Torrey officially accepted the Colorado guardsmen on 30 May 1898. While the infantry headed west, the cavalry headed east to Florida.[114] Troops A and B were not the only Coloradoans to serve in another state's unit. When Utah's governor mobilized Batteries A and B of the Utah Light Artillery on 25 April 1898, John T. Donnellan of Denver enlisted as a corporal in Battery B; the Utah guns would fight alongside the First Colorado in the Philippines.[115] Nonetheless, most public attention was focused on the First Colorado.

One young woman wandered into a company street where the men were "kangarooing" (tossing in a blanket) their newly appointed noncommissioned officers. "Oh, you horrid boys in blue, what are you doing?" she demanded. "We are kangarooing the non-coms," the men replied. "Well, I have just been appointed a non-com," she gamely responded, and so they tossed her, too.[116] Tuesday, 10 May 1898 was an especially nice day, and throngs of visitors came out to Camp Adams. Mothers and sisters showed up with cakes and pies. "Several jolly girls stayed to supper with their soldier friends, fell into line at mess and relished roast beef, potatoes, and bread with coffee, which all took without cream."[117] Such accounts indicate the sort of holiday atmosphere surrounding the encampment, but the men drilled relentlessly as well.

The Colorado guard was unusual in having full field equipment. The one aspect in which their material was deficient lay in the important area of weapons. The Colorado National Guard, like other militia units, was still armed with Model 1884 .45-70 Springfield Muskets. In 1893, after ten years of Ordnance Department testing, the Army officially adopted the .30-caliber, five-shot, bolt-action Krag-Jörgensen rifle. Of Norwegian design, the new rifle "in range, accuracy, and durability equaled or surpassed the best European military rifles of its time."[118] The modern weapon chambered a metallic cartridge and propelled its bullet with "smokeless" powder, giving the "Krag" a far greater muzzle velocity than the old Springfield with its heavy slug. Although the great advantage of smokeless powder over black powder was the new propellant's faster ignition and greater power, the men tended to concentrate on the "smokeless" aspect, probably because of the name. In truth, a volley fired from black powder weapons lay down a heavy bank of smoke, obscuring subsequent shots and preventing any chance of concealing the firing position, while the smokeless rounds carried no such liabilities. Given the tactics of the day, however, concealment was far less important than maneuver.

The real advantages of the Krag over the Springfield included rate of fire, range, and lethal effect across that range. The Springfield loaded one round at a time, through a hinged, flip-up "trapdoor" gate at the breech. The Krag loaded five rounds at once, easily moving them from a magazine to the chamber by operating a bolt action. Maximum range with a Springfield was about 1,000 yards, with bullets at that distance falling somewhere in a company front, i.e., in a rectangle forty men wide and six feet high. Because of the Springfield's low muzzle velocity, however, firing at that range required a very high trajectory, so that the heavy .45-caliber slug was above the head of a man for most of its flight, falling at an extreme angle toward the target. Even with the distance known absolutely, therefore, when firing the Springfield at extreme range, the actual killing zone through which the enemy had to advance was only about five feet deep. The higher muzzle velocity of the Krag gave not only a greater maximum range, to perhaps 1,300 yards, but also a much lower trajectory. Aimed at the belt buckle of an enemy soldier at 1,000 yards range, the Krag's bullet at the high point of its flight would still only be about five-and-one-half feet above the ground. In other words, so long as the bullet was in line with the enemy soldier, it would hit him, even if range estimates were wrong. The killing zone of the Krag, in this instance, was now 1,000 yards. In fact, the Krag's improved rate of fire was more important than its range, since engagements usually took place at 300 yards or less.

Seven regular regiments received the new rifle in November of 1894, and by 1897, the entire regular army had the new arm, along with an updated drill manual.[119] Most civilian weapons of the time still used the old black powder, however, and few factories manufactured the smokeless powder used in the military rifles. Modern ammunition was somewhat scarce, a situation only worsened as America entered the war when, on 28 April 1898, the Atlantic Powder Mills, a major army contractor, blew up in Dover, New Jersey, killing six.[120]

The First Colorado hoped to take Krags to war. So did every other volunteer regiment. Told there were no Krags available, Colorado applied to the War Department for any other comparable .30-caliber smokeless powder rifle. Washington replied that it would take at least fifteen months to get Savage rifles, and "after the first of the year before Winchester could make delivery."[121] And so, as the men prepared to leave

Colorado for the Philippines, they resigned themselves to carrying their old Springfields. A Seventh Infantry officer, asked by a reporter if the volunteers would be at a serious disadvantage if armed with the .45-70s, put the hometown audience at ease.

> I cannot believe the men will be at much of a disadvantage. It is all right for sharpshooters to be dead shots, but when it comes to the final rush, the fellows with the Springfields will get close enough to do their duty. It is not the range shooters who decide the fate of battles, and it does not take long for a great body of men in a charge to cover half a mile of ground. I still have faith in the old Springfield.[122]

Of course, his own men were regulars, and so armed with the Krag, and he could afford to be sanguine.

The shortage of modern weapons was very real. After the regiment left for San Francisco, the state organized a replacement militia to be available in the First Colorado's absence; the replacements were actually sent to Lake City for a brief period in March of 1899. Since the volunteers had taken all the state's equipment with them, Colorado ordered five hundred .30-caliber Winchesters to outfit the home guard. As the army had predicted, they only arrived in April of 1899.[123]

With orders in hand to move to San Francisco, the regiment began its final preparations. On 14 May 1898 the First Colorado paraded through Denver to the Capitol to receive its flags. The Society of the Sons of the American Revolution had ordered "the finest regimental flag that could be bought." Once that national flag arrived in Denver, the Sons placed in white letters on one of the red stripes the simple legend, "1ST. REGT. INF. COLORADO VOLUNTEERS." Governor Adams and officers of the Sons presented the flag to the regiment's officers on the statehouse steps.[124] In the tradition of the Civil War, Mrs. William Cooke Daniels presented silk regimental colors as well.[125] The First Colorado carried the two flags away proudly; over a year later, they returned their remnants with equal pride. In the morning of 17 May 1898, the First Colorado packed their tents and gear, and at noon marched through Denver's business district to the depot. The band led the way, and the cavalry troops rode alongside. Arthur C. Johnson, a twenty-three-year-old private in Company E, was also a reporter for the *Rocky Mountain News,* and the newspaper appointed him its official war correspondent. Cpl. Harry McCauley, also in E, filled the same capacity for the *Denver Republican,* but Johnson really became the voice of the regiment for the folks back home. After the war, he recalled the regiment's leave-taking as "an auspicious day, perfect overhead and underfoot, and a vast throng of thousands sent up its huzzas, said its good-byes and wished God-speed to the men."[126]

By now, the regiment had grown to 46 officers and 1,040 enlisted men.[127] As the men marched, well-wishers broke into the column and clung to "their particular boy." Guy Sims recalled one former member of Company K, rejected by the physical examination, stepping out of a bar with two glasses of beer, which he handed to the first Company K men he found. The regiment marched right through the depot and onto the platforms, where they found four trains waiting for them, locked. Relatives followed them through the depot, and so prolonged the farewells a bit longer. Sims particularly remembered Cpl. Richard Bryant's sister, almost hysterical at her brother's departure.

He tried to avoid a scene, but the only thing he could say that would quiet her was, "I'll come back all right, and then won't we be proud and happy. I won't be gone long." But Bryant was one of those who didn't come back. He was a souvenir fiend, always on the lookout for something to bring home. He got his last souvenir at Blockhouse 5.[128]

When the First Colorado's trains finally left the station, the farewells and presentations were almost over. As the regiment passed through Canon

City, Mr. Peabody gave Lt. William H. Sweeney yet another flag, which he promised to return after the war. In the Philippines, Colonel Hale borrowed that flag to fly over the regimental headquarters, but Sweeney retrieved it and fulfilled his promise.

It had taken some time to arrange the rail transportation. The First Colorado had been slated to sail on the first expedition to the Philippines, but the federal government had trouble in locating the required cars, and in arranging to hire them, delaying the trip to San Francisco enough that the regiment had to sail later.[129] The railroads carried the men at a government rate of two cents a mile.[130] For the most part, the men were oblivious to such matters. Their trip west was a great adventure. They had come from the farms and towns of Colorado to assemble in Denver. Now, in company with newfound friends, they were off for California. Arthur Johnson recalled it as a "jolly trip through mountains and across desert."[131] At 8:00 A.M. on 21 May 1898, the trains pulled into Oakland, California. The men sat in the cars until noon, and then boarded the ferry to cross to San Francisco. While the ferry provided another adventure, the men couldn't see much due to fog. Tired and hungry, the men marched off the ferry and into San Francisco's new Union Depot, to their first taste of California hospitality.[132] Arthur Johnson recalled,

> The ladies of the Red Cross Society ushered them without delay to tables groaning with palatable sandwiches and delicious coffee. California flowers were showered on the surprised, but delighted men, and they were loaded down with California fruit. Far from home and among strangers, it was an ovation they were not looking for, but it was only the initial installment of the fine treatment dealt out by the big hearted Californians to the soldier boys.[133]

Guy Sims found that California hospitality even extended to the men's weapons. As the men trooped into the depot for their "big feed,"

2. California bound. *Photo courtesy of John Stewart Post Number One, Veterans of Foreign Wars.*

they stacked their arms in one room and ate in another. When they went to retrieve their rifles, they found a beautiful lily thrust down each muzzle. "They looked pretty, all right, but boy, what a job we had getting those old guns ready for inspection."[134] After their dinner, the men marched four miles up over San Francisco to the Presidio, cheered on by crowds lining the streets.[135] Dazzled by their reception from the citizens of San Francisco, the men of the First Colorado were even more excited when, as they marched into camp, the fog cleared and they caught their first sight of the Pacific Ocean.

Until the Spanish-American War, the United States had never fought an overseas war, and at the national level, no one was really sure how to organize one. If the war was to free Cuba, then surely an expedition would have to land on that isle. The stunning news of Commodore

Dewey's victory at Manila, followed by President McKinley's decision to send an expedition to take Manila itself, only intensified Army confusion over how to organize America's first overseas war. On 16 May 1898, the War Department issued General Order No. 46, appointing Major General Wesley Merritt as commander of the Department of the Pacific. This new department, unlike the geographical ones, had no territorial specifications and no formal administrative structure. It was, in fact, only a name.[136] After a distinguished career as an Indian fighter, Merritt had served as superintendent of the United States Military Academy, and his appointment to the new post was a mark of the respect in which he was held by his peers. Although less well regarded, his second in command, Maj. Gen. Elwell S. Otis, was, like Merritt, another old Indian fighter.[137]

Late in May of 1898, Merritt arrived in San Francisco, where volunteer regiments from the western states were assembling at the Presidio awaiting transport to the Philippines. On 30 May he officially assumed command of the United States Expeditionary Forces and the Department of the Pacific.[138] At first, he assembled all his regiments into a single division, but on 13 June 1898 Special Order No. 5 divided the division into two brigades.[139] On 23 June 1898, his command became the Department of the Pacific and the Eighth Army Corps. State regiments were still arriving in San Francisco, and the Army was still contracting for and assembling shipping to carry the expedition to the Philippines. Merritt quickly realized that several flotillas would be required to transport the necessary troops. Accordingly, he placed the entire Eighth Army Corps into an "Independent Division," under General Otis, until Merritt himself arrived in Manila Bay.[140]

In San Francisco, the Army assigned volunteer regiments to Camp Merritt, named in honor of Maj. Gen. Wesley Merritt, newly appointed commander of the Department of the Pacific.[141] Located south of the Presidio between McAllister and Geary Streets, the camp was established on a windy, foggy site at the abandoned Old Bay Racetrack.[142] Each regiment was assigned to a city "square," or platted block, surrounded by a low white fence. The streets were laid out, but there were no houses on the sandy ground. City water was piped into each square.[143] In their appointed square, the First Colorado erected their Sibley tents, worn and stained from past campaigns in the mining camps.[144] They dubbed their section of the encampment "Camp Hale." Military life was not exactly what the men had expected. Officers had brought their horses, expecting to ride in the Philippines. At Camp Merritt, they discovered there would be no transport for horses, and so they had to ship their mounts back to Colorado.[145]

A photograph of the First Colorado at Camp Merritt shows them wearing the uniforms of the post-Civil War frontier army: the dark blue wool Model 1884 Blouse (also known as the five-button sack coat), Model 1883 Dark Blue Overshirt, Model 1885 light blue wool kersey Trousers, Pattern 1880 Mills canvas looped cartridge belt secured with brass H-shaped "US" belt plates, and tan broad-brimmed campaign hat with a center fore-and-aft crease.[146] While serviceable and warm, such uniforms were likely to prove rather too hot for a summer campaign in the Philippines. Former sergeant Ben Stapleton later recalled that "the blue flannel shirts started to fade before the soldiers left San Francisco."[147] In the second week of June, Guy Sims recalled that the men were issued their "fighting clothes. They were brown in color and made of canvas. . . . They were dumped into the 1st Sgt.'s tent and we just scrambled for the best fit we could find."[148] These were Model 1884 Brown Canvas Fatigue Uniforms, constructed of six-ounce cotton duck.[149] The men loved these uniforms, and called them their "pyjamas." Once on board the transport for the Philippines, they wore their brown suits exclusively. They complained of only two sizes, too-large and too-small, and the tops and bottoms never really matched, but "they were cool."[150]

The men may have thought their days of drill were over, but Colonel Hale had other plans. Each day, he drilled the men. They would storm Presidio Hill, one mile north of camp, three times each morning, march back for dinner, and then assault the hill again in the afternoon. Although

3. Uniform issue. *Photo courtesy of John Stewart Post Number One, Veterans of Foreign Wars.*

the men grumbled, they learned.[151] Arthur Johnson described the "spectacular skirmish drill, which took place on Presidio hill every afternoon under the command of Col. Irving Hale." The Colorado regiment was the first of the state troops at the Presidio to practice what Johnson called "true war drilling," but other regiments quickly followed suit.[152] Frederick Funston of the Kansas volunteers described his regiment's tactics practice in San Francisco, in which one platoon would rush fifty yards and go prone, while the second platoon would rise and pass the first.[153] The First Colorado had already learned that drill, but they continued to hone their skills as they waited for transport to the Philippines. And, really for the first time, they practiced marksmanship as well. Their approach to the subject was pragmatic, with results counting more than form. In Company K, Arthur Sims was the best shot, but he often hit the target with ricochets off the ground. The officers and sergeants divided over whether or not to count such hits. Finally, they took their argument to Colonel Hale, who ruled in favor of Private Sims, reasoning that the goal was to hit the enemy, and aiming low was probably a good fault![154]

Despite using the old Springfields, the First Colorado still had trouble drawing ammunition from government stores. The volunteers requested supplies from the United States Arsenal at Benicia, across the bay. The Army shipped 4.6 million rounds from the Rock Island Arsenal to Benicia on 10 June 1898, trying to meet the demand, and predicted another shipment could be ready ten days later, but the cartridges did not arrive in time.[155] Capt. C. W. Whipple of the Ordnance Department reported on 16 June that, while the First Expedition had been issued 400 rounds per man, the Second (including the First Colorado) had sailed the day before with only 200 rounds per man, in addition to what they might have carried with them from their home states.[156] Company A, at least, landed in Manila with only the 200 rounds they'd been issued from national stores.[157]

After supper, if the men were not on details or drills in their companies, some found time to sightsee. Camp Merritt was unfenced, and during the day, soldiers and civilians came and went relatively freely.[158] The men marched as a unit to swim at the Sutro Baths. Once they'd been paid, a number of the men dined at the Cliff House, overlooking the seal rocks. They played baseball and football among themselves. Eugene F. Bert, president of the Pacific Coast Baseball League, offered any uniformed soldiers free admission to all San Francisco ball games.[159] Thousands of citizens visited the camps each day. Women of San Francisco gave the men of the First Colorado sewing items and shoelaces. Mr. Thomas Cleary sort of adopted the regiment, and on two occasions he cooked clam chowder for the entire unit.[160] Many of the men made friends among the civilian population, which could get them in trouble. Pvt. Casper "Billy" Williams of Company D remembered,

> Every Saturday afternoon we would sneak out of camp to meet our girls in old Golden Gate Park. The girls would bring lunches. At night when we sneaked into camp we always seemed to run into MPs with bayonets on their rifles. The chase would be on.

I remember this one time when I was getting away from them when I tripped over a guy wire on one of our big Sibley tents and landed in the guardhouse.[161]

Such escapades relieved the boredom of camp life, and the men seem to have regarded the possibility of confrontation by the sentries as a minor annoyance, the price to be paid for sampling the interesting new land in which they found themselves.

California hospitality provided the volunteer regiments with other souvenirs, as well. Among the civilians flocking to the camps were a number of prostitutes, leading to a "near epidemic of venereal disease."[162] Sexually transmitted diseases were only one type of health problem. Disease was inevitable in a camp of 10,000 men with poor mess and sanitary facilities. At first, the men suffered in the damp spring weather from bronchitis and pneumonia, and summer brought both typhoid and dysentery.[163] In some respects, Colorado was better off than many regiments, for it included in its organization its own hospital corps. The regimental surgeon, Maj. Clayton Parkhill, was so competent that the Army removed him from the First Colorado for headquarters duty with the Department of the Pacific. After the Colorado unit sailed for the Philippines, the Army sent Parkhill to Cuba. Parkhill's new assignment created room for advancement in the First Colorado's hospital corps. Capt. Louis Kemble was promoted to major in Parkhill's stead, and Lt. Charles E. Locke rose to captain. Pvt. David Thornton, a doctor before his enlistment, took the promotion examination in San Francisco and secured appointment as lieutenant-surgeon.[164] Besides shifts in the officers' ranks, the hospital corps while at Camp Merritt recruited additional enlisted men from other companies of the First Colorado.[165] Counting Parkhill, twenty-two men served in the hospital corps; their number included six physicians, five druggists, ten students (one of whom was a medical student), and an insurance salesman.[166] Even with that concentration of medical expertise, the hospital corps could treat,

4. Camp Merritt. *Photo courtesy of John Stewart Post Number One, Veterans of Foreign Wars.*

but not prevent, illness. Neil C. Sullivan, the Longmont man who had accepted demotion from lieutenant to sergeant in order to accompany the First Colorado, became the regiment's first fatality when he succumbed to spinal meningitis.[167]

Despite illness and boredom, most of the men enjoyed their stay in San Francisco. The period in California cemented friendships begun at Camp Adams, and the militiamen began to think of themselves as actually belonging to their companies, instead of just being assigned to them. While still in Colorado, Second Lt. Charles Hooper applied to join the regular army, as an officer. On 1 June 1898, the Secretary of War ordered Hooper to remain in San Francisco pending orders for him to take the examination for appointment as a second lieutenant in the regulars. By that time, Hooper was reluctant to leave his regiment. After some thought, rather than be separated from Company B, on

4 June 1898 he withdrew his name from consideration for the regular commission.[168] Like the rest of the regiment, he was anxious to get to the front. The first three transports had sailed on 25 May 1898.[169] At last, it was Colorado's turn. On 14 June 1898, the men ate their breakfast at 5:00 A.M. At 7:00 A.M., a bugle call ordered the men to drop the tents. Ready for the command, the regiment struck the Sibleys as one. Baggage wagons collected the camp equipment while the men assembled their personal gear and fell into ranks in heavy marching order. After a wait of one hour, they marched back through San Francisco to the docks. Again, people cheered along the way, and again, the Red Cross supplied dinner at the docks. One last time, the men basked in the generous acclaim of the Californians, and then, beginning at noon, started to file up the gangplank of the chartered transport *China*.[170] On the docks, a band played *Home Sweet Home, Old Folks at Home, Swanee River, Auld Lang Syne,* and other sentimental favorites.[171] As they turned their faces to the west, they renewed their resolve with the slogan, "Remember the *Maine*, to Hell with Spain!"

CHAPTER TWO

To Hell with Spain

The men of the First Colorado had rallied to the cry "Remember the *Maine*, to Hell with Spain!" Expecting to liberate the Cubans from the Spanish, they instead found themselves headed for the Philippine Islands. Because the Colorado militia, unlike most western volunteers, possessed its entire complement of field gear and campaign equipage, the U.S. Army initially had scheduled the First Colorado to sail in the first fleet of transports. Delays in securing rail transport from Denver to San Francisco, however, caused the Army to relegate the Coloradoans to the second fleet.[1]

The *Australia*, *Sydney*, and *City of Peking*, comprising the first fleet, therefore sailed from San Francisco on 25 May 1898 without the First Colorado.[2] On their way to Hawaii, however, they spotted the *China* inbound to San Francisco, and predicted she'd soon follow with more troops.[3] In fact, the Pacific Mail Company leased the *China*, upon her arrival in California, to the United States Army for $1,500 a day, to help carry the second expedition to the Philippines.[4] Since the Army's prewar mission had revolved around coastal defense installations and western garrisons, the government owned no troopships, and had to rely on leased merchant vessels.[5]

On board the *China*, the Colorado men were joined by two companies of the Eighteenth United States Infantry, two batteries of the Utah Light Artillery, and detachments of United States Engineers and the hospital corps.[6] Also loaded on the *China* were some "casuals," including sailors reinforcing Dewey's squadron. By 5:00 P.M., the *China* boarded 1,800 men and fifty steers, and then left the pier and anchored in San Francisco

5. At Home on the *China. Photo courtesy of John Stewart Post Number One, Veterans of Foreign Wars.*

bay while other ships loaded.[7] The men did their best to settle into their strange new quarters, hurriedly improvised when the Army chartered the *China* as a transport. Contractors had jury-rigged wooden bunks in the holds of the ship. Pairs of bunks were bolted together side-by-side, and then laid end-to-end six bunks long. These were mounted in three levels, so that each assembled bunk unit held thirty-six men.[8] Some of the racks were stacked four high. The men slept on straw-filled mattresses and pillows, with their military blankets on top. Canvas wind funnels were supposed to vent the lower decks, but with only enough space to stand between each set of bunks and the next, the quarters were not pleasant.[9]

The enlisted men went aboard with what they could carry, which, after allowing for their military equipment and arms, was very little. Military gear was stowed away in deeper holds, but the men had to squeeze their personal possessions into, under, and over their bunks. Tight quarters didn't prevent the men from bringing their pets along. Ralph "Doc" Taylor smuggled his puppy "Dewey" aboard in bandsman

George Settle's tuba. Some of the men openly brought a water spaniel puppy named "Denver," which sported a Red Cross brassard for a collar. Company A brought its goat, "Billy," and quartered him with the steers.[10] As night fell, the ship turned on the electric lights in the saloons and covered deckways, and the "diversions commenced." Chaplain David Fleming had printed song sheets in San Francisco, which he now distributed to the men, and as a bandsman played the ship's piano, they sang both the original verses and parodies of "Hot Time in the Old Town Tonight" and "On the Banks of the Wabash." After an hour of sing-along, quartets and soloists sang, accompanied by the guitars, mandolins, and banjos of the few men who'd bothered to drag instruments along.[11]

Besides the *China*, the second expedition included the *Colon*, *Senator*, and *Zealandia*; the *China* was the fastest of the fleet.[12] By 15 June, the other three ships had embarked two more companies of the Eighteenth Infantry, another battalion of Utah artillerymen, four companies of the Twenty-Third United States Infantry, and the Tenth Pennsylvania Volunteer Infantry.[13] Finally, at midday on the fifteenth, the fleet was ready to sail. A Red Cross boat came past the four ships, carrying Mrs. Henry McCoy, wife of the regiment's lieutenant colonel, come to wave the troops off. She had already booked passage to Hong Kong on the *Belgic*, there to stay until the troops were settled in the Philippines.[14] At 1:10 P.M., the *China* blew her siren.[15] Cpl. Guy Sims recalled that she was answered by "every steamer and every tug, big and little, on the bay," as well as every locomotive and factory on the shore. Tugs accompanied the fleet through the harbor, whistling as they went, and Fort Winfield Scott saluted with its guns as the expedition passed through the Golden Gate and out to sea.[16] The public was optimistic about the war, and had not yet begun to wonder just what the American military was doing in the Philippines, and the people of San Francisco provided a grand leave-taking from U.S. soil.

The men had hoped to keep their native land in view as long as possible, but within three miles of shore, fog blanketed the sea and shrouded the fleet until the next day.[17] The seas off the Golden Gate are notorious for causing seasickness, and the Coloradoans were landsmen. Virtually all were seasick for their first day out.[18] The second day was no better for most, but in Company E, those who had gained their "sea legs" treated the miserable sufferers to a chorus, sung to the tune of "My Bonnie Lies Over the Ocean":

> O what did you have for your supper?
> O what did you have for your tea?
> Go back on the back of this vessel,
> And you will quickly see.
> Bring back, O bring back, O bring back my supper to me.[19]

The *China* was longer than the other ships, and so it seemed that her passengers suffered less from seasickness than the rest of the fleet.[20] For whatever reason, by the eighteenth of June the men were over their *mal-de-mer*, and could settle down to a busy daily routine.[21] Reveille sounded at 6:00 A.M. The seven o'clock breakfast was followed by sick call at seven-thirty. Guard mount was at 8:00 A.M.; those men not in the guard drilled from 9:00 A.M. until noon, when the regiment ate dinner. After some modest time on their own after the meal, they drilled again in the afternoon, from four until supper at six. At 6:50 P.M., "first call" assembled the men while the sergeants called the roll, in preparation for the evening retreat ceremony. Promptly at seven, the evening gun sounded and the flag came down. Then, while the men stood at "parade rest," the band played the *Star-Spangled Banner*. After inspection, the men were dismissed. Free for a time, they would climb the ship's rigging or sit on deck, wrap themselves in blankets, and smoke and sing as the sun set and the stars came out. "Church call" sounded each evening at 8:30 P.M., and those so inclined could attend the Chaplain's services. "Call to Quarters" brought the men below at 9:30 P.M., and "Taps" extinguished the lights at ten.[22]

In reality, the officers had difficulty designing any traditional drill that the men could perform on shipboard. So, the officers improvised, taking turns providing oral instruction to the men, or leading them in "setting up drill" or calisthenics.[23] The routine aimed, at least in part, to keep the troops busy. In the same way, the guard mount was primarily for the sake of form; desertion was pretty difficult in the center of the Pacific. Actually, while at sea the First Colorado discovered its only desertion of the war. Pvt. Michael O'Brien, a twenty-five-year-old miner from Boulder, had accompanied the regiment to the dock, and then slipped away.[24] Still, the regiment had embarked for the Philippines, where they would face the enemy, and the officers were determined to instill in their men the necessity for military order. One man, caught sleeping while on guard, was sentenced to two years in prison and a dishonorable discharge.[25] That frightening sentence was later overturned on the grounds that the court martial was improperly constituted, but the officers had made their point.

The little fleet reported its progress as it went. Improbably enough, on the eve of the twentieth century the First Colorado was still relying on carrier pigeons. The *China* sailed from California on 15 June 1898; three days later the officers released four homing pigeons.[26] With the *China* covering 225 miles each day, it seemed likely that at least one would get through.[27] On 21 June 1898, five days into their Pacific crossing, *China* dispatched a single pigeon to report the expedition's progress. Incredibly, the doughty bird delivered his message to Eighth Army Headquarters in San Francisco two days later.[28] The carrier pigeons eventually served civilians as well. Unable to use the military communications system in the Philippines, *Harper's* correspondent John Bass employed the birds to get his dispatches from the front to Manila.[29]

In 1898, the United States used a signal code called the "Myer System for U.S. Army and Navy Signaling."[30] Because the code used signal flags during the day and lanterns on a stick at night, the men called it the "wig wag."[31] The signal flag was "a large . . . flag with a red square in its center," waved to the left and right. As the troops boarded their transports in San Francisco, signalmen from the embarked Engineers' Corps were divided up between the four ships, to allow communication during the passage. Taking advantage of that expertise, Colonel Hale detailed three officers and three enlisted men to assist the signalmen on *China*, so that they too could become proficient in the specialized skill.[32] During the long hours crossing the Pacific, any occupation must have seemed alluring. Although not part of the signal detail assigned by Hale, on 1 July 1898 Cpl. Roy Harris carefully copied the "Myer Code System" into the back of his *Pacific Coast Diary for 1898*, a sort of Victorian day-scheduler. He attended "non-commissioned officer's school" each day, and by 5 July could record with pride that he had "held my end down with any of them in transmitting the messages" between ships.[33] The routine of drill, familiar from long hours at Camp Adams and Camp Merritt, provided some stability for the men in the midst of an environment totally alien to most. Before they truly had the chance to settle into shipboard life, however, they reached Hawaii, 2,400 miles from California.[34]

Before daylight on 23 June 1898, on the sixth day of the voyage, the fleet arrived at what the men agreed was "paradise."[35] The *China* turned in for Honolulu, while the remainder of the flotilla steamed on to Pearl Harbor.[36] At 8:00 A.M., a tug towed the *China* in to the wharf as the crew of the training ship USS *Mohican* lined her rail for three cheers. "Native boys of all ages" dove for coins thrown by the troops.[37] On the wharf, a crowd of people waving little American flags greeted the *China*, and Guy Sims recalled them crying "Oahu" (more likely, "Aloha," explained to him as Hawaiian for both the island and for "welcome") as the ship docked.[38]

Aboard ship, the First Colorado's band serenaded the crowd with the Hawaiian national anthem, after which the Honolulu band on the dock replied with the *Star-Spangled Banner*.[39] Judge Sanford B. Dole, president of the Republic of Hawaii, boarded the *China* and invited the troops ashore. The men marched four miles from the port to Waikiki Beach where, as Guy Sims later recalled, "a group of Kanaka maids and matrons in their birthday suits were riding surf boards there. They moved over and made room for us and we had a swim."[40]

6. Hawaii Beach. *Photo courtesy of John Stewart Post Number One, Veterans of Foreign Wars.*

About noon, the men marched back toward Honolulu. Pvt. W. A. Pollard of K Company collapsed from "sunstroke" as the column entered the city. As his companions dragged Pollard into the shade, two servant women crossed the street and told the soldiers "Her Majesty says to bring him over to the palace. It's cooler there." The puzzled troops saw only a dingy two-story structure, but a small detail took advantage of the offer. With some surprise, they found themselves in Queen Liliuokalani's post-coup residence, in which she had secluded herself since American missionaries and business interests had toppled her government in 1893.[41] The Queen's unjust treatment by Americans had not eliminated her sympathy for one unfortunate private. After examination by the regimental surgeon, Pollard and his friends rejoined the rest of the First Colorado, greatly impressed by the deposed monarch's solicitude.

The remainder of the troops enjoyed the Queen's other house as well, although not with Liliuokalani's knowledge or consent. The marching column turned from the street onto the grounds of the Queen's former palace, confiscated by Dole's government. Under the palm trees, to the music of an orchestra, the soldiers "ate a dinner such as man is seldom privileged to enjoy."[42] Hawaiian waiters and American women served "delicious Hawaiian coffee" and "ice cold bottled soda."[43] Baker recalled that "beautiful brunettes attended our wants."[44] Charles Mabey, one of the Utah artillerymen accompanying the First Colorado, outdid even Baker in his florid description of the lawn party.

> Then under the shading palms, amid the fragrance of flowers, with hundreds of pretty girls to wait on them the men sat down to the banquet. . . . Soldiers made love to maidens with dusky cheeks; American blue eyes told short stories of love to Kanaka brown, and the Caucasian ladies were not forgotten, for it was a feast of love. Everywhere was "Aloha, Aloha."[45]

In a sense, the First Colorado's passage to Manila represents a steady broadening of horizons: from farm to Denver, Denver to San Francisco, San Francisco to Hawaii, Hawaii to the Philippines. The men greeted each new locale with a wonder verging on childish, but in Hawaii they had their first real exposure to alien peoples in their own society. The Great Hawaiian Picnic loomed large in every man's recollections of the war, in part due to the exotic setting, and also as a welcome respite from three months of military life. To an even greater degree, though, it was the food that thrilled the men. Guy Sims recalled, "and did we ever eat?" before noting ominously "and for a great many of the boys it was the last taste of 'white folks' vittles they ever had."[46]

Then came time to "sing for their supper." The men returned to the *China*, donned their accoutrements and weapons, marched back to the capitol, and staged a dress parade for President Dole.[47] The enlisted men complained that they had been allowed no individual liberty; in a rare relaxation of military routine, the officers released the men as squads, under corporals, to visit Honolulu until 9:00 P.M.[48] After their leave, the men climbed back aboard, while the quartet of Company H sang of their "Colorado homesteads far away."[49]

As the men enjoyed their tropical idyll, stevedores labored through the day and night, loading wheelbarrows of coal into the *China's* bunkers. On the morning of 24 June 1898, the ship left the dock, while well-wishers with little flags shouted "*Aloha Oe*." The *China* rejoined the rest of the fleet as it steamed out of Pearl Harbor, and the regiment resumed its long passage to the Philippines.[50]

The First Expedition, commanded by Civil War veteran Brig. Gen. Thomas H. Anderson, had sailed three weeks ahead of the First Colorado. The transports *City of Peking, Australia*, and *Sydney* were joined by the cruiser USS *Charleston*, commanded by Capt. Henry Glass. On 20 June 1898, three days before the Coloradoans reached Hawaii, Glass's guns forced the Spanish garrison on Guam to surrender in a comic-opera attack. The American cruiser fired on the Spanish fort with such little effect that the Spanish commander expressed his regrets at not being able to return the salute. Informed of the state of war, he surrendered without resistance or casualties.[51] That bloodless "conquest" marked an important escalation of America's expansion into the Pacific. Dewey's destruction of Spain's far-eastern fleet had led in turn to American infantry being dispatched to take and occupy Manila. Now, United States forces had taken an entire colony.

On 2 July 1898, at 10:00 A.M., the Second Expedition crossed the International Date Line, and found itself on 3 July.[52] The men were amazed at the peculiarities of the International Date Line. On the next day, the nation's birthday called for a full round of patriotic observances, calculated to sustain the men's enthusiasm for the coming conflict. At 9:30 A.M., the assembled men sang "America," followed by prayer. The glee club sang the "Coronation," and Chaplain Fleming read the *Declaration of Independence*. Before the festivities were over, the band and glee club had performed "Yankee Doodle/Dewey," "The Battle Hymn of the Republic," "Dixie," "Hail Columbia," and the "Star-Spangled Banner," and the men had endured no less than three speeches, by Gen. Francis Greene and two colonels.[53] The regiment especially enjoyed celebrating the Fourth of July before anyone in the United States. The patriotic observance completed, the *China* poured on the coal, and left the rest of the transports behind.

China had a total of thirty-two boilers but had only been using one bank of sixteen, in order to keep station with her slower sisters.[54] At full speed, she quickly outdistanced the fleet, and by "midforenoon" the other ships, and even their smoke, were out of sight astern.[55] By about noon, *China* reached Wake Island, another Spanish possession. The ship anchored, and a lifeboat of officers and sailors rowed three miles to shore, where they claimed the uninhabited island for the United States.[56] After raising an American flag on a rusty flagpole, they returned to the ship, having accomplished America's second Pacific "conquest." Theoretically, Wake could serve as a coaling station for the Navy, but only if it was garrisoned, and the *China* seems to have claimed Wake "because it was there." Wake, which would play so prominent a role in the early days of American combat in the Second World War, aroused almost no interest among the troops. Cpl. Roy Harris of Company I devoted little space in his diary to the "invasion." Instead, he noted that, while the ship lay anchored, the men caught "some fine fish," and that Pvt. Johnson Shobe had landed a six-foot, 124-pound shark.[57]

One of the First Colorado officers feared that, due to the "enervating effect of climate," the motto on the *China* was fast becoming "never do to-day what you can just as well put off until to-morrow."[58] The officers began easing up on the men, at least in terms of thinking up ways to keep them busy. To be sure, a certain amount of time was occupied simply with daily housekeeping and hygiene. If they could, the men slept on deck, to escape the stifling quarters improvised below decks. Access to the evening air carried its own penalty, however, in the form of a 4:00 A.M. awakening by the Chinese crew, crying "Get up, washee deck; get all wetee."[59] After breakfast, the enlisted men formed up to wash

7. The Capture of Wake Island. *Photo courtesy of John Stewart Post Number One, Veterans of Foreign Wars.*

themselves. As the ship's crew rigged a pump from the ocean, each man reached "deck with basin in hand, towel and soap under the left arm and campaign [hat] dangling by its string from a suspender button."[60] In addition, Mondays and Tuesdays were washdays, and the rails and rigging of the *China* were covered in laundry.[61]

Colonel Hale had no intention, however, of wasting the voyage to the Philippines. Marching drill might not be practical on deck, but other military skills could be honed. As the *China* had laid claim to Wake, the remainder of the fleet had joined up. Sailing unescorted by any armed naval vessels, the ships' captains and the officers of the troops feared an encounter with any Spanish gunboats or cruisers that might have escaped Dewey's flotilla. Partly to improve the men's proficiency, and partly in what must have been the rather forlorn hope of successfully defending themselves from a Spanish man-of-war, the military commanders of the expedition ordered the Utah artillery pieces lifted out of the holds. On board the *China*, the men built an immense wooden target, and on several successive days, the fleet stopped while the target was set afloat, "and advantageous shelling practice was indulged in."[62]

Like many militia units, the Utah Volunteer Light Artillery was armed with a mixture of outmoded artillery pieces. Half of Utah's Battery B had sailed on the *China*, with two 3.2-inch breech-loading rifles, short-range cannons little changed from Civil War design. In addition, the battery had Gatling guns, chambered either for the .45-caliber infantry cartridge adopted in 1873, or for a giant one-inch slug. The other half of Battery B, with two more rifles and more Gatlings, was on the *Zealandia*; the *Colon* carried all of Battery A.[63]

On 6 July 1898, the artillery tried its hand at the floating target. The fieldpieces performed well, but the complex and venerable Gatlings did not. When the first Gatling gun clanked into action, it "discharged with barrels in every position but the right one, and the bullets struck against portions of the carriage and went flying about the deck. Several men were wounded slightly."[64] It must have been a great relief to the ship's officers when target practice concluded for the day.

Two days later, on 8 July, the infantry had their turn.[65] George Fowler recalled that:

> For target practice they put floating targets in the water for us to shoot at. We aimed a little high sometimes and by the time we got there the keels had been shot off most of the lifeboats [hanging in their davits]. The captain about had a stroke when he saw that.[66]

Lt. Charles H. Hilton complained, "we have had rifle practice several times since by the entire fleet until the artillery has shot away just half of their ammunition, which is a good scheme, nit."[67] All things considered, target practice was probably not the best use of either time or ammunition, at least while the regiment was still at sea. Despite the wear-and-tear to the fabric of the *China*, the drill continued on 11 July.[68] Mercifully, the little fleet encountered no Spanish warships, and so the First Colorado were not endangered either by hostile fire or by their own.

The drill livened up endless days steaming west. Off duty, the men still had plenty of time to try to fill. There wasn't much to see on the ocean, although they did marvel at the flying fishes.[69] They took advantage of their exotic location to affect exotic appearance. Pvt. Richard McClellan of Company E shaved his entire head, except for a braided queue on top. Men who had beards cut them off; others grew goatees and moustaches. The officers joined in the game as well, with Capt. William Cornell and Lt. Charles Lewis removing their beards.[70]

Pvt. Arthur "Duke" Rogers of Company B carried a cigar box of dirt onto the *China*. When the men got homesick, he offered to show them "land" for five cents.[71] At the officers' instigation, the men assembled a canvas swimming tank on the forward deck, and there the men took turns splashing about in six-man squads, for five-minute turns per squad.[72] They listened to the band practice. They read books supplied by the Red Cross. They played cards. And they watched the Chinese.[73]

Pvt. Henry Myers of Company F, called "Harry" or, more commonly, "Johanna" by the men of the regiment, was a notorious prankster. At one point he climbed the rigging, and for half an hour entertained his comrades by giving the crew members such pseudo-Chinese orders as "Ki yi, um la ya, ki yi." The First Colorado, and by the troops' reports, the Chinese, were much amused, although one wonders how long it took for the joke to wear thin with the industrious crew.[74] In some surprise, Pvt. Al Silverstein wrote his mother to report:

The crew is a Chinese crew, and one's ideas of Chinamen change at seeing these neat little fellows running the ship; they run the kitchen also and make a big rake-off by selling rice at ten cents a cup, fried cakes, five for ten cents, etc.[75]

The regulars and Battery B ate reasonably well on board ship, but the First Colorado suffered from insufficient and badly cooked rations, at least at first. One problem was that the *China* sailed with part of Colorado's commissary supplies still on the dock. Thomas Jefferson Tarsney, former Adjutant General of Colorado, had a brother in Congress; despite the fact that Congress had abolished the system of post sutlers, traders with an exclusive license to sell to the troops, Tarsney secured an appointment as the First Colorado's sutler. He wangled free passage on the *China* for himself, and his clerk, and his boxes of trading stock, displacing rations intended for the men.[76] Some of what food was loaded turned out to be spoiled, and Commissary Sgt. George A. Fowler dumped it overboard.[77] Making matters worse, the officer appointed to distribute the rations had no experience at the job, and consistently provided the wrong foodstuffs in quantities too small.[78] The men turned their plight to music, sung to the tune of "Hallelujah! I'm a bum!"

> Hallelujah! This is punk!
> Hallelujah! This is bum!
> Hallelujah! O for God's sake
> Let our full rations come![79]

And, in desperation, the men bought food wherever they could, spending hundreds of dollars on canned goods and other edibles purchased from the Chinese and Japanese crew, from the other military units on board, and from hated Sutler Tarsney. The ship's cooks sold entire pies for fifty cents, while Tarsney was charging twenty cents a can for baked beans.[80] Although against orders, the men also purchased from the crew Chinese whiskey, described by an officer as "a grewsome [*sic*] mixture."[81]

At last, Colonel Hale found one of the ship's ladders blocked by a line of men buying donuts from the cooks. Inquiring what they were doing, the colonel finally learned of their hunger; furious, he ordered his officers to resolve the problem. Some officers got into the hold, opened the boxes of delicacies purchased in San Francisco with company funds, and distributed the contents to the men.[82] Other officers queried the man serving as commissary officer. "Have you had any experience in the subsistence department?" "None at all," he replied. "I suppose you have an experienced clerk, then?" "No, I was unable to find a clerk with any experience in the department." Disgusted, the First Colorado's commanders relieved him of commissary duty, and prevailed upon a lieutenant from the Eighteenth Infantry to take over the responsibility.[83] To solve the food preparation problem, the regiment set up a single general mess, appointed Company A's Pvt. John Dupps as chief cook, and assigned him capable assistants.[84] Food, and morale, improved immediately.

The men did get fresh meat. Each day, the "Big Swede," Fred Springstead of Company D, would kill two of the steers. The meat would hang for thirty-six hours, "to ripen," before being served.[85] "Billy" the goat lived with the steers until the last was killed; once all the hay was gone, he took to eating mattress straw.[86] With the men placated, the officers filed their own grievance. The Pacific Mail Steamship Company was charging each officer $1.50 per day for bad food. Forty-seven of the forty-nine volunteer and regular officers on board signed a protest, refusing to pay more than $1.00 per day; Colonel Hale's signature was first.[87] The *China's* passengers were not happy, and only arrival in the Philippines would really solve the problem.

With no way to communicate with the First Expedition, the little fleet proceeded from Wake to Guam, intending to rendezvous with the USS *Boston* and take the island. Finding no cruiser, and not realizing the island had already fallen, the ships steamed on. One day after leaving the vicinity of Guam, the Second Expedition met the American cruiser. The officers of the *Boston* advised that the *China* could outrun any of the Spanish ships remaining in the Pacific. Accordingly, the *China* increased her speed again, and left the rest of the transports behind to be escorted by the warship.[88]

The fleet had been averaging 221 miles each day; on her own, at her full speed of sixteen knots, the *China* managed 328 miles per day.[89] Late in the afternoon on 15 July 1898, the ship sighted the Philippine Islands. During the night, the *China* passed around the north of Luzon and down the western side of the island. Entering Manila Bay on 16 July, the ship passed Corregidor at 10:00 A.M., and dropped anchor off Cavite at noon.[90] With the First Expedition, which had arrived on 30 June 1898, the American forces now numbered some 6,000 men with which to take Manila.[91]

That very afternoon, a Japanese cruiser entered the bay, carrying the first word of the "double victory at Santiago, Cuba."[92] On 3 July 1898, the United States Army secured the heights overlooking Santiago's harbor, forcing Spanish Almirante Pascual Cervera y Topete's squadron to leave the protection of the port.[93] On the afternoon of 3 July, off the southern coast of Cuba, an American squadron commanded by Rear Adm. Winfield Scott Schley destroyed the entire Spanish fleet.[94] Santiago was the premier city of Cuba; its surrender could not be far off, and with its fall, Cuba would fall. Since Cuba's liberation was the ostensible purpose of the war with Spain, peace could come at any time. If the United States was to take Manila, the forces in the Philippines had better hurry. As yet, though, there still were not enough American infantry to take Manila, and so the reinforcements had to camp outside the city and wait until Merritt's entire force arrived.

Cavite, occupied since 3 May 1898 by American forces, was also Aguinaldo's headquarters. The U.S. authorities set up in the old Spanish arsenal, while the Filipino leader occupied a house in Cavite proper.[95] As yet, the only American troops across the bay, where Manila lay, were a battalion of the First California Volunteer Infantry, who had gone into camp at Malate, south of Manila, on 15 July 1898.[96] One-half mile from Dewey's fleet, German, English, Japanese, and French warships lay, "apparently watching each other and awaiting developments." With Spanish control in the Philippines teetering, the archipelago might be "up for grabs" by a replacement colonizing power. Due to the unclear diplomatic situation, the American ships maintained a blackout at night, to guard against surprises.[97]

The *Boston* arrived with the other ships of the Second Expedition on 17 July 1898.[98] General Greene promptly shifted his headquarters from the *China* to the *Boston*, and the expedition set about debarking.[99] Short of off-loading the troops at Cavite and marching them around Manila Bay, there was no easy way to place the men in front of Manila, for the Spanish still held the port facilities. In the late afternoon of 17 July 1898, the side-wheel steamer *Isabella 2nd*, joined by the *Olympia*'s steam launches towing native *cascoes*, arrived to begin ferrying men to shore. Cascoes were large barge-like craft, perhaps fifty feet in length, used in the rivers and bays of the Philippines, and ordinarily poled rather than sailed. Company K filed onto the side-wheeler, while the remainder of the regiment scrambled onto the cascoes, for their voyage across the bay.[100]

The steam vessels towed the barges eight miles, to the village of Marricaban, about three-and-a-half miles from Manila. Three-quarters of a mile from shore, the *Isabella 2nd* hove to, unable to approach closer due to her draft. Company K transferred to canoes, paddled by Filipinos, and caught up with the launch-towed cascoes. The men splashed ashore through three feet of water, stacked their arms, stripped to their blue shirts only, and then waded out to offload the cascoes.[101] As dark fell, the first sergeants called the companies together, and the regiment marched 150 yards to a field. Formed up in two ranks, each rear rank man and the front rank man before him were designated as "bunkies" for the night. After a lackluster supper of hardtack and "salt horse" (tinned beef), the exhausted men collapsed on their gear, and slept in the open in a steady rain. As it turned out, 17 July 1898 was only the beginning of five days of back-breaking labor.[102]

The next morning, the men erected their tiny "pup tents" by buttoning each man's canvas shelter half to that of his bunkie.[103] The assembled tent was four feet square and three-and-a-half feet high, and both heads and feet projected from the canvas.[104] Not knowing what to expect when they landed, the First Colorado had offloaded ten days' rations. Each man landed with his rifle, cartridge belt, canteen, a blanket roll containing soap, towel, underwear, two pair of socks, a shirt, an "abdominal bandage," and a haversack containing a day's rations and his eating utensils. In case of a surprise attack by the Spanish, they could move out with short notice and "hit the hasty," reported Pvt. Arthur C. Johnson of Company E.[105]

The *China* moved to within four miles of shore; the *Boston* anchored halfway between her and the beach, to cover the landing against any Spanish assault.[106] On board the *China*, some of the First Colorado labored to swing the cargo up out of the holds and down onto the cascoes.[107] The loaded lighters could only approach to within 200 to 300 yards of the beach. Each day, the men struggled through the water, trying to carry the regimental gear ashore without soaking it.[108] The lightest of the Utah guns, little 1.65-inch Hotchkiss mountain guns, were dropped off in five feet of water and hauled out by hand.[109] While the infantry labored, the artillerymen and a detachment of U.S. Engineers improvised a "sort of dock" some 300 yards out into the bay. On 20 July, the artillery and the First Colorado transferred the battery's larger guns from the *China*, to cascoes, to the dock, to land, and then to the camp.[110]

Finally, on 22 July 1898, the Colorado hospital landed from the *China*. Less than 200 yards from the beach, one hundred infantrymen erected both the regimental field hospital and the brigade hospital, together in large tents. By nightfall, "Camp Dewey" was complete.[111]

It simply proved too difficult to unload the *China* by casco, and only essentials came ashore this way. The *China* was dispatched to Hong Kong, 500 miles away, to pick up more supplies, and return in two or three weeks. Hopefully, by her return, Manila would have fallen, and the *China* could

8. Mascot Billy in the Company street. *Photo courtesy of John Stewart Post Number One, Veterans of Foreign Wars.*

use the port facilities.[112] Such were the logistics of amphibious supply in an era before the invention of the specialized landing craft of Second World War fame. The *China* sailed away, carrying much of the regiment's baggage and a detail of her men. The men of the First Colorado had their personal military gear, but no Sibley tents and no "Buzzacot Ovens," the complete camp kitchens for preparing the rations. They could fight, and they could get wet, and they could eat out of their haversacks.

Camp Dewey lay three miles south of the line of insurrecto trenches surrounding Manila, which in turn were a mile from the Spanish defenses. The camp itself measured one mile from end to end.[113] Two companies at a time were sent on "outpost duty" about two miles north of the camp, well back from the insurrecto lines, in order to give advance warning of any Spanish breakout.[114] Enlisted men had to remain within one mile of the camp, but in truth, they had little time to stray.[115] Reveille brought them from their shelters at 4:45 A.M., and then they drilled in the rain. The monsoon season in the Philippines runs from June until September, with twenty-five inches of rain possible in a twenty-four-hour period.[116] Drill was followed by breakfast, in the rain. After eating, the men cleaned their muskets, oiling them liberally against the moisture, and then they fell in for morning drill—in the rain. Finally, they were released from duty, unless they were assigned to either the guard mount, or the "police gang" that cleaned the camp or kitchen gear.[117]

The men did their best to stay dry. They cut bamboo rods to raise their canvas higher than the regulation poles would permit. The additional headroom let them build a floor to lift themselves up out of the mud. Bamboo stakes supported stringers for the floor, and plaited bamboo strips served as mattresses and suspended tables.[118] Still, it was a losing battle.

One First Colorado officer marveled:

> It beats all creation how it can rain out here. Rain is all right in its way. Some of it is a good thing. It keeps things reasonably clean and furnishes drinking water. But one steady, undisturbed, imperturbable, unceasing flood becomes tiresome after a while, and all the time it is wet. You don't mind an occasional soaking. It gives excuse for taking a drink. But one has something to do down here besides change his clothes and drink whisky. And wet feet bring fever.[119]

Especially during the monsoons, malaria, dengue fever, and dysentery are common in the Philippines, and smallpox was an ever-present danger.[120] To combat malaria, the men lined up with their tin cups in the company streets for a daily dose of quinine, taken in liquid form and cut with water.[121] Against smallpox, the hospital corps vaccinated the men in the field, revaccinating if necessary. Back in Colorado, the women of the "soldiers' aid societies" had knitted "abdominal bandages," popularly believed to guard against tropical fevers. Each man received one on boarding the *China*; one employed his as a belt, another used his as a muffler around his neck.[122] Also, the men boiled their water to try to prevent dysentery.

Although they were waiting for the rest of the American Army to arrive, the regiment had come to the Philippines to fight the Spanish. The Coloradoans had their first alarm on 19 July 1898. After a hard day unloading cascoes, the men swam in the ocean, and then turned in. In the middle of the night, each company's bugler sounded the "Call to Arms." To the front, the men could hear a fusillade. Some of the men were prepared to turn out, and some were not. The regiment double-timed two miles through the darkness in a column, and then collapsed gasping when they reached the Colorado outposts.[123] Six weeks on shipboard had sapped their fitness. Fortunately, their haste turned out to be needless. Insurrecto forces had attacked and taken the Santolan pumping station that supplied Manila's domestic water. As the Spanish garrison from the waterworks tried to fight its way back to Manila, the Spanish lines began firing in the general direction of the Filipino trenches. Panicked insurrectos fled through the Colorado outposts. The outposts notified Col. Irving Hale. The regiment's newly acquired signaling ability proved useful. As the First Colorado rushed to support its outposts against what seemed like a Spanish attack, the regiment's signalmen used lanterns on the beach to "wig wag" to General Greene on the *Boston*. A storm was about to break, and Greene relayed his orders back to Colonel Hale by using the cruiser's searchlights to bounce his message off the low clouds.[124]

The First Colorado eventually learned that the Spanish and Filipinos routinely engaged in nighttime volley firing, to no particular purpose, but Hale did not yet know this. Unused to the pattern of Spanish-Filipino night firing exercises, the colonel called up the remainder of the regiment to reinforce the outposts; after the alarm died down, they returned to camp. The men at least had learned, however, to retire prepared to respond to a nighttime alarm.[125]

The First California Infantry felt some sense of competition with the First Colorado. As the Colorado troops double-timed past the California camp on their way to the front, the Californians fell in and followed. On discovering the false alarm, the Californians made some snide recriminations about "Colorado's panic"; the allegations would enliven the pages of newspapers in both states for a short time.[126]

Ship by ship, reinforcements continued arriving in Manila. General Merritt finally left San Francisco on 29 June 1898, sailing with an "expedition" commanded by Gen. Arthur MacArthur. The ships of that flotilla arrived at Manila on 25 July and 31 July. There, they joined the troops of the two earlier expeditions. Merritt himself landed on 26 July. The first expedition, commanded by Brig. Gen. Thomas M. Anderson, was ashore in Cavite. The second, led by Brig. Gen. Francis V. Greene and forming as a brigade under Anderson, had landed just south of Manila at Malate.[127] The First Colorado was part of Greene's brigade. With troops still on transports in the harbor, as well as on land at Cavite and outside Manila itself, and more in transit across the Pacific, Merritt needed to bring some order to his rapidly growing force. On 1 August 1898, the Department of the Pacific and Eighth Army Corps issued General Order No. 2, assembling all the American forces already in the Philippines into the Second Division, with Brigadier General Anderson, United States Volunteers, commanding. That division, in turn, was divided into two brigades. Brigadier General MacArthur, U.S.V., commanded the First Brigade. The Second Brigade, led by Brigadier General Greene, U.S.V., included Batteries A and B of the Utah Light Artillery and the First Colorado, among others.[128] To signify that the First Colorado was in the Second Brigade of the Second Division of the Eighth Army Corps, they wore a "white 8" as their insignia.[129]

Merritt's 19 May instructions from President William McKinley announced a "twofold purpose of completing the reduction of the

TABLE 2:

U.S. Army Command Structure: Philippines, 1898–1899

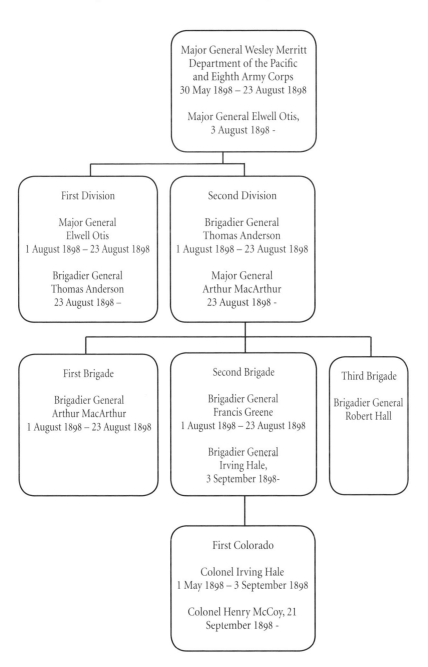

Major General Wesley Merritt
Department of the Pacific
and Eighth Army Corps
30 May 1898 – 23 August 1898

Major General Elwell Otis,
3 August 1898 -

First Division

Major General
Elwell Otis
1 August 1898 – 23 August 1898

Brigadier General
Thomas Anderson
23 August 1898 –

Second Division

Brigadier General
Thomas Anderson
1 August 1898 – 23 August 1898

Major General
Arthur MacArthur
23 August 1898 -

First Brigade

Brigadier General
Arthur MacArthur
1 August 1898 – 23 August 1898

Second Brigade

Brigadier General
Francis Greene
1 August 1898 – 23 August 1898

Brigadier General
Irving Hale,
3 September 1898-

Third Brigade

Brigadier General
Robert Hall

First Colorado

Colonel Irving Hale
1 May 1898 – 3 September 1898

Colonel Henry McCoy, 21
September 1898 -

Spanish power and of giving order and security to the islands while in the possession of the United States."[130] Those orders gave Merritt broad power and little direction, in part because the President was unsure of his own intentions. Merritt's role was to maintain American options, and any official recognition of Aguinaldo's government would restrict those options. The Filipinos were not strong enough to take Manila by themselves. If Aguinaldo's troops assisted in taking Manila, their participation would enhance the Filipino leader's authority, and it might prove difficult to eject them from the city after the victory. Given the past conduct of the insurrectos as they drove the Spanish from the countryside, the American commander feared the Filipinos would slaughter the Spanish troops and civilians in Manila, if they got the chance. Merritt even considered whether or not to wait for more troops before assaulting Manila, in case he had to fight the Spanish and Filipinos simultaneously. In the end, he avoided treating directly with Aguinaldo, while maintaining the illusion of alliance.[131]

Merritt's first step in preventing Filipino participation in the assault was to interpose American troops between the insurrectos and the city. This plan suited the Coloradoans, since they regarded the Filipino forces as a thin reed upon which to rely for any protection from a Spanish assault. The Colorado outposts were small circular depressions, scattered in front of the Coloradoans between them and the Filipino lines. Each was occupied by a noncommissioned officer and three or four men, serving as pickets to keep an eye on the enemy and provide early warning of any attack. In the event of any general Spanish assault, the Coloradoans feared the Filipinos would flee, and the First Colorado's pickets, which they called "cossack posts," would be quickly overwhelmed.[132] The Colorado regiment felt they needed more effective fortifications between them and the enemy. General Merritt refused to deal directly with Filipino patriot leader Emilio Aguinaldo, but hoped to avoid friction with the native troops. He delegated General Greene to approach Mariano Noriel, the Filipino commander closest to Manila, to negotiate a Filipino withdrawal from the trenches to the south of the city. Greene promised Noriel several "fine pieces of artillery" if he would yield the southern trenches to the American troops. Aguinaldo, twelve miles away at Bacoor, agreed, provided that General Merritt sign the request. Greene promised to send the signed paper, after the Filipinos vacated the trenches, and Aguinaldo naively agreed.

As darkness fell late on 29 July 1898, Americans took over the Filipino trenches on the south side of Manila, and promptly reneged on both the artillery and the letter. Displaying a degree of prescience, Noriel rushed to Aguinaldo and, near tears, exclaimed "Look what they're doing! If we're not careful, they will soon be replacing our flags with their own all over the country!"[133] As part of the general American movement, the First Colorado moved into the Filipino trenches adjacent to the bay, as the insurrectos vacated them. Guy Sims recalled that the empty trenches "looked and smelled too rich for us so we crept up a little closer to the Spanish line and dug in about 1000 yards from Fort San Antonio [de Abad]."[134] Half the regiment dug a new line of earthworks until midnight, and then rested while the other half dug.[135]

At dawn, the First Nebraska relieved the Coloradoans in the trench line, and the First Colorado began their three-mile march back to camp, and their breakfast. With daylight, the Spanish discovered the new fortifications and began firing in the general vicinity of the Nebraska troops. To the rear, stray Spanish rounds, fired high over the Nebraskans, began to fall amidst the Colorado troops. Pvt. William H. Sterling of Company K joked about the possibility of being wounded, exclaiming "ouch" with each overhead whine. When a Mauser bullet passed through the fleshy part of his left arm, his corporal at first refused to believe he'd actually been hit. As yet, the men had no first-aid kits, or instructions on what to do with the wounded. After some confusion, they got Sterling back to camp.[136] Because his wound was relatively minor, Sterling survived and stayed with the unit, but he had earned the dubious honor of being the first American soldier in the Manila campaign to be wounded.[137]

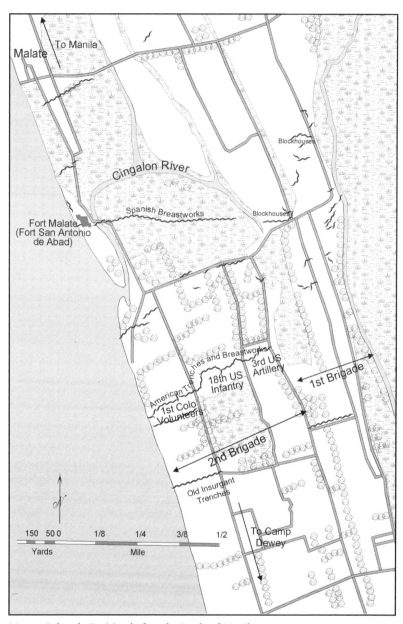

Map 1. Colorado Position before the Battle of Manila

With the Americans in new lines, General Greene removed his headquarters to the shore. He needed a system to alert his various regiments to any crisis. Overlooking the ground between the trenches and Manila, his engineers and signalmen converted a big tree into a signal tower by building a bamboo tower on top of it. Early each morning, they camouflaged the side toward the Spanish with fresh greenery, removing the wilted foliage from the day before. In the tower, men were on duty twenty-four hours each day, ready with flag by day and lanterns by night. The First Colorado's position was in easy viewing distance from the top of the tower.[138]

Utah's Battery A moved two guns into the Colorado line on the morning of 30 July. That night was marked by considerable small arms fire from the Spanish lines. Utah's Battery B, with two more guns, joined the Colorado forces on the 31st.[139] The First Utah Light Artillery left Salt Lake City with twelve guns, including 3.2-inch B.L. (breech-loading) rifles, 1.65-inch Hotchkiss Mountain Guns, and Gatling guns.[140] At the end of the Civil War, the Army had embraced the muzzle-loading 3-inch Ordnance Rifle as an effective general-purpose fieldpiece. Many were later converted to a breech-loading configuration, and relabeled as the 3-inch B.L. The gun's next evolution was the entirely new 3.2-inch B.L. Steel Rifle (Model 1891), a field artillery piece capable of firing solid shot, explosive shells, and antipersonnel canister rounds which contained over 100 small projectiles.[141] The 1.65-inch Hotchkiss Mountain Guns were small wheeled guns, designed to be hauled by one mule or packed by three. Highly mobile, they had been popular with the Indian-fighting Army, and were used by the Seventh Cavalry in the grim fight at Wounded Knee in 1890. They could fire either high explosive or canister rounds. Because the little breech-loaders used fixed ammunition, with projectile and propellant contained in one cartridge resembling a giant rifle cartridge, they were also called Rapid Fire Guns, but they were rapid only in comparison to the muzzle-loading 12-pound Mountain Howitzers they had replaced. It was the portable Mountain Guns that

Utah deployed in the Colorado line; firing canister, they would serve as giant shotguns, devastating any Spanish attack. Their firepower was most welcome. Guy Sims recalled that "Utah Battery was with us so much we came to consider them our battery and got quite well acquainted with the men. We had great respect for those 'red-whiskered Mormons' and I think the respect was mutual."[142]

By nightfall on 31 July 1898, the First Colorado's trenches were anchored on the sea, and reinforced by the four Utah guns. On Colorado's right, to the east, lay the lines of the First Nebraska, with the Tenth Pennsylvania beyond them, and Filipino forces farther yet. Perhaps to test the mettle of the newcomers, perhaps in an attempt to intimidate the Americans, the Spanish sortied from their lines at 11:30 P.M. on the 31st, attacking the Pennsylvanians.[143] Observing from the Colorado lines, Charles Mabey described the ensuing action: "The 10th Pennsylvania troops replied with their Springfields and the whiz of the '45s mingled with the keen 'twang' of the Mausers, while the 3rd Artillerymen, equipped as regular infantry, took a part in the altercation."[144]

The firing quickly spread up and down the lines. Musician George R. Fisher of Battery A of the Utah Light Artillery noted that the Colorado infantrymen fixed their bayonets "for a charge if things came to the worse."[145] Spanish artillery began shelling the American trenches. The Utah guns replied, drawing enemy attention. Spanish counter-battery fire overturned one of the guns on its crew, slightly wounding one man. First Colorado Pvt. Benjamin Lloyd of Company K, in the trenches alongside the silenced gun, suffered two ruptured eardrums in the barrage, and was eventually invalided home due to deafness.[146] Despite drawing Spanish fire, the Utah guns proved their worth, firing fifty-seven "shrapnel" antipersonnel shells before they had to be replenished.[147]

The entrenched Coloradoans fired steadily into the darkness in front of their lines, eventually forcing the Spanish to retire to their own fortifications, from which the enemy poured thousands of rounds into the American trenches throughout the night. Before dawn on 1 August 1898,

ten Americans had been killed, the first U.S. dead in the Philippines.[148]
The First Colorado was not spared. Fred Springstead, a twenty-one-year-
old private in Company D, was shot through the head by a Mauser round
and killed instantly. Among the wounded, in addition to Private Lloyd,
was Pvt. Edward L. Zachary of Company G, with a bullet through his
right thigh. The war had become real for the boys from Colorado.[149]

Despite its losses, the regiment had weathered its first real combat, and
the men were cocky. Arthur Johnson, describing the fight, told his readers
back in Colorado that "the firing was suggestive of Americanism."[150]
Each night afterwards, from then through 12 August, the Spanish fired
on the American trenches, which fire the Americans returned; each
day the First Colorado devoted to "battle practice."[151] While most of the
men drilled, those detailed to the fortifications lay in flooded trenches,
guarding against a Spanish assault. Each night, the Spanish and Filipinos
would stage half-hearted attacks on each other's lines, without any gain,
and often without any loss.[152] Arthur Sims exclaimed in disgust, "[T]hey
seem to do most of their firing in the night!"[153] The Filipinos could
threaten, but not take, the Spanish lines, and so they had no particular
incentive to risk their lives by exposing themselves to Spanish fire. For
the Spanish, posted at the farthest reach of empire, it seemed clear that
the war with the Americans was likely to result in Manila's surrender and
their eventual repatriation to Spain; it would be a shame to be the last
man killed fighting the Filipinos. Over time, the Americans accustomed
themselves to the lackadaisical course of Spanish-Filipino combat. Capt.
William Grove explained to his wife that:

> the insurgents are very poor shots, and seem to think that all
> they have to do is to point a gun toward Manila and pull the
> trigger. I don't think the Spaniards are much better.[154]

Lt. Rice Means reported, in fact, that even with the advantage of
Manila's stone walls, some of the Spanish used a "field glass of peculiar

construction" (presumably an early trench periscope) to look over the parapets without exposing themselves to Filipino fire.[155] During the day, both the Spanish and the insurrectos slept; the First Colorado quickly learned to join them in the afternoon nap.[156] The Filipinos treated the siege as a commuter war. They took their turns in the trenches, in one of three shifts every twenty-four hours, and returned to their homes in temporary villages set up by their families to eat and sleep.[157] For their part, the Spanish didn't dare issue forth from their walls to pursue the Filipinos, for fear the insurrectos would hide beside the roads and ambush the Spanish troops with their "*bolos*," heavy long knives more like a short sword, originally designed to cut bamboo.[158] Without American intervention, the stalemate could continue indefinitely, or until Manila exhausted its food supplies.

A much more vicious war developed in the bamboo thickets between the American trenches and the enemy lines, where Spanish and First Colorado sharpshooters dueled by day.[159] Exasperated by one Spanish sniper, Pvt. William Beatty removed part of his uniform, waded through a ditch, and crept to within 150 yards of the Spaniard's position. There, he wiggled a clump of grass to draw the sniper's fire, which hit a foot and a half away. Beatty shot the Spaniard, then hustled back to his own lines, under fire from the sniper's fellows.[160] By night, American volunteers crept through the no-man's land, advance scouts to warn their fellows in the trenches of any oncoming sneak attack by the Spanish. Guy Sims recalled, "Soon after landing my brother [Arthur Sims] and I settled into our nitch [*sic*]—night patrol—prowling the jungle all night five to seven nights a week. We slept daytimes."[161]

Colorado suffered no losses in the "little war" between the lines. On the other hand, the small Red Cross flag erected in front of the First Colorado's hospital tents was shot through six times by Spanish bullets, which the Americans believed indicated a deliberate disregard for the rules of war. Arthur Johnson concluded that "it is little short of jungle warfare."[162]

While men patrolled the area before the lines, other details reconnoitered the Spanish defenses, preparing for the American assault. Manila itself was enclosed by a stone wall fourteen feet high and eight feet thick. The city was partially protected on the north and west by a swamp, and on the south by Manila Bay itself.[163] Outside the city walls, at the southeast corner of Manila and directly opposite the Colorado lines, lay Fort San Antonio de Abad. Perhaps 100 yards from the shoreline at high tide, the triangular fort was old but still formidable. Its solid masonry walls stood ten feet thick and twelve to fourteen feet high; on top sat five rapid-fire three-inch guns, three of them relatively light Krupp-pattern mountain guns, the other two heavier Nordenfeldt models. At one corner stood a flagpole, proudly displaying the Spanish flag.[164] When the assault came, Fort San Antonio de Abad would have to be destroyed, or taken by storm, before the American line could pass it to advance on the city proper.

Second Lt. Rice W. Means of Company E was, at age twenty, the youngest officer in the First Colorado. Son of a Denver police sergeant, Means was an ambitious and daring young man. In part of the general reconnaissance effort, he crawled through the foliage and actually touched the wall of Manila, claiming to be the first American to do so.[165] As assault plans firmed up, Means, Sgt. Harry L. Clotworthy, and a Major Bell of the U.S. Engineers surveyed Fort San Antonio de Abad by sea, swimming to within 100 yards of the walls.[166]

Despite all the preparations, the siege remained remarkably genteel. Commodore Dewey had refrained from shelling Manila, in consideration of its civilian population. The Spanish artillery barrage against the American lines on the night of 31 July–1 August 1898 had marked an escalation of the "hostilities." To the Americans, it seemed that the Spanish were using the civilians as hostages, firing from their positions and counting on American consideration for the noncombatants to prevent any return fire. After the Spanish shelled the Americans a second time, on 5 August, General Merritt and Commodore Dewey replied on 7 August by issuing a joint demand that Jaudenes remove noncombatants from the city, preparatory to an American bombardment of Manila.[167] Obviously, the Spanish had no way to comply, but Spanish artillery barrages ceased.

Simply put, the Spanish and American authorities were engaged in a high-stakes game, to see who would flinch first. Jaudenes was under orders from Spain to hold out, and Dewey and Merritt were under orders from the United States to take Manila. Jaudenes could not simply hand Manila over, for reasons of orders and honor, but better by far to surrender to the Americans than to Aguinaldo. With food running out, the Spanish position was untenable. On 9 August, the Spanish responded to the Merritt/Dewey ultimatum, explaining that they could not evacuate the noncombatants, due to the insurrectos encircling the city. The American commanders replied with a formal demand for surrender of Manila and its garrison. Foreign warships cleared the anchorage in front of Manila, and the U.S. fleet cleared for action.[168]

The First Colorado stood guard mount at Camp Dewey for the last time on 12 August 1898. The officers ordered the men to prepare to take part in a combined naval and land battle to take Manila, beginning early the next morning. Each man was issued 200 rounds of ammunition, carrying 45 rounds in his canvas web belt loops, and 155 more in his haversack.[169] Each also received two days' field rations, consisting of a can of salmon or beef and a box of hard tack crackers. Recognizing the gravity of the next day's enterprise, the officers also distributed "first help" kits with compresses and bandages—one kit for every two men![170]

Early on the morning of 13 August 1898, while it was still totally dark, the men rolled their possessions into blanket rolls, tagged each with their name, company, and regiment, and left them in their pup tents.[171] Each man retained his waterproof poncho as his only shelter against the steady rain.[172] Except for the haversack with his extra ammunition and his meager rations, each man carried in addition only his rifle and bayonet, and a canteen. Half the canteens held cold coffee, half carried boiled water.[173]

After breakfast and roll call, the troops marched down to Colonel Hale's tent, where the regiment formed a hollow square, for prayer. Guy Sims recalled, "good old Chaplain Fleming was such a poor talker, he had to read from a book of prayers that someone else had written and that was what he did this time."[174] Concluding by leading men in the "Lord's Prayer," the chaplain closed his book and added one line of his own: "And now, Oh God, we ask thy mercy upon the souls of those among us who have just now answered roll call for the last time on Earth. Amen."[175] As the regiment marched by column out of Camp Dewey, the rival Californians, assigned to the reserve, cheered them on their way.[176]

General Greene commanded the Second Brigade on the left of the American line, touching Manila Bay. Colorado formed up at the extreme left of that line, from the sea inland. To their right stood the Eighteenth United States Infantry; together the First Colorado and the Eighteenth U.S. made up the assault wave of the Second Brigade. Behind the Colorado volunteers and the regulars, Greene arrayed the First California, Tenth Pennsylvania, and First Idaho Volunteer Infantry regiments, along with a four-company battalion of the First Wyoming Infantry, as a powerful reserve. To the right of the regulars, Gen. Arthur MacArthur commanded the First Brigade.[177]

Just before 10:00 A.M., the cruiser *Olympia* began shelling the southernmost defenses of Manila, including Ft. San Antonio de Abad, while the remainder of the fleet fired against other sections of the Spanish fortifications. From the American trenches, the Utah guns began firing as well.[178] One-half hour after the bombardment began, General Greene ordered his infantry to begin their assault, even though rain prevented attempts to signal the fleet to cease fire.[179] As the First Colorado stepped off, General Greene handed the brigade national colors to Regimental Adj. Lt. Alix McD[onald] "Don" Brooks, with instructions to raise the flag over the fort.[180]

On the right, six companies of the regiment crossed their breastworks and began firing on the Spanish from hedges 300 yards away. The other half of the First Colorado proceeded as a column along the beach, waded waist-deep through the mouth of the Rio Cingalon, and then deployed into a battle formation for the actual assault against Fort San Antonio de Abad.[181]

The First Colorado formed a skirmish line, a sort of open regimental front, in which the men from Companies C and K spaced themselves as a firing line so as to cover the rest of the regiment.[182] *Harper's Weekly* printed a widely reproduced cover illustration depicting the Colorado volunteers assaulting the fort in a column; over it, one of the veterans scrawled "Incorrect. Advanced in skirmish lines—firing line, support, reserve."[183] The fort's walls were undefended, cleared by *Olympia's* shellfire, but enemy infantry in their trenches continued firing on the Colorado volunteers. Fortunately, the American fleet ceased firing as the Colorado troops waded the river.

The only correspondent to accompany the First Colorado in the assault was John Bass of *Harper's*, and in the excitement he was actually in front of the firing line, shooting his "Kodak on the run." Colonel Hale, carrying a megaphone given him by Captain Seabury of the *China*, vehemently ordered him to get behind the ranks. The reading public back in Colorado expected their colonel to be above the use of swear words; Hale explained to Governor Adams that any reported profanity was simply a naval residue inadvertently dislodged from the borrowed megaphone.[184]

Moving forward over the bodies of Spanish defenders killed by the naval guns, the troops entered the largely abandoned fort at 11 o'clock.[185] That portion of the garrison able to flee had done so, as the American infantry advanced. Lt. Ralph Lister and Lt. Col. Henry McCoy hauled down the Spanish flag from the pole at the seaward corner of the fort's firing platform; Adjutant Brooks hoisted the American flag given him by General Greene. Thus, Colorado raised the first flag to fly over the Spanish defenses at Manila.[186]

Within the fort, Pvt. Guy Sims found a hiding Spaniard who had

9. Advancing through the Spanish trenches. *Photo courtesy of John Stewart Post Number One, Veterans of Foreign Wars.*

shot himself in the foot. Sims handed him over to a superior, and then entered a doorway. Inside, he found a Spanish surgeon wearing a Red Cross band on his arm, laboring over a room full of Spanish wounded.[187] Historian Stanley Karnow has cited the lack of strong resistance at Fort San Antonio de Abad as proof that the "assault" on Manila was in fact a sham concocted by Commodore Dewey and General Jaudenes to preserve Spanish honor.[188] Given the position of the Spanish, both globally and within Manila, such an agreement would have made perfect sense. From the casualties suffered both by the Spanish garrison and, during the day, by the American attackers, it is clear that, if such an agreement existed, news of its provisions failed to reach the troops in the opposing lines. Alternately, the Spanish and American commanders may have callously accepted such casualties as the price of credibility.

With the fort captured, the First Colorado moved on against Manila itself. Exiting the fort, the First Colorado came under a fusillade from a thicket 500 yards distant, to which the survivors of the fort's garrison had fled. The volunteers entered the Spanish trenches, now abandoned, and returned fire. The speed with which the enemy had departed is attested to by Guy Sims's discovery, in the zigzag communication trench connecting the fort to the Spanish trenches, of a "silk Spanish flag, fullsize regimental colors with number of regiment on it, still on staff."[189]

As the Spanish bullets zipped overhead, the First Colorado soldiers were amazed to hear the strains of "Dixie," followed by "Hot Time in the Old Town Tonight," as the regimental band jauntily rounded the corner of the fort! Bandmaster Harry Irvine had led his men up the beach, through the river, and toward the sound of the gunfire, playing all the while.[190] This daring exploit has often been cited as an example of extraordinary *sang-froid*, but the band's principal musician, Verner Campbell, offered another explanation.

> We were in a hurry to get there because we thought the battle was over. It wasn't until after we quit playing that we heard the bullets flying around us. We ducked behind a ridge and played some more. Then I opened a can of meat and commenced my dinner.[191]

As the men hurriedly gulped down their lunch of by-now-lukewarm water, hard tack, and canned salmon or beef, members of the Third United States Artillery brought up three one-pounder guns, drawn by water buffaloes or *carabao* impressed from the Filipinos.[192] After a ten-minute break, and supported by the guns, the First Colorado fixed bayonets and drove the Spanish from the thicket into Malate, a suburb of Manila built up against the city walls.[193] As the men advanced through the streets of Malate, bullets flying, the band gamely followed along, playing "Dixie."[194]

As the regiment entered Malate, the men passed a Spanish headquarters. Wishing Colorado to be first to raise a flag over the actual city, Lt. Col. Cassius Moses ordered Sgt. Richard Holmes, the regimental color bearer, to place a flag on the building's roof. Holmes carried the national standard, followed by Sgt. Charles Clark bearing the regimental colors. They were supported by Pvts. Alfred Miller and Claude West of Company E, the color company, and by Pvt. Charles Phenix, a sharpshooter detailed from Company I.[195] Finding no stair to the roof, the detail ascended to the top floor and displayed the national and regimental colors from a second-story window. The First Colorado had succeeded in raising the first flag over both Manila's fortifications, at Fort San Antonio de Abad, and the city itself, in the district of Malate.[196]

That triumph came at a high cost. As Holmes and Clark unfurled their banners, they drew enemy fire. Private Phenix, standing between them, was shot through the neck by a Spanish sniper and mortally wounded; he would die three days later. In addition, Pvt. Frank Smith of Company H was slightly wounded in the neck while his unit advanced up the Calle Real in Malate.[197]

The troops moved steadily through Malate, until late afternoon found them at the Puente de España, one of the entrances to Manila itself. Pvt. Carl Larsen of Company C wrote a friend, "we went across the bridge . . . a wonder nobody got killed there, the bullets came pretty thick."[198] As the First Colorado crossed the bridge, the band knew exactly the music to play while taking an enemy city: "Marching Through Georgia!"[199] The musicians followed with "Dixie" and "Yankee Doodle," and then, as the soldiers tramped through Manila's business district and linked up with other American columns in the plaza, finished up with "Hail Columbia."[200] American troops had forced their way into Manila at several points along its perimeter, although Spanish soldiers still guarded large segments of the line against the Filipinos.

Jaudenes capitulated at 4:30 P.M., surrendering not only his garrison and Manila, but 23,000 modern Mauser rifles and eighteen artillery pieces.[201] The band gave one last performance. As the American flag rose over the office of the Captain of the Port, Bandmaster Harry Irvine led the musicians in "The Star-Spangled Banner," the first time Americans ever played that tune to Philippine citizens.[202] After one hour in the plaza, the First Colorado moved into "New" or North Manila.[203] The exhausted soldiers, collapsed in the roadway by the Tondo Bridge, ate their supper of canned beef and hard tack.[204] Their day still was not over. As evening fell, they took up new posts at the eastern gates of Manila, guarding against their erstwhile allies, the insurrectos. While details guarded Sampoloc and Sebastian, the bulk of the regiment settled in on the floor of the monastery at San Sebastian, appropriated from the monks without their permission. Company H garrisoned Fort San Antonio de Abad.[205]

The victory over the Spanish was sweet, although the Colorado men mourned their casualties. In its 19 August 1898 issue, the *Denver Times* printed boxes flanking the masthead, reading:

> The flag that Colorado bore,
> Was first to float on Luzon's shore.
> Then cheers for Holmes who placed it there,
> And tears for hero Phenix's share.[206]

More poignantly, Mrs. Jane Springstead, mother of slain Fred Springstead, wrote, "all my hopes lie buried in that far distant grave."[207] The regiment's casualties aside, diplomacy also marred the triumph. In Washington, D.C., on 12 August 1898, one day before Manila's conquest, American Secretary of State William R. Day and Monsieur Jules Cambon, French ambassador to the United States, signed the protocol with Spain that established an immediate cease-fire. Manila fell one day too late, but that information only arrived in Manila on 16 August.[208] Her losses had not been necessary. Nonetheless, the First Colorado and the other American forces had accomplished their mission, and beaten the "Dons." The state volunteers had answered the nation's call, trained aggressively, and performed well in combat, and the National Guard had quickly folded into combined brigades with regular soldiers. In a letter to his father, Colonel Hale predicted:

This war will have served a good purpose in awakening the people of the United States from their lethargy, in leading them to demand a reasonably large regular army and an efficient navy. Also a national guard, with military education and perfect organization, equipment and discipline, capable of quick expansion and quick contraction when not needed, and promptly available in any emergency.[209]

Hale could be proud of the performance of his regiment.

General Merritt moved quickly to set up his headquarters in the Manila office of the Governor-General, and to establish a military government to run the city.[210] On 15 August, he appointed MacArthur to the position of Provost Marshall of Manila.[211] Almost immediately after, however, Merritt shuffled his command structure again, attendant upon his own request to be relieved. Stanley Karnow attributes Merritt's request to pique over President McKinley's refusal to let him conquer the entire archipelago.[212] On the other hand, Merritt had established a distinguished record in the Indian Wars, and may simply have wished to finish his military career on a high note. For whatever reason, late in August Merritt was ordered to Paris, to advise the commissioners working on the treaty of peace between the United States and Spain.[213] In a flurry of orders on 23 August, General Anderson transferred over from his Second Division to command the Independent Division, now renamed the First Division. MacArthur was promoted in Anderson's stead to command of the Second Division. Maj. Gen. Elwell Stephen Otis, formerly commanding the Independent (now First) Division, ascended to command of the entire Eighth Army Corps, a position Merritt relinquished to assume the title of Military Governor of the Philippine Islands.[214] The actual change-of-command was on 28 August 1898, but Merritt may only have been building his résumé, for the next day, Otis replaced him as both Commander of the Department of the Pacific, and Military Governor, and Merritt prepared to leave the islands.[215]

All those rank changes left vacancies. On 3 September 1898, in a general round of promotions, MacArthur was elevated to major general, to recognize his responsibilities as commander of the Second Division. And, in a move that caused resentment among the other state regiments, Colorado's Col. Irving Hale was promoted to brigadier general, U.S.V., and given command of the Second Brigade.[216] Hale was honored partly because of his status as a West Point graduate, and partly due to Colorado's prominent role in the storming of Fort San Antonio de Abad and of Manila itself. One suspects that his careful cultivation of *Harper's* correspondent John Bass helped, as well. His promotion, of course, left the First Colorado without a colonel.

Governor Alva Adams responded quickly to fill the vacancy, serving political expedience and at the same time rewarding men prominently mentioned in hometown news accounts. General Hale received the governor's telegram on 21 September 1898, promoting Lt. Col. Henry McCoy to colonel, Maj. Cassius Moses to lieutenant colonel, Company I's Capt. William Grove to major, Adj. Alex Brooks to captain of Company I, 2nd Lt. Rice Means to first lieutenant, and Sgt. Henry Clotworthy to second lieutenant.[217] At least in terms of their own field grade officers, this command structure would carry the First Colorado through the rest of its service in the Philippines. With Manila taken and the war over, the men expected that service to be brief. Second Lt. Ralph Lister, however, had predicted before the fight, "from the way things look now we will whip the Spaniards and then the insurgents."[218] Time would prove him right.

CHAPTER THREE

"The Worst Kind of New Woman"

America's citizen soldiers, quick to volunteer for a campaign in which they believe, have always been equally quick to demand their release from the ranks once their perceived mission is completed. Dr. Fred Anderson has detailed such expectations as far back as the Seven Years War.[1] In the Civil War, impending expiration of volunteer enlistments prompted the United States Army to launch the disastrous battles at First Manassas and Fredericksburg; the famous mutiny of the Second Maine Infantry just before Gettysburg is only one example of many such protests over what the men saw as undue extension of their term of service. Colorado's "mutiny" followed this pattern, but was marked by one extraordinary catalyst—Dr. Rose Kidd Beere.

S. L. A. Marshall has observed that "if a soldier has an initial belief in the justice of the politics of his country, this belief will be nourished in the measure that the country keeps faith with him during his service."[2] One way that Colorado kept faith with its volunteers was through private societies, organized to support the troops overseas. The Denver Soldiers' Aid Society organized on 21 June 1898, formed by 150 of the "best and most patriotic women of Denver."[3] William M. Phillips served as President, Henry Van Kleeck as Secretary, and for most of the war, Mrs. M. A. Taft led the Relief Committee.[4] Pueblo organized its own Soldiers' Aid Society. In addition, existing organizations provided assistance as well. Chaplain David Fleming was able to tap a fund supplied by the Society of Colonial Wars.[5] The problem for the voluntary societies lay in how, exactly, to assist the men overseas. The Denver Soldiers' Aid

Society found an opportunity, by sponsoring Dr. Rose Kidd Beere as a nurse in the Philippines.

In camp in Denver before the regiment boarded its train for the west coast, Surgeon General Clayton Parkhill of the First Colorado's Medical Corps was besieged by women offering to go to the front as nurses. Army regulations did not allow women to serve as nurses, and so Parkhill discussed their request with Colorado Representative John Shafroth.[6] On 28 April 1898, Shafroth introduced a bill in Congress to allow the War Department to employ trained female nurses in its general hospitals, up to half of the staff.[7] His bill went nowhere, and neither did Parkhill's nurse applicants. Parkhill himself was so competent that the regular army lifted him from the volunteer ranks and sent him to Cuba.[8]

Rose Kidd, daughter of Maj. Meredith Kidd of the Tenth Cavalry, grew up on a succession of frontier army posts, where she learned to ride and hunt. By 1898, she had married, borne three sons, been widowed, earned a medical degree from the Woman's Medical College of Northwestern University, practiced medicine in Durango, Colorado, and served as Superintendent of the State Home for Dependent Children. After the Battle of Santiago, Cuba, her father wrote her, bemoaning the absence of a Kidd in uniform. "This is the first war of our country in which our family has no part. I am too old, and your boys are too young." Raised by her father on stories of Civil War-era duty and valor, Beere replied at once. "You take care of my boys, and I'll represent our family in this war. I can't raise a regiment, or carry a gun, but I can help nurse the men who do."[9]

Armed with letters of recommendation from Colorado Governor Alva Adams and the Soldiers' Aid Society of Denver, Beere traveled to San Francisco to seek passage to the Philippines. The regiment had already sailed, but Beere, undaunted, sought an audience with Maj. Gen. Wesley Merritt, commanding the Department of the Pacific. Ushered before "The Presence," as she later described him, Beere endured his scrutiny. He asked, "Is your father willing that you should go to Manila as a

10. Dr. Rose Kidd Beere (standing left) and friends. *Photo courtesy of Bill Elswick.*

nurse?" She replied, "I am the mother of three children and am supposed to have reached the years of discretion. My father is quite willing."[10] Against all odds, the old Indian fighter, perhaps with an understanding of what the volunteers were about to face in combat, arranged for Beere's passage to Manila.

She traveled to the Philippines as a volunteer under the auspices of Denver's Soldier's Aid Society, which agreed to pay her expenses of $1 per day. Beere saw herself as a "New Woman," and took pride in Colorado's electorate having approved women's suffrage in 1893. She heralded her appointment as "a triumph for Colorado, for it is the first time that a woman has gone."[11]

She began her duties immediately. In San Francisco, Beere found 156 new Colorado recruits, like her awaiting passage to the Philippines. Many were sick with measles and coughs, and Beere bought $10 of cold cures to treat them.[12] En route to Manila, she stopped at the Honolulu Hospital to check on members of Company I of the United States Volunteer Engineers, a company recruited from the Denver area. She packed the space under her berth with cases of Rose's Lime Juice, purchased in Hawaii. And, in a letter from Manila to Emma H. Eldredge, President of

Red Cross Auxiliary Thirteen of Colorado Springs, Beere thanked her for the donation of $50 and complained that shipboard medical staff stole the fruit she supplied to the ill soldiers in the ship's sickbay.[13]

On arrival in Manila on 28 September 1898, Dr. Beere found that she was, in fact, one of eleven women sent by western states to care for the volunteers. California had supplied eight nurses, and Oregon two.[14] Despite Dr. Beere's qualifications, the Army medical establishment in the Philippines refused to recognize her as a doctor, and in fact banned any of the women from treating sick or wounded soldiers, due to their gender. Perhaps in support of their brother officers in the Medical Corps, the officers of the First Colorado snubbed Beere in a reception they themselves admitted was "frosty."[15] The California Red Cross set up a convalescent hospital as a sort of half-way house, so that soldiers released from the military hospital while still ill could recover before returning to the ranks. Chief Surgeon Lippincott coveted the Red Cross hospital and its cots, but not its personnel, and refused to send sick soldiers there unless it was turned over to the Army. The women of the Red Cross held firm; they came with the hospital. Beere joined their ranks, and with the military hospital overflowing, Chief Surgeon Lippincott had little choice but to relent.[16]

Within a week, Brig. Gen. (and former colonel of the First Colorado) Irving Hale and Col. Henry McCoy of the First Colorado had prevailed upon Lippincott to let the women into the military wards. There, Beere found conditions so bad that soldiers would stay sick in their quarters rather than risk a visit to a medical facility. She determined to create a "diet kitchen," from which to supply the men with light, digestible meals, and so nurse the ailing back to health without them entering the hospital. She secured permission from General Hale to order a $40 four-burner kerosene stove from Hong Kong, and then, while waiting for delivery, built one locally for $10.[17] Her industry and efforts on their behalf were appreciated greatly by the men. On 9 October 1898, Pvt. W. T. Byrne wrote to tell his brother that he was suffering from "a slight touch of malaria" and enjoying his rest in quarters. "Mrs. Dr. Beere of the Red Cross was here to see me yesterday, and we had a nice talk. She is the first English-speaking woman I have talked to since leaving Honolulu."[18] The men saw her as a nurse, but also, in an all-male world far from home, as a link to Colorado and their loved ones. In a conflict with their own officers, the enlisted men naturally turned to Beere to convey their message home.

The officers were less welcoming. Beere was a woman in "their" world, and at that, a woman not subject to military discipline. She pushed General Hale and Colonel McCoy to press her case with Lippincott, and while the two officers complied, Colonel McCoy didn't "push" gracefully. California's Red Cross outfitted their nurses and their hospital with a contribution of $35,000.[19] When Beere wired the Denver Soldier's Aid Society for the paltry $1,000 they had promised, the Aid Society wired only $100.[20] When she again wired the society, saying "Boys ill; wire thousand," the society instead sent $500 to Colonel McCoy, and telegraphed Chaplain David Fleming to ascertain if even that much was truly needed.[21] McCoy refused to turn the money over to Beere, claiming she had no credentials, and instead used the money for "a light diet plan" which he represented as his own idea![22] As Beere noted in an acid commentary, "Considering the fact that over $10,000 had been raised for the soldiers, it struck me as peculiar that $30 or $40 should be wasted in a cable to the chaplain telling him that I had wired for $1000 and asking if so much was necessary."[23]

Stung both by the Soldiers' Aid Society's doubting her judgment and by McCoy's questioning her status, Beere produced her "credentials"— letters praising her endeavor from Governor Adams, President William Phillips of the Soldiers' Aid Society, President Eldredge of the Red Cross, and from three patriotic societies. Above all, she said, she had her "license to die," as she called the "pewter [identity] tag we wear about our necks in battle."[24]

With Manila occupied and the War with Spain won, the men of the First Colorado felt their mission was at an end. Newly-ensconced in comfortable quarters in the city, they nonetheless chafed at the daily routine of 5:30 A.M. reveille, morning and afternoon drills, guard mount and fatigue details, and evening dress inspections.[25] The soldiers resented their isolation from their families at home. Above all, they complained about their rations. The men complained to their families and to hometown newspapers, and the officers complained to the politicians. On 30 September 1898, Captain John S. Stewart wrote to Governor Alva Adams:

> The war is over now and we all feel that to have to serve even one more year of our enlistment would be a calamity. I write you plainly and I voice the sentiments of 98 per cent of the volunteer forces here when I say they hope sincerely that within the next few months they will have been relieved by regular forces.[26]

Private Byrne echoed this view one week later in a plaintive letter to his brother, observing that "all the men and officers want to go home, as they have all they want of this place, and especially this kind of life, since we have gained what we came here for."[27] In October of 1898, their discontent flared into what the United States Army termed "mutiny."

On 17 October 1898, a committee of enlisted men came to Beere, carrying a box containing one sergeant's meager dinner ration. The men came to her since, as a representative of the Red Cross Society of Colorado Springs and the Soldiers' Aid Society of Denver, she couldn't be court-martialed. She took the box to General Hale. After examining six company kitchens, Hale reported to Beere that evening that affairs were not as bad as she had been led to believe.[28] Not all the enlisted men shared the general's optimism.

On 20 October 1898, Company G refused to drill, due to their breakfast of moldy oatmeal. A twelve-man committee of enlisted men called on Beere for help. She advised them to seek as many signatures from the men of the regiment as possible, to guard against possible official retaliation.[29] With two representatives of each company meeting in a church belfry to avoid detection by the officers, they debated the necessity of having each man in the regiment sign in order to avoid punishment. Company M's delegates held out for an individually signed letter; the rest instead voted to cast their petition as a telegraph, for rapid transmission to Colorado politicians and editors. Without Company M, they could not claim unanimity, and so they signed the petition "One thousand Colorado volunteers."[30]

Hearing of the petition, Colonel McCoy sent the popular Lieutenant Colonel Moses to reason with the men and delay the "kick." The men relented, and agreed to hear the officers out. The committee of enlisted men asked Beere to be at home at 9:30 A.M. on 21 October, to review their petition. To head off that meeting, McCoy ordered the committee to meet with him at 10:00 A.M. Stood up, she went to the hospital. At the meeting, the men presented their grievances to the colonel. In addition to complaints about rations and after expressing their desire to return home, they demanded to know why Beere had been "so badly received by the officers," and why McCoy had "refused the Denver money [intended by the Soldiers' Aid Society for her use]. McCoy replied that, since Beere brought no 'credentials,' he could not be sure she was who she said she was!"[31]

Beere returned to her quarters at noon, where she found a note from the committee. Although they had been "interfered with" in the morning, they promised to meet her at 2:00 P.M. To refute McCoy's charges of "no credentials," the men asked her to assemble her letters of introduction. She did so, and then wrote out her address to what the newspapers called "the mutiny committee." When the men arrived, she read them her "credentials," then her address, and then left the meeting. After discussion, they determined to send the cable.[32]

Lieutenant Colonel Moses visited each company, to try to dissuade them; despite his popularity, the men hissed his appearances. One explained later, "It was principally this resistance that made the men more determined to send the cable." Moses made a last, and successful, appeal to the committee at the telegraph office, urging them to adopt a cooling-off period until the following morning, before transmitting the cable.[33]

That evening, a group of three officers visited Beere and asked her to use her influence to block the petition, a power she informed them she lacked. Told she could end the message in three hours by a visit to the regiment, she asked them why, after being in the Philippines for all of three weeks, she was supposed to have more influence with the men than the officer corps? Beere refused the officers' request. She declared, "Such a *fin de fizzle* Joan of Arc would they make me out!"[34]

The next morning, the enlisted men determined to proceed with the "kick," only to find that during the night, Gen. Elwell Otis had imposed military censorship on the telegraph offices, with orders to seize any petitions from soldiers. Confident that they had headed off the petition, officers then inspected the rations, and recommended immediate improvements. One week later, however, copies of the "kick," transmitted from Hong Kong, hit the desks of Colorado's newspapers, governor, and congressional delegation. One day after that, telegrams began to land on the desk of Colonel McCoy.

The officers blamed the woman they regarded as the messenger. Beere maintained that she had not sent the petition to Hong Kong (though she may well have supplied it to a sympathetic journalist who did). Beere admitted that "outsiders who were familiar with the state of affairs, took the message to Hong Kong."[35] When Otis blocked the "kick," he censored *all* wires from Manila, angering the journalists, who began sending cables to the United States directly from Hong Kong, bypassing the Manila cable office (at the cost of a three-day ocean voyage).[36] The Denver Public Library holds the diary of Cpl. Roy Harris, which indicates that *he* sent the "kick," along with funds to telegraph it, to Hong Kong in a mail draft.[37]

However it was sent, multiple copies of the petition made it to Colorado.

Hong Kong, Oct.31—to Governor Adams, representatives to congress and the press and the people of the state. Provided peace is declared, regiment earnestly desires recall. Rations are wretched and insufficient, fifteen per cent of the regiment is sick. Will cheerfully remain for fighting. Reluctant to serve for garrison duty. Answer. One thousand Colorado volunteers. Napoleon Guyot, Chairman.[38]

The governor cabled Hale and asked for a report. Hale asked the regiment's officers to investigate. The officers assured state officials that the men of Colorado were enjoying the most wholesome rations ever served to any soldier. A furious Beere stormed the officer's mess and slammed down two just-opened cans of Argentine beef, crawling with maggots; the table cleared.[39] One evening, a group of officers was discussing the "kick," and one blamed Beere for all the trouble. Another quietly remarked, "Oh, yes and Dr. Beere issued that maggoty pork and sugar, too."[40] Hale's official response, cabled on 11 November 1898, boasted: "Sickness moderate, decreasing; nothing dangerous. Colorado rations improved." Home in Denver, readers interpreted Hale's closing assurance as evidence that, in fact, rations *had* been "wretched and insufficient."[41]

Colorado's military officers sought to discredit both the "kick" and Beere. McCoy reported that Guyot didn't reflect the sentiment of the men, and that only one man was really sick.[42] In Denver, Adjutant General Barnum of the National Guard went further, to discredit Guyot's Company G. He pointed out that Company G, while still at the Presidio, had passed a resolution condemning the governor, and that a majority of Cripple Creek citizens repudiated that resolution. "Company G had never reflected any glory upon the state since it went into the guard."[43]

In Manila, Beere was a hero, at least to the enlisted men. On 9 November 1898, Beere attended a concert at the Zorilla Theatre, escorted by a Utah artilleryman. The men's spontaneous cheer almost "ripped the canvas painting of cherubs on the ceiling."[44] Morale was obviously dangerously low, and the officers acted quickly to issue better rations. Thanksgiving was fast approaching, and cables had notified the men that holiday boxes were on the way. Ship after ship sailed in to Manila Bay, without the eagerly awaited treats. Recognizing the probable effect of a Thanksgiving "holiday" spent in a foreign land, without a special dinner, the Quartermaster and Commissary officers secured a launch and searched the anchored ships, to no avail.

Finally, each company had to do the best they could from company funds, with the regimental commissary furnishing ample canned fruit and vegetables. The company funds were used to purchase turkeys, chickens, onions, potatoes, and in one case, a pig, in the local markets. Captain Comings of Company F paid $75 from his own pocket, so as not to deplete the company funds.[45] In like manner, Lieutenant Hooper of Company B treated the company to 200 cigars.[46] The best meal the men had enjoyed since arriving in the Philippines went a long way toward assuaging their discontent, as did the discovery of their Thanksgiving boxes, buried in the holds of the *Ohio* and *Indiana*, in the first week of December.[47] As a further gesture toward the men, Thanksgiving marked the end of the pass system, and the men were allowed to come and go at will within Manila and the American lines, except that they had to show up for noon roll call, evening drills or dress parades, and any assigned duty.[48]

Telegrams could be sent between the Philippines and Colorado in one day, but ocean-borne mail could take six weeks. This lag created a sort of time-bomb effect, with responses to ancient telegrams bursting in the midst of now-peaceful ranks. Long-awaited mail arrived in Manila on 21 December 1898. In a November copy of the *Rocky Mountain News*, members of Company B read Private Todd's letter home, saying he thought the food was fine. The outraged soldiers pitched the unfortunate Todd into the company "sinks" (latrines), Todd complained directly to Colonel McCoy, McCoy threw five men into the guardhouse pending court-martial for assault, and even sent one of them to solitary confinement for "saucy speech."[49]

11. Thanksgiving boxes, with Color Sergeant Holmes in center. *Photo courtesy of John Stewart Post Number One, Veterans of Foreign Wars.*

That same mail contained another time bomb. In the first week of November, a 19 August 1898 issue of the *Pueblo Chieftain* had landed in the First Colorado quarters. It contained an article claiming that all the Colorado volunteers wanted to stay in the Philippines indefinitely. Blaming a self-serving sergeant for the article, forty angry enlisted men from Pueblo's Company C immediately cabled home a petition detailing their miserable rations, noting the number of sick, and demanding their return to Colorado. Complaining of "slow starvation since landing on Luzon," the men claimed "on the one hand are home, friends and help, on the other are starvation, sickness, and death."[50] When he read the newspaper account of the Pueblo men's "kick," the enraged McCoy reduced six noncommissioned officers who had signed the complaint to the ranks, confined them and thirty-nine privates to quarters, and assigned them extra police duties.[51] Beere's prescient fears of official retaliation against the men had been realized. The Pueblo *Chieftain* continued to receive other letters confirming the legitimacy of the men's complaints, but adopted a public policy of not publishing them until the men returned to Colorado, to protect them from official reprisal.[52] On

18 January 1899, private "Alf Alfa" reported that the Pueblo men were finally released from quarters.[53]

Against military discipline, the men could do little. They could, however, threaten retaliation against the officers when the regiment returned home and mustered out. Enlisted men wrote to hometown newspapers, pointing out that their subservience to military discipline was only temporary. Someday, they would be mustered out, and as civilians they intended to avenge themselves in Colorado upon their commissioned oppressors. Private Nason of Company C was discharged for failing eyesight. Before he left Manila, Colonel McCoy called him to headquarters and said he hoped he'd tell the truth when he got home. Nason assured him he would, but his truth may not have been what McCoy had in mind. Upon arrival in Pueblo, he reported that, before he left his comrades, they admonished him, "Don't forget to have a barrel of tar ready for us when we reach home, and be on hand for the fun."[54] McCoy had already assured Governor Thomas that "We are well aware that the regiment will return home, and we all intend to make the state of Colorado our future home."[55]

As that round of long-distance, slow-motion incendiary exchanges subsided, Beere turned out to have sparked another. Stung by official denials of the legitimacy of the "kick," she penned an angry letter to the Soldiers' Aid Society on 22 November 1898. She complained, "Of course I have been abused, but I'm the only English-speaking woman about who can stand it, and there must be the traditional female to blame. It is hard, however, to undeservedly be blamed for leading 900 men from the path of military rectitude. My fighting blood rebels."[56]

She accused McCoy of misappropriating Soldiers' Aid money to start a regimental canteen, and concluded, "With the united efforts of the enlisted men and myself, Colonel McCoy will be buried so deep that he will sleep straight through Gabriel's last trump."[57] Beere's charges, which hit the Denver newspapers on 9 and 10 January 1899, lit a firestorm.

Beere was already on shaky ground with the Soldiers' Aid Society.

She had previously received a 9 August 1898 letter from the society, asking her to account for her expenses between Denver and San Francisco. On 1 December 1898, McCoy handed her a letter from the Soldier's Aid Society, which agreed with McCoy's decision to withhold society funds from Beere. Society President William Phillips said Beere was just a nurse, with "no authority to disburse any money or contract for anything in our name." Humiliated in front of McCoy, she refused to render any accounts. "The spectacle of the finance committee squabbling over the price of my breakfast at Ogden would not be edifying. . . . No one can question my right to squander my own money on quinine and pea soup."[58]

Notified of Beere's charges, McCoy asked the society to recall Beere. Vice-President J. C. Butler of the Soldiers' Aid Society burst out, "The woman must be crazy!" and called her "a sensational woman" and "extravagant."[59] Four board members wanted to recall her immediately, but the majority instead resolved to direct her to nurse only and refrain from "inter-meddling" between officers and men, or else consider herself dismissed.[60] The board's position might have been stronger had they been paying her a salary. Beere replied that, since she was working for free, the most the SAS could do was withhold the expense money that she had been spending on the soldiers.

The SAS divided over the Beere recall, amid revelations that while the Executive Committee had begrudged Beere her $30 monthly expenses, the society's president had paid herself a weekly stipend of $40. In fact, four-fifths of all SAS funds raised in Denver for the Colorado troops were spent in Denver, aiding families of Ft. Logan's Seventh Infantry while the regulars were in Cuba.[61] In protest, reformers seceded and created a new South Side Soldiers' Aid Society.

Beere continued to nurse the sick enlisted men, and frozen Australian beef replaced the tinned Argentine maggots. Increasing strain between the American troops and the Filipinos gave promise of a new campaign in the offing, and when those disagreements burst into the Philippine-American War in February of 1899, the "mutiny" was forgotten. On the first night of the insurrection, Beere tended to the wounded on the battlefield, and then in the hospital. Arthur Johnson noted that "at the hospital, she is working like a Trojan among the sick and wounded and keeping an eye out for the Coloradoans."[62] Pvt. M. H. Maccoe, wounded on 25 March, recalled Beere working over him until 2:00 A.M. "That woman I consider one of the grandest and noblest that ever lived."[63]

Letters and dispatches still plied the waves on their one-way, six-week journey. In late March of 1899, Beere responded to continued SAS harassment with a two-word telegram, "Resigned. Beere."[64] She preceded the men's return to Colorado by five months. At their homecoming banquet in Pueblo, the men cheered loudly for Beere. To the call for a cheer for Colonel McCoy, only three voices were raised.[65] Greeley's Private Shoemaker gloated, "Didn't we sit down on Colonel McCoy hard at Pueblo?"[66] The men were proud of their service and their combat record, but not of their colonel, and the bitterness left by his attempts to silence their petition accompanied them to their homes.

Beere explained their attitude. "The American soldier can fight harder, die gamer, swear stronger and get drunker than any soldier on earth. Fancy a little thing like a censorship keeping him from saying what he has set out to say. *Viva los Americanos!*"[67]

CHAPTER FOUR

Damn, Damn, Damn the Filipinos

The men of the First Colorado enlisted to fight the Spanish, not to serve as an army of occupation. Manila's fall, cheered by the troops as the triumphant culmination of their overseas adventure, instead merely marked a passage from military campaign to a sort of peacekeeping limbo. While the United States tried to decide what to do with the Philippines, the Coloradoans turned their energies to contemplation of the strange land in which they found themselves. Their nativist attitudes, honed in Colorado labor conflicts, filtered their impressions of the peoples of the Philippines and tainted the soldiers' actions toward both their former enemies and their erstwhile allies.

Pvt. Guy Sims was perhaps one of the few soldiers who, before departing Camp Adams, had given the Filipinos any thought at all. In the summer of 1896, well before either the war or his enlistment, the young man had been intrigued by news reports of fighting between native rebels and the Spanish garrison of Manila.

> I had a long hunt in the atlas before finding the Philippine Islands, and tried to imagine what those tribesmen looked like. Best I could do was a sort of a cross between Sioux Indians and Zulus of South Africa, armed with long spears.[1]

Sims's curiosity was soon satisfied.

Initial encounters were auspicious. When the First Colorado landed at Malate, south of Manila, on 18 July 1898, the Filipinos greeted them with gifts of fruit and cries of "Americanos," "Compadres," and "Omega!" (Amigo!).[2] As the men came ashore, they stacked their arms, stripped to only their long blue shirts, and then waded out into the surf to offload supplies from the lighters. The Filipinos didn't wear clothes when they swam, and the Filipino men and women pointed their fingers and laughed at the soldiers' modesty.[3] When, their work done, the shirt-clad troops began playing leapfrog in the rain, the Filipinos could only gape in amazement.[4]

Concepts of modesty featured prominently in letters home. Band musician Verner W. Campbell wrote to his parents,

> I used to think the pictures we saw in histories, etc., were exaggerated in regard to natives, but they didn't tell half the truth. Some of them don't wear any more clothing than is necessary, and the young ones very seldom have even the traditional fig leaf to cover their nakedness. They think nothing of going naked or going where people are naked.[5]

Around Manila, Filipino men wore loose pants the Coloradoans described as "pajamas," and a shirt with a flowing tail.[6] Filipinas wore a short skirt and "a light 'waist [blouse]," and almost all men and women went barefooted.[7]

American civil and military authorities sent home glowing reports on the nature of the Filipinos. United States Consul to the Philippines Oscar Williams confidently predicted that the Filipinos would ally with the American troops to overthrow the Spanish, describing the people of the islands as "brave, submissive and cheaply provided for."[8] Brig. Gen. Thomas M. Anderson, commanding the first expedition to reach Manila, called them "industrious," and described them as "not ignorant, savage tribes, but have a civilization of their own, and though insignificant in appearance are fierce fighters."[9]

The First Colorado formed their own opinions. Given the disparity of their observations, it seems likely that each man saw what he wanted to see. Lt. Charles B. Lewis described the Filipinos as very clean, and very intelligent.[10] Conversely, Capt. William Cornell wrote his father in Denver that "they are a very dirty and ignorant class of people."[11] Captain William Grove told his wife "The natives are very ignorant and in a frightful physical condition. . . . They are a mixture in appearance between a Chinaman and a negro."[12] Pvt. Arthur Johnson informed the readers of the *Rocky Mountain News* that the Filipinos were "intelligent" and "observant," and that they only learned English slowly because the Colorado troops usually addressed them in Spanish; with each side knowing at least some Spanish, it was the preferred mode of communication. Johnson also observed that the Filipinos were fine musicians.[13]

Predictably, the soldiers applied Colorado attitudes about race to the Filipinos. Often, the soldiers called them "niggers," "coons," "chinks," and even "gugus," from the tree bark used as a shampoo by native women.[14] Private Johnson described the Filipinos as "the 'coons' of Luzon," and a family at table, eating handfuls of rice and fish *sans* utensils, as "the horde of half-naked pickaninnies."[15] Contempt and admiration could combine in the same observer. Lt. Rice Means, in a letter to his parents, called the Filipinos "a filthy set of people, having all the diseases known and some that are unknown. They rob you of everything they can." Yet, in the same letter, he told of using his penknife to remove a Spanish bullet from the leg of a Filipino boy, in a fifteen-minute "operation" in the field. "He was the gamest lad I ever saw, not making a bit of noise, only wrenching his face now and then, for it must have hurt him very much."[16]

In the days before the assault on Manila, the Coloradoans took a professional interest in their potential allies, the insurrectos. They got their first view of rebel troops on 20 July, when "quite a number of Insurgent Battalions marched past our camp."[17] Irregular troops, the Filipino soldiers wore blue madras uniforms taken from Spanish prisoners. They carried a variety of weapons, including a fair number of modern Spanish Mauser rifles. The enlisted men were barefooted.[18]

Filipino officers, the Americans noted, could be distinguished by the fact that they wore boots.[19] Maj. Cassius Moses told his wife that "insurgent soldiers are funny little men. I have met a lot of the higher officials of their army and find many of them intelligent, brave men."[20]

The soldiers of the two armies fraternized openly at first. "To the Americans, the members of the insurgent army are deferential, and there seems a desire to have them considered as comrades in arms, which is checked by the inability to make themselves understood in the native language." Spanish was the only common language, and few Filipinos knew Spanish, and even fewer of the First Colorado, although Johnson boasted of "a few first-class Spanish interpreters in the regiment."[21] The Army had no system of training or designating interpreters. The First Colorado would have seemed likely to have an edge in Spanish-speakers, but the social, economic, and power relationships in 1898 Colorado meant that the state militia had failed to enlist a single Hispanic in its ranks. Dropped into a country that spoke either Tagalog or Spanish, the unit searched its ranks for anyone possessing twenty words of Spanish. Cpl. John S. Airheart served as Lieutenant Colonel Moses's interpreter. The regiment also turned up Pvt. John Salisbury, who had learned Spanish in Florida; he became General Hale's interpreter. Pvt. William Thompson, Colonel McCoy's interpreter, had gained a knowledge of the language working as a cowboy alongside Mexican and Spanish *caballeros* in Colorado and New Mexico. Pvt. William Curtis learned Spanish working around Mexicans and Spaniards in Pueblo. The great linguist of the regiment, however, was Pvt. George Lynch. The California native had served with the British army in Africa, India, Hong Kong, and Singapore, and spoke Malay, Spanish, Irish, and Chinese.[22]

Inevitably, the soldiers compared rations and equipment. The Coloradoans were especially interested in the Filipinos' Mausers.

There was a family of brothers in the native army named Del Pilar. All were officers and all were fighting fools and the

12. Teaching the Filipinos to set their sights. *Photo courtesy of John Stewart Post Number One, Veterans of Foreign Wars.*

fightingest fool of them all was Gen. [Gregorio] Rio Del Pilar, who commanded the brigade directly between our camp and Manila and his men when off duty used to visit our camp. They nearly all had Mauser rifles which were better guns than we had by far. And they all had their sights set as high as they would go, 2200 yards. A lot of our Colo. boys spoke Spanish and they told these natives how to set their sights. A little over 7 months later 125 of us bumped into Rio Del Pilar's whole brigade at Marriquina [*sic*] in a desperate and one-sided encounter and discovered, to our sorrow, how well they had learned their lesson.[23]

General Del Pilar eventually gave his life to ensure Aguinaldo's escape from pursuing American columns.

While the American enlisted men blithely instructed their Filipino counterparts, a *New York Sun* article of 16 July 1898, reporting on the Filipino soldiery, said, "It will be hard work to subdue men like them.

Godsend we don't have it to do!"[24] Colorado officers shared that premonition. Lieutenant Means predicted that, once Spain was defeated, the Americans would have to fight the Filipinos.[25] While there was no official word about the intentions of the United States regarding retention or liberation of the Philippines, it seemed likely to the men that they had not been sent across the Pacific to seize Manila, only to hand it over to the Filipinos. 2nd Lt. Charles O. Zollars believed, "The Filippinos [sic] like us all right now, but I am afraid we will have trouble with them later, as they don't want to belong to the United States, but have a republic of their own."[26] Farther up the chain of command, Maj. Gen. Wesley Merritt, commanding the entire American military force, agreed. To President William McKinley he suggested, "it seems more than probable that we will have the so-called insurgents to fight as well as the Spaniards."[27]

While Merritt and Aguinaldo maneuvered, Filipino-American relations broke down at the person-to-person level over simple mercantile transactions. Pvt. Johnson called the Filipinos a "nation of yellow Yankees" for their enterprise.[28] After weeks of shipboard rations, the Coloradoans were eager to trade for fresh foodstuffs. They found the Filipinos to be good businessmen and women. The first day, a penny would buy five bananas; by the second day, the price had risen to a penny each, or two cents for a large banana. At first, unfamiliar with American money, the Filipinos thought that the larger the coin, the greater the value, and would give more produce for a nickel than for a dime. "For a short time there were some wonderful bargains driven and some of the men carried off more change than the money laid down."[29] The Filipinos quickly figured out they were being cheated, and refused any payment except Spanish money or "dollars Mex," coins minted in Mexico and in wide circulation in the Philippines.

The Filipinos charged three cents for an egg. Soldiers would simply put down the money they thought fair, grab the eggs, and walk off grinning.[30] The soldiers did not seem to think it dishonest to cheat a non-White foreigner. They also do not seem to have considered that, if

13. Filipino "Vino" stand. *Photo courtesy of John Stewart Post Number One, Veterans of Foreign Wars.*

they earned a reputation for cheating the Filipinos, the Filipinos would quit showing up with items to sell. Trade nearly broke down, until the troops and the Filipinos discovered a form of currency the soldiers were eager to part with, and the Filipinos eager to receive: hardtack! The virtually indestructible crackers, despised by the men but issued in their military rations, proved extremely popular with the Filipinos. One tin of the soldiers' hated canned "hoss" (really stewed Argentine beef) was worth four dozen bananas in barter.[31] Quartered near the First Colorado, the Utah artillerymen "adopted" by the Coloradoans as their organic artillery, even used hardtack to buy native alcoholic "vino."[32]

Enterprising troops also began bartering government-issued materials for personal services. Issued military soap by their commanders, individual privates traded it to Filipina washerwomen in return for laundry services. Both parties were pleased with the bargain.[33] Again, however, American dishonesty could poison such transactions. One Filipino presented a promissory note to the regimental headquarters. "Colonel Douzenberry: Sir—Please give this nigger one peso (one dollar) for wood delivered. Signed I. McCorker, Private." The private rested while the Filipino toiled, and "paid" with a worthless order.[34] Ironically, Johnson reported in the same article, "There is a growing feeling of disrespect and contempt for the natives in the regiment, probably for the reason that the latter have insisted in playing the Americans as 'good things' instead of lending aid."[35] Given the near-glee with which the Colorado soldiers cheated the Filipinos, Johnson's surprise at Filipino intransigence seems particularly ethnocentric.

The First Colorado settled into a sort of wary co-existence with the Filipino troops, suffering their presence rather than actively fighting with them against the Spanish. Col. Irving Hale discounted any cooperation between the Filipinos and the Americans during the period before the assault on Manila. "On the contrary, their presence in this vicinity was more of a nuisance than otherwise, as they interfered with our operations and frequently drew the Spanish fire."[36]

To fight the Katipunan rebellion, the Spanish had attempted to augment their forces in the Philippines by recruiting and arming Filipino auxiliaries, often from tribes hostile to Aguinaldo's Tagalogs. Aguinaldo's exile and return had helped turn his Tagalog-based revolt into a more general movement for independence, and Spain's auxiliaries switched sides, often killing their Spanish officers in the process. In the countryside, the rebellion often led to the murder of Spanish priests, as well.[37] American authorities feared a Filipino slaughter of the Spanish within Manila. On 14 May 1898, two weeks after Commodore George Dewey's United States Navy squadron destroyed the Spanish fleet at Manila, a newspaper report explained, "there is a strong force of insurgents back of the city, and some fears were entertained on board the warships that they would attempt to enter the city and massacre the Spaniards." Dewey was prepared to land "bluejackets and marines" to, if necessary, defend the residents of the city.[38] When the American fleet shelled the Spanish arsenal at Cavite, ten miles southwest across Manila Bay from the city, Filipinos looted the facility as the Spanish withdrew. Taking that as evidence of Filipino lack of discipline, the American leaders therefore were determined to control the Filipinos during the assault on Manila.

On 13 August 1898, as the First Colorado marched into Malate, Filipinos began to loot the abandoned houses. Accordingly, when the Colorado troops entered Manila itself, they posted guard details to keep any Filipinos from following. As the Coloradoans occupied Fort San Antonio de Abad, a Filipino tried to cut the throat of a wounded Spaniard. The American troops stopped the Filipino from his assault, and Chaplain Fleming gave the wounded Spaniard water.[39] The Colorado men barred the Filipinos on their own initiative, but their instincts anticipated their orders. At 6:00 on the evening of the Manila assault, Maj. Gen. Francis Greene ordered Hale to ban armed Filipinos from entry to Manila.[40] The Spanish had surrendered, but Spanish troops remained in their defensive lines around the north and northeast ends of the city, holding back the Filipino army. "Thus the problem took the phase that was not unexpected. The Spaniards should be conquered first and then the insurgents."[41] At 9 P.M., the First Colorado marched to the east side of Manila and entered the Spanish trenches, taking up position against the Filipinos.[42] In one long day, the Americans had defeated the Spanish garrison, and then joined them to defend Manila against the insurrectos.

The troops took very seriously this mission, that of safeguarding the civilian and military population of Manila from vengeful Filipinos. As one of the Coloradoans' Utah artillerymen explained it,

> Their leader [Aguinaldo] had with subtle diplomacy urged on his wary braves with the thought that when they battered down the walls of Manila all that it contained would be theirs to loot and ravage. They loved liberty, but they loved the gold which it would bring still more. So they looked with hungry eyes when they saw the Americano enter the city of their dreams and close the gate against the black hosts who sought entrance to plunder and steal.[43]

By calling Aguinaldo's troops "braves," the westerner clearly compared the conflict in the Philippines to the Indian Wars in the American West. At the same time, within the phrasing limits imposed by Victorian sensibilities, he raised the specter of European women being "ravaged" by "black hosts," and that would not happen while American troops guarded Manila.

On 14 August 1898, Capt. William Cornell and eight men of Company K were on "outpost" duty at Manila's gates, having camped in former Spanish positions the night before. They were fired on by some 300 Filipinos, two companies under an officer of General Rio del Pilar's Regiment, who thought they were Spanish. The Americans retired from their position, and then made a stand on the road as the insurgents fired. Maj. Cassius Moses led Capt. Kyle Rucker and forty men from Companies B and E to the rescue. Once each side had identified itself, the fifty nervous Coloradoans, with fixed bayonets, ordered the Filipinos to lay down their arms before passing into the city. With some grumbling, the native troops complied. The Coloradoans kept the confiscated weapons, as Colonel Hale said, "as a lesson not to monkey with the buzzsaw when in motion."[44] The Colorado detachment detained the Filipinos for two hours before releasing them; the weapons were actually returned at a later date, when the Filipino force left the city.[45] Unarmed Filipinos could come and go freely, but the Americans allowed no troops bearing weapons into Manila.

While the American and Filipino forces awaited diplomatic developments, each strengthened its position. The Filipinos saw the Santa Mesa Road as the entry to Manila, and its San Juan Del Monte Bridge had been a conflict point with the Spanish. The Utah battery emplaced one of its guns in the Spanish gunpit there.[46] To support their outlying trenches around Manila, the Spanish had built fourteen blockhouses around the city's perimeter. Blocked by the Americans from entering Manila itself, the Filipinos occupied the old Spanish trenches and the line of blockhouses, and fortified them against the Americans.[47]

The trenches that had once held the Filipinos out, now hemmed the Americans in.

In July of 1898, after Dewey's victory but before the American soldiers arrived in force, the Filipinos had captured Manila's waterworks, located east of the city. At Commodore Dewey's insistence, they had continued to supply Manila with water. As part of the 13 August 1898 assault on Manila, the Filipinos again shut off the water as the Americans stormed the city. Gen. Wesley Merritt convinced them to restore water service, but the Filipinos remained in possession of the critical facility.[48]

The Colorado troops settled into quarters in the city. From 14 August until November, the First Colorado guarded a portion of the Manila defenses, at the Balic Balic Road and Sampaloc Cemetery. It was a strange situation. In some ways, a declared war between the Filipinos and the Americans might have been easier. Not quite enemies, and with no common foe, the Americans and Filipinos regarded each other warily. Every twenty-four hours, two new companies marched from the First Colorado barracks to take position on the line and relieve the previous day's watch.[49] After reporting from quarters at 5:00 P.M., the men would occupy small "cossack posts" every few hundred yards, three men to a post. One man stayed alert at all times, guarding against a possible insurrecto attack. Marching picket posts protected the telegraph line. The farthest outpost lay only one hundred feet from the closest part of the Filipino line. Each army decreed that no one was to pass their lines under arms, but unarmed Americans and Filipinos were free to tour each other's territory.[50]

Lt. Charles Hooper told his wife, "the insurgents, however, are ugly and we may have to give them a 'swipe.'"[51] Colonel McCoy, less pessimistic, predicted several months of rest, broken only by the rotating outpost duty, and felt that it was "useless to send companies daily to these posts, as the insurgents are showing only the most friendly spirit."[52] And so, after initial tension, relations between the Americans and the Filipinos improved for the fall of 1898, and when not on outpost duty

14. Captain John Stewart marching Company A to outpost duty. *Photo courtesy of John Stewart Post Number One, Veterans of Foreign Wars.*

or drilling, the men of the First Colorado had an opportunity to explore Manila and its environs.

The city was filled with paroled Spanish prisoners of war, soldiers who had surrendered but not yet been repatriated. There was a certain degree of resentment of the Spanish by the Coloradoans, whose rations were still insufficient. The Spanish received the same daily rations as the Americans, but in addition also got donated rice contributed by the Spanish civilian inhabitants of Manila.[53]

In general, however, the Spanish and Colorado troops cheerfully fraternized. Pvt. Guy Sims found them friendly, and glad the war was over.[54] The Spanish, after all, were on their way home. Arthur Johnson reported the bars full of Spanish uniforms, the parolees drinking "gin" at one centavo a glass, playing the guitars available in each establishment. "The [amateur] performers seldom seem to mind an audience and they usually send forth a cordial invitation to what Americans there happen to be in it to come inside, drink, sing, and be happy." Johnson also remarked on the homogeneous nature of the Spanish army, in which all soldiers were of the same "race"—Spanish. Their army contained no Germans, no Irish, no red-heads, "not like that of the United States."[55]

The Coloradoans enjoyed exploring the exotic city, although it was not without perils. In Manila, transport was on the left, and the Americans were constantly having to scuttle out of the way of horse-cars traveling the opposite direction to those at home.[56] The *Escolta* was the primary business street. The principal time for commerce, the Americans found, was between 6:00 and 9:00 in the morning. From 11:00 A.M. to 3:00 P.M., shopkeepers closed their storefronts with large shutters for *siesta*, although with the Americans in town merchants often left a small door open. At 5:00 P.M. the Escolta filled again, with a rush of carriages headed for the *Luneta*, Manila's historic parade ground. The Spanish had cut down all the trees on the Luneta in order to observe Dewey's fleet, but it was still the place for Manila's elite to see and be seen. The carriages promenaded from 5:30 until 7:30 in the evening, and then the wealthier Spanish civilians repaired to the second-story Japanese and French restaurants lining the Escolta, where they took the heaviest meal of the day. Many of the restaurants backed on the Pasig River, with rear "porticos" actually hanging over the water to catch the breeze.[57]

With their first payday, the American volunteers descended on Manila's merchants, who they found eager to sell. The port of Manila reopened the day after the city fell, and commerce in the city quickly returned to normal. All told, military authorities estimated that United States forces would spend half a million dollars in September of 1898 alone. According to Johnson, the universal Filipino cry was "*Mucho bueno Americano.*"[58] As time wore on, the Americans wore out their welcome, by running up bills on credit. Three March 1899 was a bi-monthly payday. Eighth Corps commander Maj. Gen. Elwell S. Otis took advantage of the occasion to order his soldiers to pay their debts to civilians. So many foreign merchants had been cheated by the troops that American honesty was in question, and Otis was determined that the Americans should be regarded as stable governors.[59]

In the Philippines, much of the merchant class was either Chinese or of Chinese descent. The evening of Manila's fall, Lieutenant Hooper washed down his hardtack with a bottle of champagne bought from a "friendly Chinaman."[60] Probably anyone bearing champagne would have been considered "friendly" at that point. The First Colorado's attitude toward the Chinese shows more clearly in Capt. William Cornell's observation that "Manila, for the most part, is very similar to that part of Denver which lies under the Sixteenth Street viaduct and along the Platte." It had, he found, "a great many Chinese and Japs."[61]

Improbably, General Otis attempted to ban any Chinese from the Philippines! His official United States Customhouse Notice, posted 24 September 1898, stated, "The Laws of the United States which prohibit the entrance of Chinese will be enforced here."[62] Hong Kong lay only three days away by steamship; Otis was fighting a losing battle.

Another doomed campaign swirled around what might as well have been the Filipino national sport, cockfighting. Filipinos so enjoyed cockfighting that the *New York Sun*'s reporter, granted an audience at the headquarters of Filipino General Mariano Noriel, had to wait for his host to finish watching a bout before the meeting could begin.[63] Cockfights in the Philippines had only one survivor. Unlike the gaffs used in American cockfights, which were rounded and only sharp on the end, Philippine *cuchillos* were two-and-a-half-inch-long hollow-ground razors, tied to each bird's right heel.[64] Under Spanish rule, cockfighting was legal, and 1,000 gamblers were out with their cocks each day. The Americans prohibited cockfighting, and so the Filipinos simply gambled on the edge of town, or just into the countryside.[65]

In a public relations ploy, the First Colorado's band would perform on the Luneta each Tuesday evening, beginning on 6 December 1898.[66] In fact, they played their favorite, "There'll Be a Hot Time in the Old Town Tonight," so often that Filipinos assumed it was the American national anthem, and bared their heads in respect.[67] The Coloradoans delighted in teaching the Filipinos another popular song. "In the amusement halls and saloons of Manila the Spanish and Filipino piano players render 'All Coons Look Alike to Me' in rag time."[68] An American civilian set up the "Circo Filippino" within two weeks of Manila's fall, complete with a minstrel show, and Johnson observed that "the American soldier boys think it funny to see 'coon' clowns with white powder on their faces."[69] Perhaps the Americans believed the Filipinos would not understand the racist joke; surely the Americans did not care.

Given the official American concern to prevent Filipino looting, it is ironic that the greatest source of conflict between the Filipinos and the Americans, both before Manila's fall and after, lay in the Americans' disrespect for Filipino property. In the weeks before they stormed the city, Americans seeking a temporary resting place would simply occupy the *nipa* huts of the locals. Johnson cheerfully reported:

> It was not always discoverable whether the Filipinos "allowed" the usurpation of their premises, for the US soldier in the Philippines never asks permission to enter a hut or get out of the rain to get at ease. Grunts of dissatisfaction from the occupants of the place are generally drowned in a scraping of muddy boots and a rattle of belts, canteens and guns as the men "peel off" their heavy equipment and settle down with all the noise and bustle of the "go-as-you-please" American.[70]

Johnson's willingness to share such attitudes with the readers back home clearly indicates the degree to which the Americans felt entitled to at least short-term use of the property of the Filipinos; the First Colorado's officers did nothing to interfere.

With Manila taken, the First Colorado abandoned Camp Dewey and relocated the five miles to quarters in the city. Filipino teamsters refused to transport the soldiers' baggage, due to the loss of fares in the city while they were so engaged. The Americans simply "impressed" the teams at bayonet-point, declining to pay any rent at all in view of their trouble.[71] Once in Manila, the soldiers settled into rented quarters, but despite orders against looting private residences, trouble quickly followed.

Much of the First Colorado initially was quartered at the largely empty Convent of San Sebastian, while a handful of priests continued to occupy the remainder. On 24 November 1898, Ayaria Francisco of the Convent of Recoletos demanded of the Provost Marshall General that the troops be evicted, since they were expanding beyond the quarters originally agreed upon. Investigating the claim, the Inspector General, Maj. John Mallory, found that Company G had required a dining room. Discovering that three priests were using three or more rooms, Colonel McCoy had authorized the men to move into one room. One week before the move, and again a day before, an interpreter told the priests to vacate the room. Corporal Brown's men moved the priests' crockery to an adjoining room and, when one priest refused to leave his chair, "tipped [him] out of it and . . . half led and half pushed [him] out of the room."[72] After reading Mallory's report, Gen. Arthur MacArthur agreed that the soldiers had not employed undue force, but noted that Colonel McCoy could not simply occupy the convent. The general ordered the room returned to the priests, and the troops to vacate.[73]

From Eighth Corps funds, regimental officers leased barracks for the enlisted men and rooms for themselves. Filipino landlords, willing to rent their quarters for use by officers, feared damage by enlisted men. Capt. Raymond Sulzer, Assistant Quartermaster, found that members of the First Colorado had intentionally destroyed mangers and a coachman's hut in a stables, to make room for their company mess, and he recommended partial reimbursement to the landlord.[74] Dominguez Santiago complained that the lease on his rental property at Calle Alix specified officers-only, and enlisted men were moving in; he demanded indemnification.[75] His concerns were borne out by Army investigations. Assistant Adj. Gen. Thomas H. Barry, seeking to settle all Spanish or Filipino claims against the Army, issued Paragraph 10, Special Orders 98, requiring receipts for any Spanish property appropriated by the soldiers. Assured by General MacArthur that all the troops of the Second Division had complied with the request, Barry responded:

> The quarters occupied by a portion of the 1' Colorado Volunteer Infantry on Calle de Orix No. 66 was used by the Spaniards for a storehouse, and it was reported to me verbally by Lt. J. H. Gowdy when I inspected the house that beside the property in the building a good many articles were in use by the balance of the regiment but as yet I have received no receipt for any of it.[76]

The Coloradoans' cavalier attitude toward civilian property extended even to Colonel McCoy, who was directed by Brig. Gen. B. P. Hughes, Provost Marshall General, to return to Gen. Ricardo Monch of the Spanish Army "certain furniture" from the house at No. 1 Calle Alix, which had been taken over by McCoy.[77] McCoy had leased the house, and simply appropriated the general's personal property for his own use.

As the American officers set up housekeeping, they looked for servants to take care of their needs. Some of the First Colorado's officers brought black civilian servants to the Philippines with them. Capt. C. E. Locke, regimental surgeon, noted that "we have our negro servants with us and when we landed the natives gathered around them and were much excited."[78] George Hopkins, Colonel Hale's servant, was the "genuinely black Southern negro" who presided over the kitchen of the regimental officers' mess.[79] After Hale's promotion to general, Hopkins stayed on cooking for regimental headquarters. Although a civilian, he was quartered with Company E (and would fight alongside E against the Filipinos on 5 February 1899).[80] Hopkins's status was further blurred, in that he supervised enlisted orderlies, detailed from the ranks to assist him in the kitchen.[81]

Hopkins may have enjoyed the esteem of his employers; other imported servants were less highly regarded. Lt. Charles Hooper wrote to

15. Irving Hale in his Manila quarters, with his Filipino "boy." *Photo courtesy of John Stewart Post Number One, Veterans of Foreign Wars.*

his wife that "we have fired the 'coon' as utterly useless, and a native 'boy' comes to work for us tomorrow."[82] Having been carried across the Pacific by the regiment's officers, one has to wonder how the discharged servant was supposed to make his way back to Colorado. The "boy" was, in fact, surely an adult Filipino. Hooper neatly embodies, in one casually racist phrase, the Victorian master-servant power disparity, and a common tendency of colonizers to juvenilize those they conquered. In *The White Man's Burden*, Rudyard Kipling's famous defense of imperialism, he referred to the Filipinos as "Half devil, and half child."[83] If the conquered population consists only of juveniles, then they deserve the discipline and tutelage of the conqueror.

Many of the Colorado officers, either individually or as a mess, hired servants, paid for from their own pockets. From the ranks, Pvt. Herman Heim ran the company officers' mess, assisted by a "squad of Pedros and Tomases."[84] Colonel and Mrs. McCoy resided in the house formerly occupied by Spanish General Monet; the corps of servants included one who pulled a rope to operate a punkah fan over the table at meals. Mrs. McCoy was attended by her own personal maidservant, Rosa. Not one of the servants received more than $10 Mex per month.[85] With labor so cheap, it did not take the enlisted men long to realize that they, too, could enjoy the efforts of others. The most hierarchical social system in Victorian America was the military, but in the Philippines, even the lowly private outranked the Chinese and Filipinos. "Company E was the first to discover that Chinks like to work for soldiers and the price of their labor don't amount to much."[86] Since soldiers called any non-Spanish resident of the Philippines "Chinks," the ethnicity of the natives is unclear, but their function is not. Cpl. Winfield Scott Grove directed the operations of three "slant-eyed hustlers," dubbed "Hard-tack Jim," "Sam Kee," and "Malate Mike" by the troops. The three "Chinese" handled Company E's entire wood, water, and cooking details, in return for which each man contributed fifty cents per month from his pay.[87]

Company E was not alone. Company F employed "two bias-eyed bucks" in its kitchen, and Company A had "El Señor Mauser," a Spaniard who had deserted from both the Spanish and Filipino armies.[88] Company G's "horde" of Filipino servants worked just for the leavings from the mess.[89] Fatigue details, the bane of any soldier in any army, were no more!

Colorado troops were accustomed, from life in Colorado, to Chinese working in service positions. In a land already full of Chinese immigrants, General Otis's Chinese exclusion policy had no visible effects. In the Philippines, the soldiers found that Chinese barbers charged two cents for a shave.[90] Capt. E. E. Booth recommended hiring a Chinese contractor to establish and operate a regimental laundry, rather than having the men or companies negotiate on their own for laundry services.[91] Booth's suggestion eventually was adopted, though not without some difficulty. On 6 July 1899, Captain Hilton reported to the adjutant that "one of the Chinamen assigned to me by the Quartermaster department ran away on June 25."[92]

Chinese provided other services as well. As is true any time an army is posted amidst a civilian population, the men's thoughts quickly turned to lust. While officers were free to import their wives, if they could afford it, they expected the enlisted men to remain celibate. The officers did their best to bar the men from houses of prostitution. Years later, Pvt. William S. Watson recalled his arrival in Manila.

> When we got there, we discovered that girls had come down from Hong Kong to entertain the troops and the commander put some of us on guard duty to keep the soldiers out of the places. I thought to myself I'd come a long way to walk guard duty in front of such a place.[93]

Such attempts at suppressing prostitution probably worked about as well as they usually do. In fact, well before the fall of Manila, the Army had recognized the probability of sexual activity between the men and local women. As the American regiments disembarked outside Manila, the Chief Surgeon called "attention to the great danger of syphilic infection of the men of the command."[94]

Sexual encounters aside, many of the men of the First Colorado simply hungered for some female companionship. In an all-male society, a woman is a rare and wonderful creature. After Manila's fall, the Coloradoans first tried to meet the Spanish women of the city. The European women, on the other hand, only warmed slowly to the *Americanos*. By the end of September of 1898, the Spanish women still seemed reluctant to even come outdoors and be seen by Americans.[95] By November, they were out on the streets in their carriages, although Arthur Johnson felt that the women remained far more anti-American than the Spanish men.[96] Finally, at year's end, when the Third Battalion officers held their Christmas Ball on 28 December, many Spanish women attended.[97]

In October of 1898, Lt. Gowdy complained to his mother that

There are few American women here as yet, and it makes one homesick to see some of them. I have failed to find any of the Spanish beauty you read about. Every woman you see has about a dollar's worth of powder on her face and neck. Their complexions are a muddy white.[98]

Perhaps Lt. Gowdy was simply trying to reassure his mother of his chaste existence, for other Coloradoans found the Spanish attractive enough. Captain Booth reported that "many of the young men have taken up the study of the Spanish language with an ardor which is unexplainable until one sees them casting longing looks at some beautiful senorita."[99] It is unlikely, however, that any such longings were fulfilled, for as the young Spanish women promenaded in Manila, each had a chaperone in attendance.[100]

With the Chinese prostitutes off-limits and the Spanish women relatively unavailable, that still left the Filipinas. One correspondent tried to calm home-front fears by writing "well, girls who have sweethearts in the Philippines need not worry about losing them, or rather their affections. The women look about as well as our Indian women and no better."[101] Pvt. W. G. Lumbard wrote that "the women—natives I mean— are very ugly, and the men don't get much ahead of them."[102]

On the other tack, one of the First Colorado's infantrymen penned an anonymous poem, published in the *Denver Post*, praising his Filipina girlfriend.

I would like to write a sonnet and put loving trimmings on it,
To the pretty little girl I left behind me.
But she's got another feller, and I simply want to tell her
That her loss with bitter tears will never blind me.
Here in beautiful Manila, far across the bounding billow,
I have found another sugar plum. God bless her!
And although she is the color of fried New England cruller,

It will never drain my pocketbook to dress her.

Hers a figure like a Juno, doesn't try to hide it, you know

With the finery our Yankee girls so covet;

And her mouth is a creation built for blissful osculation,

With the cutest nose on earth, above it.

And her smile! O! holy Moses! What a vision it discloses

Of a rosy portal gemmed with grinders pearly.

O! there are no flies upon her, and I fear I am a goner

To the wiles of this sweet Filipino girlie.

So the girl I left behind me isn't very apt to find me

Shedding tears of disappointment should I lose her.

For I'm really quite enraptured with the native belle I've captured

And she's gone upon her Colorado snoozer.

So exultantly I tell her, that her once best steady feller,

Whom she thinks she's downed forever in the soup,

Has been happily re-lovered, has quite easily discovered,

That she's not the only chicken in the coop.[103]

This version, appropriate for publication in Denver, still hints at the sexual liaisons common between occupying soldiers and local women. Seventy years later, Guy Sims recalled, in answer to a U.S. Army questionnaire, no more consorting with native women than by a "like number of young civilian men."[104]

The Thirteenth Minnesota Volunteer Infantry Regiment was responsible for duty as town guard. Relations between the Minnesota troops and the Coloradoans were usually excellent, with one notable exception. As Minnesotans Tom Graham and John Dallam, the regiment's "preacher soldier," were patrolling one day,

they were hailed by a half-dozen Colorado boys who had somehow or other got possession of a keg of beer and insisted upon the patrol drinking also, and made their demands so strong that John Dallam gave them a little lecture on the evils of intemperance.... When he got done speaking, he took the keg and was pouring the beer upon the ground when the Colorado boys made at rush at him and soon there was something doing.

Armed with clubs, and with the Coloradoans somewhat "dopy" from their repast, the patrol won the fight, but allowed the Colorado men to go free, the lost beer being punishment enough.[105] Such altercations aside, the First Colorado eventually took their turn helping out for a month on town patrol, garrisoning Bilibid Prison, used for both civilian and military malefactors.

The men's brown canvas uniforms, issued just before boarding the *China*, were worn out after one month in the Philippines. On 25 August 1898, Arthur Johnson was able to report that every man in the regiment had been issued a third uniform, consisting of white duck trousers and sack coats, along with an anti-mosquito head net. The uniforms had been ordered up and manufactured in Hong Kong.[106] It is unclear whether the new uniforms were Model 1886 Summer Garments, or simply replicated from the existing brown canvas uniforms but in the lighter material and shade. What is clear is that the men liked their white suits, although steady service meant that they didn't stay white for long.

Off-duty, the men amused themselves with their pets. Company A's goat Billy and Company I's dog Dewey successfully made the move into quarters in Manila, although Dewey had been wounded in the Manila assault, losing one toe on his left front foot.[107] Most memorably, the regiment had a total of seven monkeys, bought from the Filipinos for a dollar each.[108] The monkeys of Manila are Long-tailed Macaques, about two feet tall. The band had a monkey, and the drums had two: Fairchilds, a.k.a. Zeke Spivens, and Dickey, a.k.a. Josh Spruceby.[109] Pvt. Bernardt Altmeyer of Company H had a monkey named Sambo, who would pick up a stick and shoulder arms with the men when they drilled. Sambo also learned to go to the position of "present arms," or at least

16. On guard duty at Bilibid Prison. *Photo courtesy of John Stewart Post Number One, Veterans of Foreign Wars.*

"sticks," whenever he saw an officer.[110] Color Sgt. Dick Holmes's monkey "Dick" had his own tin cup, and would line up with the men for rations. On the day the officers issued the first quinine ration, the color sergeant manfully went first, to inspire the men. "Dick" the monkey was next, but as he swallowed the bitter potion, he screwed up his face, fled to the nearest tent, and tried to wipe out his mouth with a gun rag, as Company I collapsed in helpless laughter.[111]

As they settled into garrison duty, the men and officers of the First Colorado speculated freely upon their nation's potential retention of the conquered islands. Gen. Irving Hale wrote to Governor Alva Adams, advising that the United States should keep the Philippines until "the natives . . . are sufficiently educated in the ways of civilization," and that once an American-controlled government was established, the Filipinos could "pay us a sufficient revenue to compensate us for our trouble in acquiring, fumigating, civilizing, and governing the country." He concluded that "it would be barbarous and a breach of faith with the insurgents, nuisances though they be, to give it back to Spain."[112]

At least one enlisted man shared that sense of reluctant duty, explaining in a letter to his parents that the regiment could not return home "until the job of preaching Liberty, Union, and Religion to these poor ignorant heathen [was] accomplished."[113] Many in the regiment shared Hale's distaste for the islands and their inhabitants, but felt no sense of paternal responsibility to uplift or protect them. Those soldiers rejected any notion of retaining the islands. Pvt. Martin Scheidig of Pueblo left the Philippines on 26 September 1898. To a Colorado reporter's question, he replied, "they can have my part of the islands. They are a miserable place to live in."[114] William Currier concurred, telling his parents "this country is not what it is cracked up to be."[115] Other members of the regiment were not unaware of larger considerations. While not impressed with the islands themselves, Oliver Lomax recognized their strategic value. "If I had my way I would auction the group off to the highest bidder, keeping only a naval station at this port."[116]

Pvt. A. G. Baker differed from many of his fellows by praising the Filipinos. He found them to be skillful farmers, artisans, and merchants, "as efficient as the Americano." He also noted, however, that they were willing to work for extremely low wages, a circumstance against which he warned. Baker opposed annexation of the islands by the United States, for fear that statehood would flood and "demoralize our already overcrowded labor market. Thus again would we have a repitition [sic] of a Dennis [sic] Kearney agitation, a Coxey and Kelly invasion, and it would take a thousand Altgelds and Tanners to keep the labor element from an intervescent [sic] and continual struggle."[117]

As a force originally organized to quell labor disputes, the Colorado militia had certainly had occasion to reflect on the origins of labor unrest. Baker's perceptive analysis, while perhaps unusual in a lowly private, makes sense in this context. Colorado had been hard hit by the financial Panic of 1893, and the state had been alarmed when, inspired by Ohioan Jacob Coxey, unemployed miners marched on Washington. Baker's reference to the "Coxey invasion" would have struck a ready chord with Colorado readers. In citing Denis Kearney, Baker warned of the fiery leader of California's Workingmen's Party, prominent in 1877 and 1878, who had demanded the expulsion from the state of all Chinese.[118] Largely in response to the political and labor unrest caused by Kearney's agitation, the United States Congress had passed the Chinese Exclusion Act in 1882, a measure extended for an additional ten years in 1892 by the Geary Act.[119] It was these acts that General Otis sought to extend to the Philippines with his 24 September 1898 order banning Chinese from the archipelago, and Baker merely expressed a Colorado viewpoint on official fears of both Asians and labor competition.

One soldier saw the Filipinos as fellow workers. Harry Westfall, Company K's bugler, had been the youngest conductor on the Denver Tramway lines before his enlistment. Among the staunchly anti-labor militiamen, it was "whispered about that [he had] union ideas."[120] Westfall was so proud of his profession that he wore his Denver Tramway badge No. 64 from Denver to the gates of Manila. Insulted to find that *Tranvias de Filipinas* paid its conductors a mere fifteen dollars Mex per month (and its drivers only twelve), Westfall apparently led the Filipinos on strike. Three days into the strike, as townspeople struggled to operate the cars themselves, Westfall's only response to requests that he end the strike was to grin, and blow his bugle in salute to the chaos.[121]

There are few accounts from the other side—of Filipino perceptions of the Coloradoans. John M. Bass, correspondent for *Harper's Weekly*, was the dean of the American press corps in the Philippines. Hale recognized the value of a friendly press, and always reserved a bunk at headquarters for the reporter. One of Bass's dispatches, dated 30 August 1898, sheds some light on the attitudes of both peoples.

> The Filipino is the true child of the East. His moral fibre is as the web of the pineapple gauze of which the women make their dresses. He will cheat, steal, and lie beyond the orthodox limit of the Anglo-Saxon. His unreliability and the persistence with

which he disobeys orders are irritating beyond description; besides this, his small stature and color invite abuse. There can be no doubt our soldiers are spoiling for a fight. They hate and despise the native for the manner he has lied to and cheated them, and on the whole they are inclined to treat the Filipino the way a burly policeman treats a ragged street urchin. The native is like a child, unreasonable, and easily affected by small things. Unable to appreciate the benefits of a good government, he fiercely resents the rough manner in which the soldier jostles him out of the way.[122]

Filipinos resented American mistreatment, but since the Americans viewed them as "children" who "disobeyed orders," their "small stature and color invited abuse." Clearly, at least some of the Americans had had enough of duty in a foreign land, and were irritated to find that land full of "foreigners." W. T. Byrne confirmed the reporter's observations when he told his brother that "there are about 10 natives to every foot of ground, and down in town one has to knock them off the sidewalk to get along, and we have just got disgusted with them."[123]

If other Americans and Filipinos still hoped for amicable relations, political developments worked to the contrary. In the late summer of 1898, Aguinaldo moved his headquarters from Cavite to a monastery at Malolos, twenty miles north of Manila. On 15 September 1898, in a church next door, he convened a national assembly, attended by 100 delegates. The delegates, westernized Filipinos, addressed each other as "citizen," but such egalitarianism was limited entirely to language. Most of the delegates were drawn from the class of rich intelligentsia called by the Spanish the *ilustrados*, long used by the Spanish to administer colonial edicts among the population. Whatever Aguinaldo's vision of an independent and democratic Philippine nation, the ilustrados intended that new country to confirm and protect their status. Expecting the position to be cosmetic, the ilustrados voted Aguinaldo president.[124]

A rich attorney, Felipe Calderon, drafted a Filipino constitution that vested most power in a legislature run by ilustrados, an "oligarchy of intelligence." Only the landed upper class could vote, and there would be no agrarian reform or redistribution of land. The "Malolos Constitution" divided the Filipino Congress into a conservative faction supporting it, and a radical faction in opposition. That division lasted through the Philippine-American War of 1899–1902, with many of the conservatives siding with the Americans as being most likely to maintain the status quo.[125]

In any event, the United States did not plan to recognize any constitution developed by Filipinos. President William McKinley seems initially to have regarded the Philippines simply as a combat theatre. On the other hand, simply to have sent infantry to the islands after Commodore Dewey's naval victory carried with it an implication that the United States did not intend merely to destroy the Spanish fleet and then relinquish the islands, either to Spain or to the Filipinos. Early in September of 1898, *Literary Digest* published its survey, indicating that the vast majority of American newspapers favored retention; only six suggested an American withdrawal.[126] Aware of at least editorial support, on 16 September 1898 McKinley informed the Spanish that, at minimum, the United States had to acquire Manila and Luzon as permanent outposts, as an aftermath of the war.[127] The President toured America in October, and found great public acceptance of his pro-annexation speeches.[128] By late fall of 1898, McKinley believed that the American people and the Republican Party favored annexation of all the Philippine Islands, and directed America's peace commissioners to secure them.[129]

McKinley explained to a group of clergy his decision to keep the Philippines. After "prayer," he concluded that Filipinos "were unfit for self-government [and] would soon have anarchy and misrule." So, the United States would keep the islands "to educate the Filipinos and up-lift and Christianize them, and by God's grace do the very best we could by them, as our fellow men for whom Christ died."[130] Private Baker's self-published book had argued against keeping the Philippines, but he may have best summed up the issue when he noted, in resignation, "we must not take down our flag when once it has been planted."[131]

Since Manila fell one day after the cease-fire, the United States agreed to pay Spain $20 million for the archipelago.[132] The representatives of the United States and Spain signed the Treaty of Paris, relinquishing Spanish control of the Philippines, on 10 December 1898. But, the United States Senate would not meet to ratify the treaty until February of 1899.[133] While the Philippines' final fate hung in the balance, awaiting Congressional action, tensions steadily increased between the Americans and the Filipinos, as the Americans made no move to depart from the islands. News of the treaty did not improve the situation. On 12 December 1898, Hale warned the Adjutant General of the Second Division of the Eighth Army Corps that "the insurgents are becoming so restless and aggressive that unless they are strictly required to be behind their line there is liable to be a collision with our Outpost at any time."[134] Two days later, Cpl. Roy Harris filled his diary with routine details of fatigue duty, battalion drill, policing the grounds, and family correspondence, and then, as an afterthought, noted that "there is some talk of trouble with the Philippinos."[135]

The Filipino and American officers had been sizing each other up, in a professional sense, literally since the Americans took Manila. During the actual assault, the American right flank was occupied by the Thirteenth Minnesota. Immediately to the right of the Americans, Filipino Gen. Mariano Noriel commanded the Philippine insurgents. He detailed Lt. Col. Juan Cailles to analyze the Americans' performance in combat. Son of a French father and an Anglo-Indian mother, Cailles would rise by 1899 to the rank of brigadier general and *Jefe Superior Politico-Militar* (Governor) of Laguna Province in southwestern Luzon; he was a capable and informed observer.[136] He reported to Noriel that the Minnesotans had faltered under fire. According to Cailles, many of the officers hid behind the church, while the enlisted men hid in the grass or ran away.[137] Whatever the truth of the information, the colonel's report led the Filipinos to underestimate the Americans' fighting ability.

The First Colorado's officers did their best to gather intelligence as well, in preparation for what many supposed to be the coming conflict. On 3 October 1898, Capt. Kyle Rucker and 1st Sgt. Adelbert West of Company E reconnoitered the village of Pandagan, across the Pasig River from the Manila suburb of Malabon. The captain smiled and introduced himself to the Filipino garrison, and an insurgent captain conducted the two Americans through the defenses. They counted 200 insurgents, and secretly mapped the town, before returning to their own lines. In conversation, Rucker found that the Filipino captain and his men were among those disarmed at bayonet-point by Company E on 14 August 1898, near Malabon. The American did not mention his role in that affair. "It may have been the smiling faces of Capt. Rucker and Sgt. West that dissipated the suspicions of the native soldiers when they arrived; or, perhaps, it was their Camp Dewey Spanish."[138] The First Colorado regarded this reconnaissance as a particularly clever ruse.

Because of the perceived insurgent threat, the First Colorado was shifted to outposts near Balic Balic Cemetery, opposite Filipino (formerly Spanish) fortifications designated Blockhouses Number Five and Number Six. Tension mounted in the Philippines in mid-December when the terms of the American treaty with Spain came out, but the Senate had yet to ratify the treaty. Aguinaldo and his ministers were well aware of sentiment in America opposing annexation, and hoped that when Congress finally came back into session, the Senate would refuse to acquire the Philippines. As Col. Henry McCoy, commanding the First Colorado after Hale's promotion to general, explained to the *Rocky Mountain News* correspondent, "the insurgents are around the city in great numbers and are acting ugly. It looks like they mean business."[139] An exasperated infantryman sighed, "nothing would be finer that [*sic*] a good lively tussle with those natives right now."[140]

Despite the alarms, there was no "tussle"—yet. As the United States

Senate debated the merits of Philippine annexation, Rudyard Kipling's famous poem "The White Man's Burden" circulated informally through the nation, even before its official publication in *McClure's Magazine* in February of 1899.[141] Theodore Roosevelt sent advance sheets of the poem to Massachusetts Senator Henry Cabot Lodge on 12 January 1899; Lodge read them and replied favorably on 14 January.[142] Kipling himself subtitled the poem "The United States and the Philippine Islands," clearly linking it to the debate. In the Senate debates, Lodge led the charge for annexation; Maine's Republican Senator George Hoar fought it, as placing the United States over a subject people. In the end, Nebraska's William Jennings Bryan, although opposing annexation, urged ratification of the treaty with Spain, suggesting a later referendum on keeping the Philippines. Bryan's support turned the tide, and on 6 February 1899 the Senate approved the treaty, and annexation, by two votes.[143] By then, however, independent of any Washington vote, the Colorado troops had been fighting the Filipinos for two days.

After the initial alarms following the treaty's announcement, the last two weeks of December remained tense, but quiet. The First Colorado's officers used the lull to survey the terrain between the lines and the Filipino blockhouses.[144]

Maj. Gen. Elwell Stephen Otis, commanding in the Philippines since General Merritt was ordered to the Paris peace talks shortly after Manila's fall, fractured that lull.[145]

Frank Dickey wrote to his parents that

> Tuesday night [3 January 1899] orders were issued for every man to sleep with his clothes on and gun handy. Nothing happened however. Last night appeared Major General Otis's Proclamation to the Philippinoes.[146]

Otis issued his general proclamation on 4 January 1899, asserting American sovereignty over the Philippine Islands, and signing his name as "Military Governor of the Philippine Islands."[147] As evidenced by putting the men on alert, Otis clearly expected Filipino reaction. The next day, 5 January, Aguinaldo responded with his own proclamation, issuing a formal protest and insisting on Filipino control of their own country, and the diplomatic lines were drawn.[148]

These were just the opening salvoes in a war of dueling proclamations. On 7 January, two Colorado soldiers arrested a Filipino for tearing down a posted copy of Otis's proclamation.[149] On 9 January, Aguinaldo's second proclamation reached Manila, terming any American advance beyond the walls of the city an act of war and a declaration of war. Otis forbade its publication or posting in Manila.[150] Col. Juan Cailles explained in his own 10 January 1899 missive to the U.S. Secretary of War, "war, war, is what we want."[151] Private Dickey was too busy to mail his 4 January 1899 letter, and managed an 11 January update before sending it out. Soldier mail moved by ship, a six-weeks' passage; war news would go by telegraph. He predicted ominously that "long before you read these lines you will know whether we have 'met the enemy and they are ours' or not."[152]

The regiment's officers also anticipated immediate conflict. They were especially concerned about the possibility of a general uprising within the walls of Manila. Each night, sentries guarded the entrance to each company quarters, as a precaution against assassins.[153] The soldiers tightened their guard at the gates of town, as well. Marveling at the sudden increase in the number of coffins being carried into the city, when all the cemeteries lay outside the walls, the watch stopped one party to inspect their burden. In front of the guard, the bottom of the coffin fell out, dumping its load of Mauser rifles! With the possibility that Manila was already full of "secreted arms and ammunition," the troops began inspecting churches and other public buildings for cached weapons.[154] Boasting of U.S. sentries' prowess, Arthur Johnson noted that in mid-January, "Smith of the South Dakota regiment inaugurated the custom of making good Filipinos . . . when he bagged two 'hombres' who tried to slay him with machetes."[155] In Johnson's slang, a "good Filipino" was akin to Gen. Phil Sheridan's famous quote about "the only good Indians I ever saw were dead."

Colorado was responsible for a segment of the American line defending Manila. In case of a fight, the First Colorado's officers planned to send eight companies out into their lines opposite the Filipino blockhouses. Expecting fierce street fighting against the Filipino population of Manila, the officers planned to retain four companies in Manila, to defend the barracks.[156] The Coloradoans also began conducting mock street-fighting tactical exercises. "Then perhaps the command 'charge' is given and shouting and howling they sprint down the road and make an imaginary routing of a group of banana girls, to the decided fright of the same."[157] The sinister purpose of the drills cannot have been lost on the watching Filipinos.

The long-awaited Malolos Constitution was distributed on 27 January 1899, intensifying nationalistic feelings among the Filipinos.[158] By the end of the month, Nebraska troops guarding the San Juan Bridge were reporting attempts by Filipino sentries to intimidate their pickets. On 30 January, General Hale requested permission to use force against bullying Filipino sentries, without advance notice.[159] In an undated field signal, filed under one dated 1 February 1899, Hale noted that "in case trouble arises during night it is Genl [Arthur] MacArthur's plan to burn all on Lico Road and some other streets in bamboo districts."[160] Apparently, MacArthur intended to destroy Filipino neighborhoods on Manila's outskirts in order to eliminate potential cover for the insurrectos.

At this critical juncture, the First Colorado finally learned that six regiments of regulars were on the way to the Philippines to relieve the volunteer troops who had, after all, enlisted to fight the Spanish. As the third regiment to arrive in the Philippines, Colorado was sure to be replaced. But, Colonel McCoy pointed out, "if there is to be trouble between the insurgents and the American forces we sincerely hope that it will occur before our regiment is ordered home, as we are anxious to do our share of the work."[161] The regiment had come a long way from the welcoming cries of "Amigo!" that had greeted their arrival less than a year before.

Each soldier assumes his war is the most important war. On 1 February 1899, Private Johnson confidently predicted that "the initial blow will be struck where the Colorado and Nebraska regiments cover the line."[162] On that day, the officers doubled all the outpost details, and that night, the men slept in their uniforms, with one third of the company awake and under arms at all times.[163] Each man abandoned his "white suit of the tropics for the blue shirt, brown trousers and leggings used in the field."[164] Even so, after so many alarms, Cpl. Harry McCauley was able to write his weekly *Denver Republican* column on 2 February 1899, explaining that "the [men] will not believe any 'nigger scare' is the real article until they see Springfield-made Filipino funerals wending their way down the street."[165] The First Colorado ended up conducting those Filipino funerals themselves.

CHAPTER FIVE

Civilize 'Em with a Krag

Months of rising tension between the Americans and the insurrectos, fueled by uncertainty over the intentions of the United States regarding eventual Philippine independence, exploded into war on 4 February 1899. Each side expected a conflict. Neither side ended up with the conflict it expected. The fighting both intensified and polarized the Coloradoans' attitudes toward the Filipinos, and called into question the First Colorado's role in the front lines of America's empire.

American authorities termed that conflict "the Philippine Insurrection," to imply unjust rebellion against legitimate authority; Filipinos call it "the Second Philippine War for Independence." If the war between the United States and Spain is called the Spanish-American War, perhaps the most even-handed appellation for the conflict between the United States and the Filipinos is the Philippine-American War. As Eighth Corps commanders plotted their strategy in the days just before the outbreak, they assigned eight companies of the First Colorado regiment to service in the trenches. There, Col. Henry McCoy apportioned them between a firing line, a support detachment, and a reserve. In front of the trenches, between the American lines and the Filipino positions, the regiment established outposts, from which to keep an eye on the enemy.[1]

The insurrectos had moved into Manila's outlying Spanish fortifications as the Americans entered the city on 13 August 1898. In addition to the Spanish trenches, the Filipinos also occupied the fifteen Spanish blockhouses that ringed Manila.[2] Each of these two-story structures, approximately twenty-four feet by twenty-four feet by twenty-four feet,

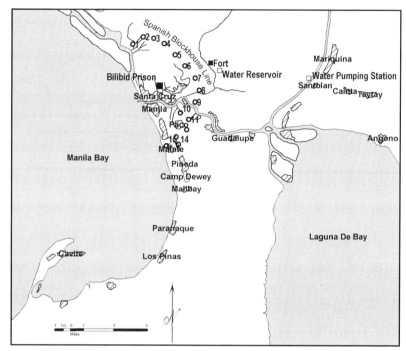

Map 2. Map of Manila and Environs[3]

was built of two-inch-thick planks, and featured firing slits and, on top, an observation cupola. Like the Spanish blockhouses in Cuba, the fortifications had been built to counter the insurrectos. They offered their garrisons, Spanish or Filipino, ample protection from small arms fire; since the Spanish artillery had been vastly superior to the insurrecto guns, the blockhouses were never intended to resist shellfire.

Colorado's segment of the line fronted on Blockhouses Number Four, Five, and Six. Number Four sat to the north, at the point where Colorado's position adjoined the First South Dakota Infantry. Four hundred yards south, centered on Colorado's section of the line, lay Number Five. Another 750 yards to the south, where the extreme right of the Colorado line touched the First Nebraska Infantry's trenches, sat Number Six.[4] Unlike the Colorado troops, comfortably quartered in Manila, the Nebraska garrison had been camped in the field, 200 yards behind their

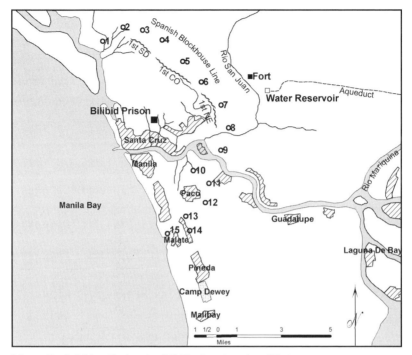

Map 3. Battlefield at Outbreak of Philippine-American War[5]

outposts, for several months.[6] Depending on location, four to eight hundred yards separated the American lines from the Filipino fortifications.

On 4 February 1899, night fell black, starless, and cold.[7] Companies B and K manned the outposts in front of Colorado's lines, without expecting any immediate trouble. The remainder of the regiment retired to the barracks along Calle Alix and in the Plaza Santa Ana; because of the general air of tension in the preceding weeks, the soldiers slept in their clothes. Colorado's officers, attired for a social evening, in their white uniforms, sat down for a game of "progressive whist" (bridge).[8]

At the Nebraska position to the right of the Colorado outposts, in Manila's eastern suburb of Santa Mesa, First Nebraska Pvts. William W. Grayson and Orville Miller patrolled their camp perimeter. At 8:30 P.M., at the bridge over the San Juan River, they heard low whistles. Investigating, the two men saw four Filipinos in the darkness. Grayson called out "Halt," to which one of the Filipinos responded, "*Alto.*" Again, Grayson demanded, "Halt!" Again, perhaps in mockery, the insurrecto patrol responded with "*Alto!*" Grayson fired his Springfield, killing one of the Filipinos. Two of the other Filipinos jumped forward; Miller shot one, and Grayson, quickly chambering another round, shot the other. The fourth Filipino escaped, as the two Americans ran back into their own camp, Grayson crying, "Line up, fellows, the niggers are in here all through these lines."[9]

The Nebraskans may or may not have overreacted to the supposed insurrecto provocation; the Colorado troops certainly approved of their response. Arthur Johnson, described the action two days later:

> When the barefooted sentinel of old gold color attempted to do duty at the Nebraska end of the bridge he was promptly shot dead by the Nebraska man. Another shell went into the Nebraska man's gun, and he made another good Filipino out of the comrade of the sentinel.[10]

Grayson's words and deeds, while not exactly immortal, triggered the "Philippine Insurrection." In response to the shooting at the bridge, the insurrectos in Blockhouse Number Seven returned fire, triggering a Filipino fusillade against the American outposts. This was followed by calm.[11] As the sound of firing reached Manila, the officers sounded the "call to quarters," the command for the men to gather their weapons and prepare for action. Ironically, Lt. Charles Haughwout of Company F, before even taking the field, received Colorado's first wound of the Philippine-American War. As he dressed in his room, preparing to move to the front, he was wounded in the right calf by a bullet that came through his window.[12]

A second outbreak of firing sent the troops into action. "Each company filed into the street, received the order, 'Fours Left' or 'Fours Right,' and was off to war."[13] Four companies—A, H, C, and M—

remained behind, to guard the barracks.[14] As they formed up in the Plaza Santa Ana, some of the Spanish residents cheered them on from second-story windows; others just looked on in seeming indifference.[15] As the Colorado ranks swung around the corner into Calle Alix, their column fell alongside the First South Dakota Infantry, coming in from their barracks in the San Miguel district. The Coloradoans were marching "at route step," requiring them to maintain their alignment but allowing them to carry their arms at will and to talk. Moving down the Balic Balic Road beside the Dakotans, the excited troops gave vent to a series of "yips" and "hoorays."[16]

The American column deployed behind the outposts, the South Dakotans leaving the road to take up position on the left of the Colorado line. Backing up the two outpost companies, the Colorado troops moved onto ground they had already prepared and surveyed, along a small ridge facing the Filipino blockhouses. By 11:00 P.M., the First Colorado, eight companies strong, covered a one-mile north-south line from the Balic Balic Road south to the pipeline connecting Manila to its waterworks.[17]

Companies F and G, under Captains Ralph Comings and David Howard, respectively, deployed behind the brush on the ridge over-looking the rice paddies, but lower than the opposing hill surmounted by the enemy blockhouses. Company E, under Capt. Kyle Rucker, lay in the swamp fronting Blockhouses Five and Six. Companies B, L, and K, commanded by Captains Frank Carroll, William Cornell, and David La Salle, went on line directly opposite Blockhouse Five; Maj. Charles Anderson commanded that battalion. The remainder of the regiment fell in on the left, toward the South Dakota lines opposite Number Four.[18] Lt. Col. Cassius Moses commanded the Colorado regiment from the center; Maj. William Grove directed the left flank.[19] As the American forces settled into their new positions, their Filipino counterparts were reinforcing their own lines. Just before midnight, the insurrectos commenced heavy firing against the United States troops. As shooting continued in front of the Nebraska positions on Colorado's left, Companies

F, G, L, and B joined in the firing, blazing into the darkness in support of their prairie comrades.[20]

While the Americans in the lines deterred any projected Filipino assault, their nervous colleagues on guard in Manila itself encountered no organized uprising. Nonetheless, there were some scattered Filipino attacks on individual Americans, quickly suppressed by the provost guard.[21] At the first firing, Muriel Bailey, the *San Francisco Examiner's* intrepid reporter, had armed herself with a pistol and headed to the front in a rented carriage, passing the Colorado troops in the Calle Alix. Ordered back to Manila by the military commanders, she arrived at her hotel only to find men carrying in a soldier wounded in a street fight. "Four niggers jumped on him with knives below here in this alley," one of the men explained.[22] Individual Filipinos may have assaulted lone American sentries, but the American guards never had to face the nightmare of concerted attacks in the streets of Manila.

Each man carried forty-five rounds in his looped cartridge belt, and another 105 rounds in his haversack.[23] Out on the firing line, the First Colorado began to run low on ammunition. Pvt. Frank Lyons, Company K, detailed to the regimental quartermaster's detachment, coolly rode up and down the Colorado positions with a box of cartridges on the pommel of his saddle, dispensing fresh rounds.[24] Despite the heat of battle, the men shivered in the cold night, having turned out lightly dressed for combat.[25] For all that, the men were in good spirits. In some satisfaction that the expected conflict had finally arrived, one Coloradoan stated, "they've started something they can't stop this time," as he loaded another round into his rifle.[26] Like most of the Americans, he automatically assumed that the Filipinos had instigated the conflict, and that the Americans were only defending themselves, albeit in someone else's country.

Lieutenant Colonel Moses, rather than letting the men fire at will, ordered them to fire measured volleys at the blockhouses and the huts between. With each volley, the Filipinos would shout back defiantly, "*Viva la Republica Filipina*," or "*Malo*," to signify a miss.[27] At one o'clock in the morning on 5 February, Brig. Gen. Irving Hale and Col. Henry McCoy began to ride the line, checking the security of the Colorado defenses. In quarters before the outbreak, the men had taken to requesting "seconds" of food with the borrowed phrase, "*mucho bueno, uno mas*," (very good, one more), an expression which had found general use for other occasions as well. When their colonel inquired as to their progress, the men told him of their volleys against the Filipinos. McCoy replied, "*mucho bueno, uno mas*," to the laughter of the men. After that, each Filipino volley was met with an American cry, "*mucho bueno, uno mas.*"[28]

At 3:00 A.M., McCoy detached Companies D and I, under the command of Major Grove, to support the hard-pressed Nebraskans.[29] Through the rest of the long night, the American troops all around Manila traded shots with their new enemies; in the darkness, with both sides sheltered by breastworks, it is unlikely that either did much damage.[30] With dawn, the Americans prepared to break through the insurrecto encirclement at the blockhouse line. Rice paddies, punctuated with low dikes or ridges every twelve feet, lay between the American and Filipino fortifications.[31] The Spanish-built Filipino blockhouses, impervious to rifle fire, dominated the field. During the night, the American fleet had been unable to lay the insurrecto lines under its guns. With daylight, Dewey's ships maneuvered to each side of Manila, and began shelling the Filipino positions.

In the early 1880s, the United States Navy had begun its first tentative efforts to build a modern "steel navy" with the so-called "ABCD ships," the steel cruisers *Atlanta*, *Boston*, and *Chicago*, and the dispatch boat *Dolphin*.[32] Commissioned in 1885, the *Boston* was already outmoded, but her two eight-inch guns could still throw 250-pound projectiles well inland.[33] She took up position off Malate, south of Manila, and shelled the insurrecto trenches by the sea. Commodore George Dewey had wrecked Spain's Pacific fleet with his own flotilla of cruisers, armed, like the *Boston*, with, eight-inch guns.[34] Anticipating that the reduction of Manila might require more firepower, the Navy had dispatched two powerful monitors, the *Monterey* and *Monadnock*, armed with ten-inch and twelve-inch guns. Superficially akin to the "ironclad" monitors of the Civil War, these all-steel "New Navy" monitors were thoroughly modern ships.[35] Basically low-freeboard vessels each equipped with twin two-gun turrets, they resembled disembodied battleship batteries mounted on rafts. Alexander C. Brown described them as "designed to combine heavy striking power with concealment and the presentation of a negligible target area."[36] In fact, the *Monterey* had water-ballast tanks to allow her to partially submerge to even further reduce her target area in combat. Actually, submerging was an all-too-real possibility. The two ships were the only monitors ever to cross the Pacific. With less than three feet of freeboard, the ungainly craft shipped heavy seas over their decks the entire way, and only made the crossing with extreme difficulty.[37] Wisely, the Navy decided to leave them in the Philippines. *Monadnock*, as of 1919, was the Submarine Depot Ship for the U.S. Navy's Asiatic Fleet.[38] Ironically, like their stateside sisters, the monitors ended their days as mother ships for the Navy's World War I-vintage submarines, their low decks offering easy access to the weapons system that most closely replaced the monitors' role of heavy hitting power and concealment.

Whatever the monitors' seaworthiness, the soldiers of the First Colorado were keenly appreciative of the Navy's gunnery support, and eagerly anticipated the additional strength of the monitors. Company F's Sgt. Edres Herbert noted, "every soldier in the army is interested in the arrival of the *Monterey* and every salute we hear, everybody shouts the *Monterey*."[39] The *Monterey* finally steamed into Manila Bay on 4 August 1898, with the *Monadnock* close behind.[40] Between the *Boston* and the monitors, the insurrectos could not remain in the open along the coast. Unable to flee south along the coast road, the hapless insurrectos took shelter in the old American trenches, where the naval artillery sought them out; the Filipinos then fled east along the Pasig River, behind Aguinaldo's lines around Manila. The soldiers' faith in the peculiar ships was justified. They called the projectiles from the big guns "soul-searchers," and on 5 February 1899 the *Monadnock* lofted 500-pound shells against the Filipinos all the way from Manila Bay to the Laguna de Bay.[41] Over the course of the day, the monitor fired over 400 ten-inch and four-inch shells at the Filipinos.[42] Muriel Bailey saw a ten-inch shell from the *Monadnock* sail straight into Blockhouse No. 14, leaving only three different corner posts to mark the former location of the fortification.[43]

North of Manila, the navy inflicted the same damage. San Francisco's Union Iron Works launched the cruiser *Charleston*, the first "New Navy" steel ship built on the West Coast, in July of 1888.[44] Like the *Boston*, the *Charleston* carried two eight-inch guns, with which she shelled the town of Caloocan approximately three miles above Manila.[45] The *Charleston* was assisted by the *Callao*, an 1888 Spanish gunboat captured by the U.S. Navy and converted to American use.[46] The *Callao* mounted one-, two-, and three-pounder guns, and machine guns; between the cruiser and the gunboat, the Filipinos along the coast had no choice but to flee inland.[47] While the Navy played an important role in supporting American troops along the coast, however, the First Colorado found themselves fighting without assistance from naval gunnery, since the City of Manila blocked the fleet from firing at their opponents. And so, while the naval guns, and the threat they represented, had silenced Spanish artillery in the days before the fall of Manila, in fighting against the Filipinos the First Colorado would have to depend upon the Utah Light Artillery.

By sunrise on Sunday, 5 February 1899, Captain Wedgewood of the Utah Light Artillery had led the first platoon of his Company A into the Colorado lines, placing its two 3.2-inch B.L. rifles on Balic Balic Road near the Sampaloc Cemetery.[48] The artillery pieces could hit whatever their gunners could see, but at the close range between the American lines and the Filipino lines, so could the insurrecto riflemen. The Utah guns had to move into the cemetery, firing through gaps in the wall, in order to shelter their crews from Filipino marksmen. From that position, the guns could not fire on Blockhouse Number Six, as Colorado's Company E lay between the artillery and the enemy, but the Utah battery shelled Blockhouse Number Seven, on Colorado's right. The Utah guns also fired on Blockhouse Number Five, only 300 yards in front, and on a little fortified stone church immediately to the blockhouse's right.[49] The blockhouse itself was only hit once, by a shell striking its foundation, and the Filipinos within continued firing.[50]

Frank Lyons, the faithful quartermaster, handed out the last of the ammunition he'd been able to carry on his horse.[51] At 8:10 A.M., Colonel McCoy ordered his infantry to take Blockhouse Number Five. While other companies continued firing on the insurrecto fortification, Companies B, K, and L, and part of E advanced in rushes, moving from "one vantage point to another."[52] The Colorado soldiers took ground by platoons, with one platoon firing while the other attacked.[53] As the Colorado assault neared the blockhouse, its garrison tried to flee, only to fall to the guns of the rest of the regiment. A Utah gunner recalled, "as the Tagalans moved from their cover they fell many deep before the blasting volleys of the invincible Coloradoans."[54] "The orders were to let no Filipino live."[55] Arthur Johnson gloated, "to shoot down human beings like pigeons as they are hurled from the trap has surely been a dream of every warrior."[56] The Filipinos had been reduced to objects of sport!

Colonel McCoy and Lt. Tingley Wood were the first Americans to enter the blockhouse, with Company K hot on their heels. A detail rushed up into the cupola on top of the structure, the better to fire upon the fleeing Filipinos.[57] By 8:15, Blockhouse Number Five had fallen to the Americans.[58] The victory had come at some cost: As Company L rushed the blockhouse on the left of the attack, Pvt. Charles Carlson was killed by a shot through the head, and Pvt. Charles Boyce was wounded in the left knee. Company K's Pvt. Harry "Joe" Wheeler had a finger nearly severed.[59] In Company B, Pvt. Charles Morrison was hit in the left hand, and Pvt. Orton Weaver received a wound in the left thigh, causing a compound fracture.[60] Company B's Pvt. Maurice Parkhurst was also wounded.[61]

While Colorado stormed Blockhouse Number Five, the Utah battery shifted its fire to Blockhouse Number Four, 1,700 yards distant, with

17. General Irving Hale (second from left) and his staff in front of Blockhouse Five.
Photo courtesy of John Stewart Post Number One, Veterans of Foreign Wars.

devastating effect. The South Dakota troops quickly took it.[62] With the Colorado regiment in motion, the way was now open for the guns to fire on Blockhouse Number Six, but as the battery trained its weapons in that direction, they found "the insurgents had disappeared into the woods with the swift-moving Colorado infantrymen hard on their track."[63] Along with some of the Nebraska men, Companies F, G, and the remainder of E took Blockhouse Number Six; from the captured fortification, they then fired on the fleeing Filipinos.[64]

Companies D and I had reinforced the First Nebraska Regiment at 7:00 A.M., and accompanied the Nebraskans as they attacked and captured Number Seven. During that charge, Company I engaged in a "hard fight" in the small village between Blockhouses Number Seven and Eight.[65] A shot from uncaptured Number Eight, to the right of the action, killed Pvt. Elmer F. Doran, and Cpl. William H. Earle received a "light bullet scratch" on his left cheek.[66]

In the months between the fall of Manila and the outbreak of hostilities between the Americans and the insurrectos, the Filipinos had built small villages along the blockhouse line, temporary communities providing shelter for the insurgent garrisons. East of the fortifications, behind the Filipino trenches, sat the permanent communities of Balicbalic and San Juan. The *nipa* huts of the villages provided cover for Filipino marksmen, but not for long. Shortly after securing the blockhouses on the morning of 5 February, Companies F and G burned the little village between Blockhouses Number Seven and Number Six; the troops burned the latter fortification as well. Company E passed through the blockhouse line and over the ridge, and burned the village of San Juan, before returning to the American positions. E, F, and G then settled in at the blockhouses, ate breakfast, and waited for orders.[67]

On the left of the line, Companies B, K, and L consumed their breakfast, and then began firing on the insurgents in Balicbalic, driving the insurrectos from the town. One hundred yards separated the Filipinos from any cover to their rear. As each man would run, the Colorado soldiers, including Company E, would fire at them. The fleeing insurgents would crawl behind the dikes of the rice paddies; the First Colorado would shoot them as they crossed over the dikes. Arthur Johnson described "the fine sport of scaring out the prey and then leisurely pulling it down in its vain attempt to get away."[68]

Finally, Colonel McCoy asked General Hale for permission to take and destroy Balicbalic, by now abandoned by its inhabitants. After receiving authorization, Companies B, K, and L rushed the village and burned it to the ground, leaving only the ruined stone church.[69] All told, the First Colorado burned twelve villages, of various sizes, on 5 February. In one, Company E found a sick old Filipina. They burned everything in the town but her house. Late in the afternoon, the Hospital Corps collected the old woman, and then Company E put her house to the torch as well.[70]

Colorado was not alone in its incendiary fervor. In Paco, just northwest of Malate, 100 insurgents got into the stone church, and from there and huts along the road, fired on the First California, and then on the ambulances that came to retrieve the California wounded. California's Colonel Smith held his men back, while the Sixth United States Artillery brought in fieldpieces and shelled the church. After the guns killed half the occupants, the California regiment stormed the insurrecto position and burned Paco; there was no more firing from Paco's huts.[71]

By late morning, most of the First Colorado had settled in along the blockhouse line. Companies A, C, and H marched out from Manila and relieved Companies B, K, and L. The fresh troops stacked arms and busied themselves, turning Blockhouse Number Five into a regimental headquarters.[72] On the right, however, Companies D and I continued to fight alongside the Nebraskans, as they advanced along the pipeline that supplied Manila's water.

Manila's waterworks consisted of a pumping station located on the Rio Mariquina at Santolan, seven miles southeast of the city.[74] There, pumps pushed water through an aqueduct up over the ridge separating the Mariquina Valley from Manila Bay, down across the Rio San Mateo, then over the Rio San Juan and into Manila, entering through Sampaloc, the city's easternmost district. The aqueduct crossed the San Mateo near the stone bridge of the Santa Mesa Road. Just upstream, to the north of the stone bridge, a frail bamboo span crossed the river. East of the river, on a hill behind the insurrecto lines, the aqueduct fed a Spanish-built reservoir called the *depósito [de agua]*, intended to supply Manila for two days if the pumps failed. The Spanish had guarded that facility against sabotage with

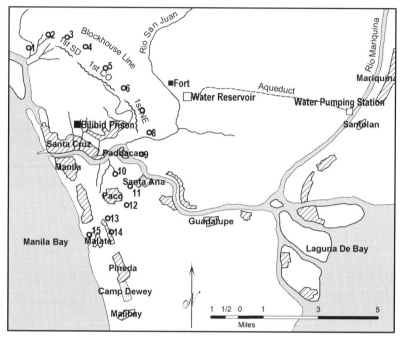

Map 4. Map of Mariquina and Waterworks[73]

a fortified barracks, built of stone. The little fort was surrounded by high stone walls, with lookout towers on each corner, and the only gate to the east, away from the river. After the Spanish departed, the insurrectos converted the barracks into an arsenal, guarded by a small garrison.[75] This stronghold overlooked the Nebraska lines, and the depósito held water critical to Manila.

At 11:30 A.M., a time later determined precisely by examination of watches stopped by immersion in water, the First Nebraska and its attached Colorado companies stormed over the two bridges. The bulk of the men went over the stone bridge; the Colorado troops crossed on the bamboo structure. The spindly bridge, carrying fourteen enlisted men and Lieutenants Harry Clotworthy, of Company I, and Albert Luther, of Company D, failed and sank to the surface of the river. As the men tumbled into the Rio San Mateo, Pvt. Cass White of Company D was shot in the head; his body was lost and not recovered until the Nebraskans found it floating in the river on 7 February 1899.[76] By the time the men extricated themselves from the twenty-foot-deep waters, the remainder of the soldiers were advancing on the arsenal.[77]

The arsenal's stone walls effectively protected its garrison from rifle fire, and from its shelter the Filipinos poured a devastating fire into the advancing infantry. Six Nebraska companies, supported by two big Utah guns, advanced on the right, while the other two Nebraska companies and the two Colorado companies, reinforced by two new Utah Nordenfeldt guns liberated from the Spanish, moved up on the left. The artillery forced the insurgent garrison to abandon the arsenal.[78] By then, the infantry had flanked the position on three sides; as the fifty defenders exited the one gate, each was shot down by the Americans. The fighting was over by noon, and the Americans held the depósito.[79] The Colorado troops finished their day's work by dumping several thousand insurgent Remington rifle rounds, unusable in American weapons, into the Rio San Mateo.[80] By about 3:30 P.M., after nineteen hours of continuous combat, the firing had stopped all along the lines, ending the first day of the "Philippine Insurrection."[81] With pride, Arthur Johnson reported that "the First . . . now has numerous scalps dangling at its belts," a chilling figure of speech given the Colorado militia's Sand Creek legacy.[82]

Two Colorado civilians fought with the First Colorado on 5 February. One was H. G. Shockley, son of William Shockley of Denver, who had arrived in Manila in October as a deck hand on the *S.S. Condor*. Since then, he had been working on the staff of the newspaper *The American*, and living with Company E.[83] The other was

> George Hopkins, colored, who formerly cooked for Gen. Hale and who still directs the kitchen at the Colorado regimental Headquarters. He took his place in E company's ranks Feb. 4 and claims that he killed at least one "nigger."[84]

Blacks couldn't enlist in the First Colorado, but as a civilian, Hopkins at least was welcome to fight alongside the men of Company E.

Along the entire perimeter of Manila, American forces killed approximately 3,000 Filipinos on 5 February; depending upon the estimate, the Eighth Army Corps lost fifty-one (some reports say fifty-nine) dead, and almost 300 wounded.[85] In their sector, the South Dakota, Colorado, and Nebraska troops killed over 100 insurrectos in what came to be called the Battle of Sampaloc or, variously, Balicbalic.[86] In front of their lines, the First Colorado found forty-nine Filipino dead, and captured fifteen wounded and six unwounded prisoners.[87] It seems that, in order to survive, an insurrecto had to avoid being shot in the thick of battle; once the shooting had stopped, the militiamen would accept a surrender. The regiment had suffered three men killed in action and, counting Lieutenant Haughwout's injury on the evening of the fourth, seven wounded.[88] The First Colorado's low casualty rate, according to one member, was because "from the way the cowards fired, [they] couldn't hit a balloon ten feet in front of them."[89] The Filipinos may simply have been surprised. In months of skirmishing with the Spanish, the Europeans had never attacked the Filipino trenches on a broad front. Accustomed to a static war in which opposing soldiers simply fired at each other from fixed fortifications, the insurrectos may have been caught off-balance when, instead of defending Manila, the Americans took the offensive.

When the Coloradoans hit the line of insurrecto blockhouses on 5 February 1899, they employed their by-now familiar tactics of advancing in rushes by platoons, one platoon firing while the other attacked.[90] Once the Filipinos were forced from their fortifications, however, the men abandoned the discipline of the drill. As they pursued the insurgent forces, the volunteers were apt to forego the prone firing. In the shock of the first action of the insurrection, before the Filipinos had come to expect the Americans to advance against them, the guardsmen could risk the upright charge. From the sidelines, a pipe-smoking corporal of the regular infantry, commenting on the performance of the volunteers, judged them "a little bit unscientific, but successful as hell."[91]

It is entirely possible that Aguinaldo's military commanders had not intended any battle, given that Grayson fired the first shot. American commanders interpreted the immediate Filipino response, in the form of volley firing all along the lines, as evidence that the insurrectos had in fact planned an assault. If so, the Filipinos clearly anticipated an easy victory. As the Coloradoans examined the bodies of the slain Filipinos, neatly uniformed in blue and white, they found the enemy's haversacks, rather than carrying rations, instead filled with clean clothes. Apparently, the insurgents expected to dine in Manila![92]

In assessing their opponents, the Coloradoans concluded that the *insurrectos* were "plucky" adversaries.[93] Guy Sims "found them *brave stubborn* fighters but very ineffective."[94] Most died of head shots. They would run across a rice paddy and drop behind a dike; when they raised their heads to survey the situation, they would be shot. And, many of the Filipinos were found behind the dikes, crouching facing forward in the midst of a pile of spent cartridge brass, hit in the face while still firing at the advancing Americans.[95] In such combat, the insurgents received few nonfatal wounds.

During the day's fighting, Company E cornered a Filipino sniper in a thicket and fired into his bush. The insurrecto feigned death, with closed eyes and protruding tongue. He seemed unwounded, and to be breathing well. General Hale rode up to the troops, and ordered them to take the Filipino to the rear as a prisoner. The men didn't want to carry him, if he could walk. So, 1st Sgt. Cecil West and Cpl. Howard Edwards tried to revive the Filipino with a switch, to no avail. They kicked him in the ribs six times—nothing. They poured water down his throat—still, nothing. Finally, as the Americans shouted "No Muertes," the enemy soldier opened his eyes. He was convinced that the Americans crucified prisoners of war. The Coloradoans escorted the lucky insurgent to the rear; finding another such role-player, and with no officer around, Cpl. Benjamin Holly simply killed him.[96]

After all the American wounded had received treatment, the Colorado surgeons cared for the Filipino wounded. Steward Alexander McAllister treated one boy, shot by his own officer when he tried to flee Blockhouse Number Five. The insurrecto wounded were stoic, and exhibited few signs of pain.[97] Once the medical staff was through, the Colorado soldiers had no intention of expending their own efforts on the wounded insurgents. They impressed gangs of Filipino civilians to care for their countrymen, tapping each on his shoulder to signify his selection. Accepting no excuses, they held the unlucky Filipinos to their duties with armed guards, finally releasing them just before mealtime. After the meal, the Americans would round up a new group, saving themselves both rations and labor.[98]

The practice of impressment had actually commenced immediately after the outbreak of the insurrection. At 1:00 A.M. on 5 February, American authorities realized they needed transport, as their forces advanced beyond the city and through the insurgent lines. Filipino draymen refused to rent their carts and teams to carry ammunition and food, and so the Americans simply commandeered them without pay.[99]

In like manner, Filipinos made up the burial details. Most of the American dead were placed in black coffins and, pending eventual shipment home, buried for the time-being in numbered graves in Paco Cemetery. The graves were dug by "an impressed detail of Filipinos, gathered up around the city."[100] Privates Carlson and Doran lay there with the dead of other American regiments; Private White's body, retrieved from the river on 7 February, was buried on its banks.[101] With the Americans interred, the Filipino dead came next. Along the coast, the Americans rolled the bodies of insurrectos killed by the naval guns into the shattered trenches, and covered them over.[102] The First Colorado made similar use of the earthworks along the blockhouses. Over one mass grave stood the placard, "Twenty-four good Filipinos lie here."[103]

The depósito lay in American hands, but the Santolan pumping works that supplied it, four miles away on the Rio Mariquina, were held by the insurrectos. As fighting began between the Americans and the Filipinos, Aguinaldo's men turned off the pumps, and the depósito only held enough water to supply Manila for two days. Accordingly, the First Nebraska advanced on the waterworks, starting from the depósito at daylight on 6 February. The Nebraska regiment was still accompanied by Companies D and I of the First Colorado, commanded by Maj. William Grove, and by a detachment of the First Tennessee Infantry; the Utah guns followed along.[104] Within half a mile, the soldiers began skirmishing with insurrecto riflemen, slowly pushing them back.[105]

Assistant Surgeon Harry Young, of the Utah artillery, had tried on Sunday evening to join up with the battery's Major Young at the depósito; becoming lost, he blundered into the insurrecto lines and was captured early on 6 February by the insurgents.[106] As the infantry advanced on Monday morning, driving the Filipinos before them, one and a half miles beyond the depósito, the Americans came across Dr. Young's mutilated body. According to General Hale's official report, the Filipinos had executed him with a shot to the head. This may have been a fiction designed to spare the sensibilities of Dr. Young's family. Certainly, the insurrectos chopped up his corpse with *bolo* knives, which would seem an extraneous activity in the face of advancing American forces.[107] The Spanish had learned to expect such actions from their Filipino opponents, but the Americans were only now fighting the insurrectos for the first time.

Doctor Young had been a popular officer, with both the Utah and Colorado units. Enraged, the combined regiments rushed the Filipino lines, routing the insurgents and killing an estimated eighty of them. By late morning, the infantry reached the western heights of the Mariquina Valley, overlooking the waterworks and the town of Mariquina. Utah set up its guns and, using the steeple of the Mariquina church as its aiming point, bombarded the town, as the occupants fled.[108] The Tennessee troops had separated from the column in the rush through the insurrecto lines; as they rejoined, the Tennesseans sang "Marching through Georgia." The Utah artillerymen saluted them with a chorus of "Dixie."[109]

While Utah shelled Mariquina, the Colorado detachment charged into the waterworks across the river from nearby Santolan late in the afternoon, dispersing the Filipino garrison. Arriving ahead of the accompanying Nebraskans, Color Sgt. Richard Holmes, "true to his flag raising instinct," whipped a pocket-sized American flag from inside his uniform and raised it on a small bamboo pole. The Nebraskans attempted to replace it with a larger flag of their own, but the Coloradoans declined to relinquish the place of honor.[110]

Unfortunately for the population of Manila, the Americans found the pumps not only shut down, but sabotaged. Control of Manila's water supply had been Aguinaldo's strongest bargaining chip, and the Filipinos would not surrender that advantage easily. Four big cylinder heads from the pumps, and several valve heads and rockers from the engines, were completely missing. Company I's Lt. Charles Hilton set his men to searching for the parts early on 7 February. They combed the fields, clambered down into wells, and dove the river, to no avail.[111] By noon, the water was giving out in Manila, and the situation was critical.[112] A detachment of U.S. Army Engineers came out from Manila and took measurements of the existing equipment, and then set out for the naval machine shops at Cavite, intending to replicate the missing components. They estimated ten days, however, to replace the castings.[113] Manila could not wait ten days.

Each company of the First Colorado included one artificer, a skilled mechanic. At 10:30 A.M., Artificer Guy B. Hayes of Company I called Lieutenant Hilton's attention to a pile of coal in a large coal shed. Several pieces of clay dirt lay on the floor, two feet from the coal pile. The artificer confidently predicted, "it's buried under that pile of coal." The men secured shovels and, buried three feet below the coal, found the missing parts, coated in white lead and undamaged.[114] An observant enlisted man had saved the day! The engineer detachment was quickly recalled, and the parts were installed and operating by 8 February 1899.[115] Manila was saved, or at least able to get a drink.

In the afternoon of 7 February, while the Colorado troops rested after their hunt for the missing machinery, General Hale and several companies of the Twenty-Third United States Infantry entered the deserted town of Mariquina. From each structure, white flags, white curtains, white underwear, even, the men joked, white dogs, fluttered to proclaim the town's neutrality. Under more white flags, a group of civilians approached Hale to see if he intended to destroy the town. Through his interpreter Johnny Saulsbury, Hale assured them that Mariquina would not be torched, if in return the townspeople would keep all insurrectos out. Hale did not yet understand the nature of the insurrecto army. Aguinaldo had raised a Republican Army, some of whose uniformed bodies the First Colorado had buried at the blockhouses. But, the *sandahatan* local militias were just as much a part of Aguinaldo's forces, and much more difficult for the Americans to locate. It is not at all clear exactly how civilians were supposed to resist infiltration by armed insurgent soldiers, especially when those soldiers were not infiltrators at all, but the Filipinos readily agreed.

Mariquina would remain the largest contested town in close proximity to the Americans, and a continual irritant. For the time, Hale and the Twenty-Third Infantry recrossed the Rio Mariquina, and camped in reserve of the Colorado and Nebraska troops guarding the waterworks.[116] One of the regulars grumbled, "we haven't even had a chance for a shot, and the volunteers have got the coons on such a run now that there seems to be a poor show for us."[117]

The American forces were nearing the limit of the territory they could police and defend with the available men. The bulk of the First Colorado regiment remained encamped along the blockhouse line outside Manila, ready to reinforce the detachment at the waterworks. From that vantage point, they observed the consolidation of the American position. The Manila and Dagupan Railway ran north along the coast from Manila. Once outside the city limits, the next town to the north was Caloocan, seven miles distant. On 10 February, the cruiser USS *Charleston* and the monitor USS *Monadnock* began shelling Caloocan from three miles out in Manila Bay. Under the command of Gen. Arthur MacArthur, a force composed of the Twentieth Kansas, First Montana, and the Third United States Artillery (fighting as infantry), with the Utah battery in support, stormed Caloocan. As the Americans entered the town, in the railroad's roundhouse they found five locomotives, disabled by the evacuating Filipinos. From the Montana and Kansas ranks, MacArthur recruited former railroaders to repair the locomotives. After moving the rolling stock to safety, the troops fired the town, and withdrew. Until more regiments arrived, American forces could go no farther, since insurrectos could stage attacks inside the American lines if the United States troops expanded the perimeter.[118]

On the other side of the world, the hostilities provoked immediate reactions. At 9:00 A.M. on Sunday, 15 February 1899, the *New York Sun*'s correspondent walked into the Manila telegraph office and filed his report on the outbreak of hostilities between the Americans and the Filipinos. In New York, it was 8:00 P.M. on Saturday, due to time zone differences. There was no telegraph cable under the Pacific, due to the technical difficulty of spanning the Marianas Trench; the message had to go the long way around the world, 14,311 miles from Manila to New York City. First, it went from Manila to Hong Kong, 529 miles underwater. From Hong Kong, it ran 460 more miles under the South China Sea to Saigon. Another 630 miles took the dispatch to Singapore, and then 288 miles around the Malay Peninsula to Penang on the west coast of Siam. From Penang, the cable ran 1,498 miles under the Bay of Bengal to Madras, in India. From Madras, 800 miles of telegraph wire carried the news overland to Bombay, where it dropped back into the ocean for the 1,851-mile run under the Arabian Sea to Aden. The cable ran from there 1,403 miles up the Red Sea to Suez, then 200 miles overland to Alexandria. Another 913 miles of underwater cable took the dispatch to Malta, and then 1,126 more, to Gibraltar. From "The Rock," the line ran 337 miles to Cascaveltos, near Lisbon, and then 856 miles under the Atlantic to Land's End, England. Western Union's

Transatlantic Cable carried the message 2,531 miles to Dover Bay, Nova Scotia, and a final leg of 888 surface miles brought it to the *Sun* in New York City—at 11:00 P.M. on Saturday, 4 February 1899, three hours after it was sent from Manila![119] In Congress, the Senate at last voted on the Peace Treaty with Spain. Article III of that treaty required that "Spain cedes to the United States the archipelago known as the Philippine Islands."[120] On 6 February 1899, the Senate approved the treaty on a vote of fifty-seven for, and twenty-seven against, gaining the necessary two-thirds in favor with a margin of only one vote to spare. President William McKinley quickly signed the measure.[121] The United States at last had accepted Rudyard Kipling's challenge, to "Take Up The White Man's Burden," with far-reaching consequences for both America and the Philippines. The *London Morning Post* of 6 February 1899 noted smugly that "the white man's burden is not an empty phrase."[122]

Claiming to speak for the American soldiers who would in fact have to carry that burden, the *New York Sun* explained that "our troops . . . were glad to have an opportunity to square accounts with the natives, whose insolence of late was becoming intolerable."[123] The troops themselves were less sanguinary. One First Colorado soldier worried, "it looks to me very much . . . like our grand 'War For Down trodden Humanity' will end up in a war of conquest, and here, conquest means extermination."[124] Pvt. Carl Larsen wrote:

> The situation here is awfull [*sic*], and what seems to me to be the worst thing, is, that it is to a great extent our own doings. If U.S. intended to do the right thing to these people—give them their Independence, and told them so, they would, instead of being our enemies, been our best friends, and if we are going to hold these Islands, the Insurgents ought to been disarmed at the time we took Manila, as it could have been done very easy at that time. I do not criticize our government, but there certainly has been made some terrible blunders here what will

cost the lives of thousands of soldiers, but I don't know who is to blame. Of course, now we have to kill all the Insurgents we can. But as far as I am concerned, and I know it is the same way with many others, I fight these people with a very difference [*sic*] feeling from what I had toward the Spainiards [*sic*]. Then we was fighting for a good cause, and now? The fact is, I don't know what we are fighting for now.[125]

Pvt. Guy Sims summed up years later:

Soon as the Spanish War ended what we wanted most was to come home. We liked the natives and didn't want to make war on them but when they attacked us we had no choice. It was their lives or ours. We had to fight them. They were brave and patriotic. We respected their courage and favored their independence.[126]

The ambivalence of their situation, in the midst of a civilian population that concealed active enemies, is revealed in the First Colorado's sardonic use of the term "*amigos*" to describe the Filipinos. General Hale noted on 2 March 1899 that "we have been having quite a lively campaign against our Philippine 'Amigos.'"[127] Greeted with cries of "*Amigo!*" when they first set foot on the islands, the First Colorado had now come to use *Amigo* to denote the treacherous enemy.

After the first shock of combat, both the Filipinos and the Americans settled into a sort of "phony war." For the most part, the First Colorado suffered no further casualties, although on 7 February Company A's Pvt. Clyde McVay accidentally shot off the little toe on his right foot with his own rifle.[128] As they cleared away the villages in front of their lines, the Coloradoans industriously rounded up any stray livestock or poultry that might improve their rations. Years later, an anonymous Colorado veteran recalled that "the food wasn't too bad when you think of the chickens and pigs we stole."[129]

Some of the scavenging was officially sanctioned. As the villages burned, Company E gathered up forage, horses, and carts and turned them over to the quartermasters. But, Arthur Johnson observed Company G as it re-entered Manila on 7 February, pockets bulging with "relics" from the villages, and the men laden down with poultry. That evening, they feasted on a turkey dinner, and turned a young pig into roast pork.[130] Harry McCauley confirmed Johnson's account of looting, while blaming it on the black servant George Hopkins, at least in jest.

> Whether or not the presence of Hopkins had anything to do with it, it is certain that some chickens, turkeys, horses and carriages were captured by the Colorado regiment in the native villages.[131]

Pvt. Carl J. Larsen of Company C told a friend that

> Gen Hale with about five hundred men went out to a town called Maraquina several miles ahead of our line, there was no one in town. there was a house what had been used as an Insurgent headquarter [*sic*]. From there the officers took a lot of truk [*sic*] as I had to bring back for them. I got a few trinkets myself. I got a d[r]esswaist as the ladies use them here. If you are a relic fiend I will keep it for you, if I ever get back to gods country again, a thing what is very uncertain under present circumstances.[132]

The men of the First Colorado shot enough poultry for their mess pots that Nebraska's Colonel Stotsenburg was moved on 7 February to enjoin Colorado's Maj. William Grove,

> Please have your men stop all shooting at chickens, or anything but known enemy. Do not allow them to destroy any private property under any circumstances.[133]

By that time, there was very little private property left to preserve. The *Manila Times* reported on 8 February that "the South Dakota and Colorado men have cleared away all the native houses for half a mile in advance of the outposts."[134] The huts provided cover for Filipino snipers, and could house civilians; with the huts gone, the men could separate insurrectos from noncombatants.

The arson at Caloocan marked the end of active hostilities, for a time. The First Colorado camped on line about two-and-a-half miles from Manila, east of the blockhouses, in a three-mile arc running from Balicbalic to San Francisco del Monte. Their orders prohibited their permanently occupying the ground east across the Rio San Juan, and so the men patrolled that territory by day, and watched it by pickets at night.[135] And, they maintained a watch on Manila as well.

At first, eight companies guarded the blockhouse line, while four patrolled Manila itself.[136] Within three days, the officers shifted that ratio, putting ten companies on line and leaving only two in Manila; at intervals, the line companies would rotate through the town patrol.[137] The men were bivouacked in the trees, behind the trenches, and so did not bother to erect their tents. Instead, they slept on blankets, and each kept his shelter half, poncho, blanket, haversack, and canteen packed and ready for a march.

Between the trees and the trenches, the regimental and national colors stood in bamboo supports, marking the line on which the men could assemble in an emergency.[138] Next came the trenches, with Utah guns interspersed. Expecting the insurgents to move away from the coastline and Dewey's guns, General Hale reinforced the Colorado and South Dakota positions with additional artillery manned by the Utah volunteers, including three Gatling guns at the Colorado headquarters.[139]

From its trenches, each line company detailed half its complement for "Cossack duty" in front of the line. At eight o'clock each morning, the men would change positions with the other half of the company as they

18. Outpost under fire. *Photo courtesy of John Stewart Post Number One, Veterans of Foreign Wars.*

returned from their twenty-four hours on guard. As Arthur Johnson put it, "vigilance is the price of liberty."[140] Each company's pickets assembled in a "cossack post" a quarter-mile in front of the trenches; from that point, "outposts" or observation posts were thrown still farther forward. At night, each outpost had two men awake at all times; by day, each had at least one man. In the event of an insurrecto attack, the outposts were to fire and fall back on the cossack post, where all would make a stand while the remainder of the regiment came to the rescue. If the Filipinos kept coming, the "Cossacks" were to retire to the regimental trenches.[141]

Coupled with roving patrols, this deployment created a formidable defense, in depth, with plenty of warning of any assault. As a result, the First Colorado and the Filipinos avoided any further major conflicts for about six weeks. Occasionally, the insurgents would try to ambush a sentry in the night, or send some volleys into the American lines at extremely long-range.[142] In the midst of war, the Coloradoans and their former allies were able to maintain some sense of mutual respect. Guy

Sims related an incident that occurred one morning when, heading back to camp for breakfast after a night of outpost duty, he came to a hill exposed to Filipino fire.

> Before stepping out on the bare hillside I looked back. The plum thicket (containing an insurrecto outpost) was about 400 yards away, and it didn't seem reasonable that the natives would let our fellows walk up and down that hill-side in plain sight, and not do something about it. But I didn't know any other route, so I took a long breath and stepped out and right now rifles began to spatter behind me and bullets to snap and whine overhead. Within a few seconds not only the outpost but also a long sector of their mainline was firing at me. Of course my first impulse was to see just how quick I could streak it up the hill, but I had never made a homerun so far (that was before Mariquina) and hated to spoil my record. I noticed, too, that the bullets were all far above my head, none were close down, so I maintained the regulation military cadence—120 per minute—but gosh, how I stretched the stride! As I neared the shelter of the hedgerow at the top of the hill, I noticed that it was literally snowing green leaves that the bullets were cutting from the bamboo. When I was within 20 feet of the hedge the firing ceased like turning off the switch, and the Little Brown Brothers gave me a rousing cheer. They hadn't been able to either drop me or make me run. Very few lone soldiers have ever received a cheer from the enemy and fewer still have lived to tell about it. I have regretted ever since that I didn't think to turn and wave to them before stepping out of sight, but I was so intent on getting out of sight I never thought of it till too late.[143]

In spite of the casualties already incurred, the Filipinos could see the war as a cockfight, and cheer a brave contestant.

Unable to assault the American lines, the Filipino forces instead attempted to infiltrate Manila itself. Since the majority of the city's population was in fact Filipino, this was a very real possibility. Insurgents set fire to East Paco, just south of Manila, on 20 February.[144] Seeking to cow the insurrectos by threats of retaliation, General Otis warned a former insurgent officer, General Torres, that if the Filipinos launched a "throat-cutting expedition" in Manila, he would lose control of the Eighth Army Corps, and "the slightest insurrection would mean a slaughter of natives in the city."[145] The same word went out to the American soldiers. On 21 February 1899, Arthur Johnson reported to his Denver readers that:

> The bastilles in the walled city, by the way, are full to overflowing, and the fiat is said to have gone forth that no more prisoners are to be taken. In the next engagement the Filipino death list promises to correspondingly increase.[146]

This might seem like a bold admission of official intent to violate the accepted rules of war, but in fact, American troops had already done so. In the 10 February assault on Caloocan, the First Colorado had been chagrined when ordered to remain behind and guard the waterworks, while other units carried the war to the rebels. Fortunately, though, that meant that they were not in any way implicated when the Twentieth Kansas Infantry, apparently under orders from its commander, executed Filipino prisoners of war taken in the Caloocan advance.[147]

General Otis's threats were insufficient to deter the arsonists. Aguinaldo might eschew attacks on Manila, but any one of his principales could initiate his own policy. On 22 February 1899, "a bold and gallant chief named Zandico" led insurgent raiders through the American lines and into Manila.[148] At approximately 8:30 P.M., the insurrectos successfully set fires in the Tondo, Santa Cruz, and San Nicolas quarters of the city. Tondo, described by Muriel Bailey as "crowded with native shacks built on the maze plan," was a northern suburb of Manila lying along the bay, north of the Binondo business district. Built almost entirely of nipa huts, Tondo lost its marketplace and over 1,000 homes.[149] If the insurrectos couldn't have Manila, neither could the Americans! The provost guard, consisting of the Minnesota and Oregon volunteers and the Twenty-Third Infantry, ended up fighting the fire and, hand-to-hand, the insurrectos. In the early morning of 23 February, a coordinated Filipino attack against the northern American lines caused sixty Kansas and Montana casualties before it was repulsed. The two companies guarding the Colorado quarters in the city were not involved, and the men on the line had a spectacular view of the conflagration.[150]

During the twenty-third, as the provosts hunted insurgent snipers, the military evacuated all American women from Manila to transports in the bay. Those women included nurses, wives of businessmen and officers, and reporter Muriel Bailey. Insurgent forces moved across in front of the Colorado line, and the men fired upon them from the trenches.[151] Insurrectos shot at the South Dakotans from the stone church at San Francisco del Monte, and so the next morning, on 24 February 1899, the Utah battery shelled it.[152] At the same time, the First Nebraska defeated an insurgent party north of the Mariquina Road, marking the last Filipino attacks on Manila.[153] To prevent any recurrence, the Americans imposed an absolute 7:00 P.M. curfew on Manila; that measure was successful, because infiltrators no longer could hide among the crowds.[154]

On 13 March 1899, the First Colorado received orders to exchange places with the Nebraska regiment guarding the waterworks and the pipeline. The men welcomed the new assignment, feeling that their original positions were so impregnable as to make any chance of action unlikely. "'No fight, no joy,' is the motto of our regiment."[155] On 14 March, Companies A, E, and M relieved the Nebraskans at the depósito; the remaining companies moved on 15 March, one at a time, to replace the Nebraskans at the waterworks and along the pipeline, with the First Nebraska moving into the abandoned Colorado positions.[156] Supported by four of Utah's 3.2-inch guns, the bulk of the First Colorado settled into a new camp some eight miles from Manila, on a hill overlooking the Mariquina Valley and the Santolan pumping station. Having called their Denver campsite "Camp Adams," in honor of Governor Alva Adams, they now named their new home "Camp Alva."[157]

From 15 March until 2 June 1899, the First Colorado remained on line at Camp Alva.[158] Below the camp, on the near or west side of the Rio Mariquina, sat the pumping station, opposite the hamlet of Santolan on the east bank of the river. North of Santolan, the much larger town of Mariquina lay in "no-man's land" on the far side of the valley.[159] Mariquina's fortunes offer some measure of the Coloradoans' increasing frustration with the character of the war. Mariquina lay exactly 3,350 yards from the pumping station, out of rifle range but completely within view. General Otis had taken part in Army campaigns against the Sioux, in which converging columns tried to trap and engage a mobile enemy. He now applied that same strategy to the Philippines.

From 11 March until 17 March, a "provisional brigade" composed of both volunteer and regular infantry, and United States cavalry and artillery, carried out an expedition up the Pasig and Mariquina Rivers.[160] In support of that effort, four companies of the First Colorado moved one mile north of Camp Alva on 16 March, to the Mariquina Road.[161] At noon, Companies B and K and part of I crossed the Mariquina River and probed into the town, seeking to intercept insurgents fleeing from the American advance on nearby Cainta. As the First Colorado advanced, the left platoon of Utah's Battery A sent three-inch shells into Mariquina. Using their Mauser rifles, the Filipinos fired volleys, at the limit of their sights, into which zone the Americans had to advance, still outranged.[162]

All told, 150 men took part in the advance. One of those was Company K's Pvt. Edward Pynchon, a renowned Denver bicycle racer who had traded his picket duty with another man so as to participate in the action. Seeking shelter from the Filipino fire, 1st Sgt. Clifford Bowser and his squad, including Pynchon, took cover behind a dike in one of the rice fields. A plunging bullet grazed Pynchon's shoulders and buried itself in his lower back. "Fellows, they've got me!" he cried. Bowser admonished him, "Don't let 'em know you are hit." "All right, I won't," responded Pynchon, as two privates carried him to the rear.[163] Bowser's concern seems inspired less by any tactical consideration, than by a sort of schoolboy "don't let them see you cry" ethic. The men could not stay behind the dike, and so they rushed on toward the town. In the assault, Company L's Cpl. Charles Haskell (an Annapolis graduate) was shot in the left groin, Company B's Pvt. Henry Haymus was slightly wounded in the left calf, and Maj. Charles Anderson was shot through the flesh above his left ankle.[164] All told, it was an expensive little engagement.

An aggravated First Colorado took the town, clearing the streets by volley fire. "The fight lasted until 2:30 PM, when the Coloradoans retired, after setting fire to the town."[165] The rebels successfully withdrew to the northeast, but Mariquina's days were numbered.[166] Pynchon lingered on for four more days. At first, he and the doctors were hopeful, but the surgeons couldn't find the bullet; apparently it fell out as the private was carried to the hospital. The wound had injured his intestines, and he developed peritonitis. On the nineteenth, he told his nurse that the end was near. Lt. William Vannice sat with the private until he died on the morning of 20 March; the twenty-nine-year-old private was buried the next afternoon.[167]

Arthur Johnson complained of Hale's initial decision to spare Mariquina,

> The leniency which was displayed when it was not reduced to ashes to keep the Filipinos from coming back to make it a stronghold has since been greatly regretted. The policy of doing away with habitations in the Filipino territory is at this day more generally followed.[168]

Clearly, the Mariquina Valley was likely to prove a very active theater. On 17 March, the First Colorado's officers halved the town guard back in Manila to a bare minimum of one company to watch the barracks, freeing one more company to add to those on the line.[169] As they moved to strengthen their regiment's position, however, General MacArthur was preparing for a major campaign, to strike north and seize the insurrecto capitol at Malolos. MacArthur's plan called for a general breakout through the Filipino lines, along the coast, the railroad, the San Mateo Valley, and up the Mariquina Valley.[170]

In preparation for the Malolos strike planned for March of 1899, Gen. Irving Hale reinforced the importance of offensive maneuvers and the 1891 tactics. His General Orders No. 4, issued on 24 March 1899, directed his commanders to "impress upon the men that against the present enemy the charge is the safest form of attack." He went on to insist, "when under fire, advance by alternate rushes of companies or platoons, thus keeping the enemy down by a practically continuous fire, to proper distance and then charge." Finally, he enjoined his company commanders strictly to control their men in the attack. "Controlled volley firing by Company, platoon, or squad will be used, except when the enemy is scattered and retreating, and individual firing, when necessary[,] will be closely regulated."[171] That last instruction, requiring officer-directed volley firing, cost Company A's Capt. John Stewart his life the next day at Mariquina. Command-and-control dictated that he be on line with his men, and there he was killed.[172]

The First Colorado was ordered to stay behind and guard the waterworks, due to its "reputation for absolute reliability." Col. Henry McCoy appealed to his superiors for the right to be included in the Malolos strike, directing his request first to General Hale and then to General MacArthur himself. MacArthur refused, explaining, "I consider the pumping station one of the most important points on the line and it must be held at all costs."[173] Completing their distress, the men of the First Colorado found themselves transferred from General Hale's Second Brigade, into Brig. Gen. Robert Hall's Third Brigade, an adjustment dictated by their garrison role at the waterworks. Hall was new to the campaign, and freshly promoted, having only recently arrived in the Philippines as a colonel of regulars.[174] Adding injury to insult, on 24 March Utah's Battery A was pulled from the Colorado lines, in order to reinforce the coming assault.[175]

The First Colorado need not have worried that they would be left out. The breakout began at 5:30 A.M. on 25 March 1899, with firing along a front from Mariquina to Manila Bay. Hale's brigade led off, with the Filipinos contesting the American advance every step of the way. Brig. Gen. Harrison Otis's brigade flanked Hale's men on the left, along the coast road, while Brigadier General Wheaton's brigade formed a reserve.[176] Hall, with the Fourth and Seventeenth United States Infantry and the Thirteenth Minnesota Volunteer Infantry, dropped down into the Mariquina Valley and marched north, protecting Hale's right flank. Perched above the valley, the First Colorado had a good view.[177]

By 6:30 A.M., the Minnesota regiment was hard-pressed, and the Coloradoans received orders to reinforce them on their right. Just as Hall's Third Brigade was covering the main column's right flank, the First Colorado would cover Hall's right flank. At 6:35 A.M., Lieutenant Colonel Moses led Companies A and M out from Camp Alva.[178] The rest of the regiment remained behind to guard the pumping station. As Moses and the two companies moved forward, a half company of insurrecto soldiers, ensconced on a rocky hill one and a half miles in front of the Colorado trenches, opened a steady fire on the advancing troops. While A and M continued forward, Colonel McCoy ordered Company E's Sgt. Albert Givens to take a detail of nineteen men and storm the hill. They took the hill in an hour's time, but then were stranded there.[179]

Companies A and M advanced across the rice fields, firing a volley and then rushing. Maneuvering against them was the 1,500-man *Batailon de Kawite*, a crack insurgent division personally trained and led by Major General Montenegro. Unable to credit Filipinos with military prowess, Harry McCauley attributed their proficiency to a mercenary Englishman called "Wistar" by the insurrectos, and to three renegade Americans. Guy

Sims blamed the First Colorado themselves, for having explained the use of the sights to their Filipino "amigos" back in July, before Manila's fall.[180] Whatever the source of the enemy's training, the Coloradoans found themselves for the first time fighting against Filipino riflemen who knew how to set their sights, and who fired low, at the correct range. By 6:55 A.M., Privates Charles Brill and Malcom Maccoe, both of Company M, had been wounded, Brill through the right thigh, and Maccoe through the intestines. Bandsmen carried them to the rear.[181]

As Company M moved out on the right, Capt. John Stewart of Company A deployed his men in skirmish formation and headed for the Minnesotans.[182] Company A advanced perhaps 500 yards, over rice paddies and through bamboo hedges, before the insurgents saw them.[183] As Company A prepared to charge the last enemy trench, Captain Stewart joined them in the battle line and, at 7:15 A.M., gave his last command. "There they are boys, give them lead!" Immediately after, he gasped, "I'm hit," followed by "Right here." Wounded through the abdomen, the captain collapsed in a faint and died twelve minutes later.[184] Company A's Pvt. Edwin Pitts was wounded in the right lung in the same volley.[185] The Coloradoans "gave a cry of rage and dashed forward with such a rush that the yellow-skinned natives turned and fled."[186] Hall's column pushed on, forcing the Filipinos up the Mariquina Valley and then west toward San Francisco del Monte and the San Mateo River.[187]

Stewart's death was only one of many casualties the First Colorado sustained at Mariquina on 25 March. For the first time in the insurrection, they were fighting well-trained insurrectos who knew how to aim and fire their Mauser rifles effectively. This was the "European"-style enemy the 1891 tactics manual addressed, and against which the First Colorado had trained. The men fell back on that training. Harry McCauley recalled that "the fight was of the old style, to which frequent practice had accustomed them: some volleys fired while lying down, and then with a yell a charge on the next trench."[188] In this instance, the regiment was attacking in the open over rice paddies, and "trench" refers to the small dikes that separated the fields. As they charged, they would shelter behind one of the dikes, drink from their canteens, and refill their cartridge belts from the loose rounds carried in their haversacks.[189] Although they suffered six casualties, the First Colorado's training paid off. Even against trained marksmen armed with magazine rifles, they were able, using the 1891 tactics, to advance against the insurrectos and drive them from the field. The volunteer guardsmen relied upon tactical reforms instituted by professional military officers since the Civil War; those reforms, when put to the test, proved an effective response to the threat posed by modern small arms.

Meanwhile, Sergeant Givens and his detail remained holed up in the rocks on their little hill. Finally, as the battle advanced up the Mariquina Valley, Lt. Rice Means and twenty men from Company C were able to reinforce the tiny detachment; finding the rocks pretty much impregnable, the entire command simply settled in, to prevent insurgents from reoccupying it.[190]

Colorado suffered two other casualties in the day's fighting, although the regiment didn't find out about them until later. General Hale, commanding the Second Brigade, was shot through the fleshy part of his leg below his left knee, while his orderly, Pvt. Harry Kerr of Company H, was wounded in the left lung.[191] It had been a sad day for the First Colorado. The casualty list was almost as high as that of 4 and 5 February, and included the loss of a popular and respected officer. Unlike the first battle of the Philippine-American War, the losses of 25 March achieved no great goal, at least that the men could see.

Despite their anger and frustration, the First Colorado turned to caring for the Filipino wounded. That charity was rewarded when one of the patients, in gratitude, told Surgeon Lewis Kemble of two wounded Americans, concealed about three miles away. A squad rushed down the valley and found two Minnesotans, who had lain there from 7:00 A.M. until found at 1:00 P.M. Another Colorado man collected another Minnesota soldier, shot through both legs, and sent him two miles to the rear on an old horse.[192]

John Stewart had been the senior captain of the regiment, and often had acted as major of the first battalion.[193] Trusted by the men to safeguard their interests, he had served on the Council of the Regimental Canteen.[194] As they carried the officer's body by horse litter to Paco Cemetery in Manila, marching men saluted by coming to the position of "Port Arms," while those standing came to the "Present Arms."[195] On 27 March 1899, half of Company A was released from duty to attend his funeral; the entire half-company insisted on serving on the firing detail.[196]

In part, the First Colorado blamed its losses at Mariquina to inferior weapons. The Colorado volunteers bitterly resented having to fight with the old Indian Wars Springfield rifle. According to Guy Sims,

> It was a crime to send men into battle armed with the obsolete .45 caliber Springfield against an enemy armed with Mausers, about the best gun of the time. . . . The one thing both the Spanish and Filipino lacked was marksmanship. If they had been marksmen, none of us would have come home.[197]

Arthur Johnson felt that the Colorado troops were at a disadvantage because the Spanish had smokeless powder weapons, and the .45–70s gave away the American positions. But, he did allow that the heavy lead slug of the Springfield could do horrendous damage when it hit a man.[198] Looking over the Filipino dead after the fighting of 5 February 1899, Harry McCauley determined that "the frightful wounds which the injured bore suggested that a man wounded seriously by a Springfield bullet is almost as good as dead in any case."[199]

Another benefit of the Springfield was its reliability. During the Indian Wars, the Ordnance Department found that the Springfield could be fired with 50 percent of its parts missing, if one chose the parts judiciously. In the steady rains of the Philippines, the First Colorado paid scant attention to the niceties of appearance. At "Inspection Arms," the inspecting officers would examine the weapons' firing pins, triggers, hammers, and sights, and nothing else.[200] Still, the men complained that "the enemy had much better rifles than we did."[201] Guy Sims summed up their disgust when he referred to his .45–70 as "a cross-eyed old bitch" (a line borrowed from Rudyard Kipling's description of the British Army's Martini-Henry rifle).[202] In recognition of the disadvantage the men faced in fighting opponents armed with superior weapons, on 27 February 1899 Colonel McCoy announced to the men that the First Colorado's regimental badge, approved by Division Headquarters, would be a Mauser cartridge, positioned ball to the front, worn in the left side of the hat band and held in place by the bow of the band. The cartridges had been picked up in the insurrecto trenches outside Blockhouses Number 5 and 6, after the 5 February fighting. The First Colorado was the first regiment to adopt a regimental badge, and the only one allowed to use the Mauser cartridge.[203]

When Manila surrendered, the American forces captured 23,000 Mauser rifles, along with eighteen pieces of artillery.[204] Given the inability of the United States Army to modernize the arms of the volunteers, it would seem that reissuing the captured rifles to the American guardsmen would have been an easy and effective means of upgrading their weapons. Unfortunately, in a face-saving gesture, the Spanish troops were allowed to carry their Mauser rifles with them when they were repatriated to Spain. The Army chose instead to modernize their ammunition. Against the Spanish, the volunteers had used black powder cartridges in their Springfields, the ammunition for which the weapons were designed. On the morning of 4 January 1899, each man in the First Colorado was issued forty-five smokeless .45-caliber rounds, enough to fill his cartridge belt. The Cuban war was done, and smokeless powder production had caught up to the point that the Army produced special smokeless rounds for the Springfields. The new cartridges were an expedient to bridge the gap until Krags could be issued to volunteer regiments. Even so, the supply of smokeless .45-caliber rounds was limited; on 9 January 1899 each man in the First Colorado received a further issue of 105 of the old black powder rounds, a full load for a haversack.[205] And so, although the First Colorado still carried their Springfields into the first battle of the "Insurrection," they fought the Filipinos with smokeless powder. Given his fixation on the importance of "no smoke," it is little wonder that Arthur Johnson credited Colorado's low casualties on that day to the new rounds.[206]

The more powerful smokeless powder also increased the Springfields' range. On 5 February 1899, a squad of Company G took aim at a fleeing Filipino, setting their sights at 1,200 yards, and fired in unison, killing the insurrecto.[207] Since they could not have recalibrated their sights to accommodate the new ammunition, their success must surely be attributed to luck, but this still represents a record for the .45–70 Springfield rifle. Even with the new ammunition, however, the Springfield was outranged by the Mauser. Not all Filipinos were unskilled as marksmen. Even such a behemoth as the USS *Monadnock*, protected by nine-inch armor plate, could be threatened by insurrecto snipers. On 6 February 1899, two of the monitor's crew were wounded by Filipino marksmen, firing from shore.[208] The Mariquina fight of 16 March 1899, in which Edward Pynchon was killed and three others wounded, demonstrated to the Coloradoans the inferior range of their own weapons.[209] Later that month, Filipino snipers began systematically picking off members of Company E in their outpost camp, firing from the hill 1,000 yards away, beyond the range of the Springfields. Artificer Archie Aldrich was shot in the left shoulder on 20 March; his wound eventually proved fatal.[210] On 23 March, firing from the same hill, the insurrectos shot Pvt. Merton Esshom through the leg as he sat in front of his tent, reading the 18 February edition of the *Rocky Mountain News*.[211]

The Filipino post in the rocks on the hill dominated the Colorado outpost and commanded the rice paddies in between. Whether he succeeded in his request because of the 16 March Mariquina fight, as Arthur Johnson believed or, as Colonel McCoy told the men, because of Artificer Aldrich's wounding, on 23 March the colonel was able to distribute to his men their first 300 Krags. They were the first volunteer regiment in the Philippines to get any.[212] With only 300 of the new weapons, each company received twenty-five, which most reserved for "outpost duty."[213] The exposed outposts, closest to the insurrecto lines, could now more effectively return fire. Johnson noted that "a decided improvement could be seen in the outpost work, as the men were able to retaliate now and then by picking off an insurrecto."[214]

When the men of Company E stormed the sharpshooter's nest in the rocks, they solved most, but not all, of their sniper problem; they thought themselves secure until Pvt. Charles Carty was hit in the shoulder by a Filipino marksman on 30 March.[215]

Even when the treasured Krags were assigned to outposts, the troops on outpost duty didn't always receive them. In Company K, Sgt. Clifford Bowser had taken a special dislike to two brothers, Guy and Arthur Sims, and so he had assigned them permanent outpost duty. The two privates had been vociferous in their hatred of the Springfield, and the Sergeant denied them Krags out of spite, even though they were constantly on patrol. Lt. Charles Lewis, temporarily assigned to K, ordered Bowser to provide Arthur Sims, the company's best shot, with a Krag, but Bowser delayed. The next day, seeing Sims still carrying a .45–70, the officer inquired why. When the private reported that Bowser had snarled, "Keep your shirt on," in response to Sims's request for the new rifle, the lieutenant ordered Bowser, in front of the entire company, to go to his tent and get a Krag for Sims. It was a sweet victory for the abused private. His brother Guy finally got his own Krag when Cpl. Alvin Moore, headed for the hospital, handed his to Sims to safeguard.[216]

As the First Colorado licked its wounds and guarded the waterworks, the offensive rolled north without them. And, insurrecto forces filtered back into Mariquina and the surrounding valley. On 30 March 1899, McCoy received orders to prepare five Colorado companies to move the next day as part of the "flying column" in the Mariquina valley. McCoy pulled in all the Krags from all the companies, and redistributed them to

Companies C, D, E, and G, so that he had an entire battalion equipped with the new rifles. Adding McCoy's battalion to four companies of the Twenty-third Infantry and four companies of the Fourth Infantry, General Hall was able to assemble an entire regiment armed with Krags. But, McCoy's orders had specified five companies, and even by gathering every Krag in the First Colorado, he could only outfit four companies with the new rifle, and as a consequence, Company A had to accompany the "flying column" once again carrying the hated Springfields.[217]

On 31 March, MacArthur's division occupied Malolos, Aguinaldo's government evacuating in disarray.[218] On the same day, to prevent insurgents from concentrating in the vicinity of Taytay, near the Laguna de Bay at the mouth of the Mariquina Valley, General Hall launched his own drive.[219] At 4:00 A.M., he struck the town of Mariquina in a surprise pincer movement, with the Fourth Infantry and Twenty-third Infantry attacking from the south, and Minnesota troops and the First Colorado hitting from the north. Colonel McCoy personally led the Colorado detachment.[220] Supported by a 3.2-inch field gun and a Nordenfeldt gun of the Utah Light Artillery, the "flying column" took Mariquina without loss. Then, Companies G and C roared up the Mariquina Valley after the insurrectos, chasing them from position after position for a total of six miles.[221]

The insurgents fought desperately to hold back the pursuing Coloradoans, inflicting heavy casualties on the Americans. Company G's Cpl. Leonard Phillippi, a twenty-six-year-old druggist from Cripple Creek, was mortally wounded by a shot through his brain; he died on 1 April. Also from G, Cpl. John McCorkle was wounded through the right thigh, and Pvt. Charles Dennis was shot in the left side of his neck and in the right shoulder. In Company C, Pvt. Henry Redmond received a wound in his mouth and neck; Pvt. George Dickinson was shot through the left shoulder; and Pvt. Charles Hutchinson was shot through the left thigh. Major Kemble, operating under fire in the front lines, attended to the wounded men.[222]

In what came to be known as the "Mariquina Dash," the volunteers quickly outdistanced the regulars. One young U.S. Infantry officer complained, "My men can never keep up with that charge."[223] The Colorado advance reached Bayanbayanan before being recalled, and then the tired infantrymen retraced their route back down the valley.[224] Along the way, they collected Company E, left behind to screen the advance column's flank as it moved forward. Always expert foragers, Company E had found and looted a watermelon patch as they skirmished along the river![225] By 12:30 P.M. the four companies were back at their starting point, expecting a well-earned rest.

Instead, Gen. Elwell Otis ordered them to reinforce Manila's northern defenses. The four companies immediately marched west nine miles overland, fording the Rio San Mateo several times, and took up a defensive line running from the La Loma Church to Caloocan. By late night, some of the detachment had gone into action at 4:00 A.M., stormed into Mariquina, fought a heavy engagement, and marched thirty miles![226] The weary campaigners collapsed without shelter in a pouring rain, and took their rest.[227]

Captain Ewing Booth congratulated Company C for its

> gallant work on March 31st and April 1st. Your bravery, discipline, and endurance won favorable comment from Brigade and Regimental Commanders, and have added laurels to the already fair name and reputation of your company.[228]

After the Mariquina dash, reflecting on the performance of the Krags, McCoy reported "the superiority of this rifle for this sort of work was so apparent, and the work done by these four companies so excellent, that I immediately decided to make requisition for these rifles for the entire regiment, they having fully demonstrated their ability to use them to good advantage."[229] McCoy may have wanted Krags for the entire regiment, but the supply was still limited. Pvt. Harry Doxsee was killed on 23 May 1899, still carrying his Springfield.[230]

The detached companies quickly returned to the rest of the regiment at Camp Alva. In the coming months, however, it was fairly common for selected companies to be detailed for temporary duty on the Manila lines. For a time, at least, the First Colorado was spared any active campaigning.[231] But while the regiment guarded the pumping station, Mariquina, for just a while more, remained a focus for insurrecto activity.

Arthur Johnson noted, "During the month of April things went peacefully in this vicinity, the only remarkable event being the disappearance of the muchly conquered Mariquina in smoke."[232] On 15 April, a Utah artilleryman, sightseeing at the deserted church, was captured by a band of Filipinos. Company G of the First Colorado deployed to rescue him. As they approached the town, the artilleryman escaped his captors and fled to the protection of the infantry.

> The insurgents were driven out of the city, and simultaneously the thatch of the nipa huts that remained, and also the roof of the big church began to smoke heavily and lurid flames burst forth. When Capt. [David] Howard returned to Camp Alva he reported that he had done all in his power to stop the conflagration, but the village was then totally destroyed. No one seemed to care whose fault it was that the village was finally destroyed, but there were remarks of satisfaction at the disappearance of one of the insurgents' particular strongholds.[233]

The smirking tone of the official history leaves little doubt that Company G deliberately torched Mariquina. In his newspaper column, Johnson boasted that "Company G would rather fight than eat ice cream and it takes pride in doing its work well."[234] A Utah man tried to explain Mariquina's fate.

> The encounters which took place between the Americans and the Tagals at this place are illustrative of the peculiar mode of

warfare carried on by the natives. Not a few times our forces made invasions in the enemy's country at Mariquina under the protection of the guns and drove his army into the foothills on the opposite side of the valley, only to find him back in his old position before nightfall with his camp fires piercing the gloom of the valley as darkness settled in. These successive defeats seemed to have no power in dampening the ardor of the ducky warriors of the plains. They continued to make invasions on the American territory, and frequently waylaid belated American troops. Up to March 25th the infantry force was not sufficiently large to hold the country which had been taken. Four times the town of Mariquina was captured in this style. Finally, by some peculiar decision of fate, a battalion of Coloradoans descended into the valley and after dislodging the enemy set fire to the hideous *nipa* huts. Thereafter fewer skirmishes occurred in the locality. The white and shining church steeple arose above the blackened ruins as a ghostly monument of the work of war.[235]

Still, while the First Colorado might take out its frustrations on Filipino property, it conducted its war against the Filipinos by the accepted standards of the day. In their relatively static lines, that war settled down into a pattern of long-range sniping punctuated by periodic forays in strength into the Philippine countryside.

Ambush remained a very real danger. At Quingua, near Malolos, insurrectos led by Gen. Gregorio del Pilar ambushed a cavalry detail on 23 April 1899. The cavalrymen deployed as infantry and held their ground. When battalions from the First Nebraska and the Fifty-first Iowa came to the rescue, eight Americans were killed in action, including Nebraska's commanding officer, Colonel Stotsenburg.[236] The men called such "gorilla" [*sic*] encounters "smokers," and they became used to them.[237] Colonel Stotsenburg was remembered in the name of a United States Army cavalry post established in the Philippines in 1903, and in a twelve-inch seacoast mortar battery at San Francisco's Presidio.[238] Most victims were less famous, and their deaths far more private.

First Sgt. Clifford Bowser signed Company K's morning reports for the last time on 1 May 1899.[239] While on reconnaissance, Sergeant Bowser was wounded in the left arm.[240] Following the same advice he had given Private Pynchon at Mariquina on 16 March, Bowser crawled unaided a mile to the rear. Unable to go any farther, he hid himself under some brush. His men found him by following the blood trail.[241] Bowser died on 9 June 1899, while undergoing an operation to amputate his injured arm.[242]

The nature of the First Colorado's war against the Filipinos was in large part determined by Aguinaldo's military strategy. Aguinaldo was militarily inept, and relied upon Antonio Luna, his primary field commander. Luna's only military knowledge, which was very slight, came from classic military texts. As a result, Aguinaldo initially fought a European-style campaign against the Americans. The Filipinos incurred tremendous losses in the early part of the war, as they tried to defeat the well-trained Americans in conventional combat. Only after the First Colorado had returned home did Aguinaldo switch, in desperation, to the much uglier guerrilla war that made the Philippine-American War synonymous with brutality on both sides.[243]

The insurrectos dared not attack the American trenches in frontal assault; the Americans could not find concentrations of insurrectos against which to focus their artillery and massed infantry. As a lieutenant colonel, Maj. Gen. Elwell Otis helped pursue Crazy Horse in the late summer of 1876. While chasing the Sioux around Wyoming, Otis had learned the use of, and the limitations of, multiple columns against an irregular enemy. Otis had actually fought Sitting Bull and Gall, with some effect. The Hunkpapas, Miniconjous, and Sans Arcs taught Otis the futility of trying to operate a column with a heavy logistical train far from its base of operations. That lesson seemed relevant to fighting Tagals as well.[244] The old Indian fighter applied the frontier army's strategy of multiple columns to try to defeat the insurgents, but ran them as light "flying columns," with the men carrying most of their own supplies. The Malolos and Mariquina offensives of late March had been examples of that strategy. Colorado would participate in two more such campaigns before leaving the Philippines forever.

The First Colorado's toughest campaign may have been the grueling four-day march they later called the "Antipolo Hike."[245] As part of a much larger force, they set out on 3 June 1899 northeast from Santolan toward Antipolo, seeking to form the second pincer of a campaign in Morong Province, north of the Laguna de Bay. Colonel McCoy led Companies A, C, F, G, K, and L, organized into two battalions under Majors Charles Anderson and William Grove.[246] The men left Camp Alva at 4:00 A.M. on 3 June 1899—and moved quickly against what was left of Mariquina, but found no insurgents there. After the remainder of the column had passed, the First Colorado fell in at the rear. The front of the column had to fight its way through Filipino pickets, but the Colorado men saw no real action. The terrain, however, was extremely rough, and progress much slower than projected. After a bivouac in the forest, the First Colorado moved out at 5:00 A.M. on 4 June. Within one mile of camp, they fought their way through an insurrecto ambush, with only one casualty.[247]

Pvt. Charles Hickman of Company A suffered a severe gunshot wound to his left foot and, with the wounded from other units, was transported by "Chinese coolies" and litters to the nearest road, there to await an Army wheeled ambulance.[248] The regiment moved into Antipolo from the east and north at 10:00 A.M., without any real resistance.[249] There, they encountered refugees fleeing other American columns.

> None of these natives were molested, although it was plainly evident that many of the able bodied men had been fighting in the insurgent army. The Filipino is adept at throwing away his gun and donning the clothes of a 'mucho pobre' peasant.[250]

In Arthur Johnson's official accounts, the insurrectos always "skulked,"

19. Slogging uphill on the Antipolo hike. *Photo courtesy of John Stewart Post Number One, Veterans of Foreign Wars.*

whether in the 26 March 1899 Mariquina Road fight, or the 4 June 1899 Antipolo advance.[251] The men of the First Colorado especially despised, however, this practice by the Filipinos, of fighting and then blending into the civilian population.

Leaving Antipolo, the men soldiered on through fifty miles of what they called the "boondocks" (from the Tagalog word for the mountain jungles, *bundoks*) for three more days, through Teresa, Morong, Binangonan, Angona, Taytay, and Cainta. By 12:15 P.M. on 7 June 1899, most of the regiment had completed a big circle back to camp at the waterworks.[252] While not further engaged in combat with the Filipinos, they suffered from "exhaustion." Out of a total force of 2,576 officers and men, eighty-four were disabled by heatstroke.[253] Colorado didn't count heatstroke as a true casualty, and so records are incomplete, but Company A alone sent eleven men back to camp, besides Private Hickman.[254] In Company K, Guy Sims claimed they left with fifty-five men, and returned with thirty-five; the thirty-fifth, Cpl. William Keogh, finally crawled into camp, on all fours, six hours after the rest of the unit.[255]

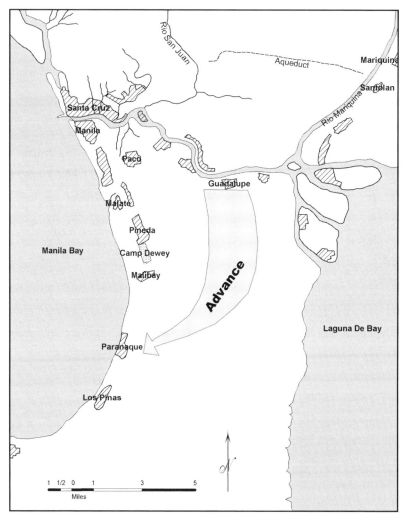

Map 5. Map of Guadalupe Heights and Parañaque [256]

Improbably, on 9 June 1899, Colonel McCoy led six more companies out on another "flying column." This time, he selected fresh companies, B, D, E, I, and M, along with poor Company F, just returned from the Morong Expedition two days before. Lt. Col. Cassius Moses and Major Grove served as his battalion commanders. In concert with other units, they crossed the Pasig River at San Pedro Macati and advanced toward the rebel town of Parañaque. On 10 June, serving in the brigade of Brig. Gen. Lloyd Wheaton, the First Colorado and First Nevada charged insurgent trenches at Guadalupe Heights, flanking the enemy on the left of the American line. At 6:30 A.M., they "swung around a hilltop above Guadalupe yelling and screaming at the top of their lungs and opened the battle."[257] Here, Colonel Moses's arm was nearly severed by a bolo; eleven enlisted men suffered wounds as well. Despite their losses, the First Colorado drove the enemy from their trenches and pursued the Filipinos for approximately five miles.[258]

Again, Arthur Johnson provided a vivid account of tactics in the field. On 10 June 1899, Johnson was with Company E when they took part in the assault on Guadalupe Heights.

> The sun was just rising when columns of fours were broken and the bugles rang "deploy as skirmishers." Colorado took the extreme left and started its long line over hill and into gully, through grass waving waist high and drenching one to the skin with early dew. Jungles had to be penetrated and rocky ridges climbed in order to make an even advance upon the enemy. . . . A mile of this progress and the enemy, entrenched on a heavily wooded hill 800 yards ahead opened up. Down on their knees went the skirmishers, cartridges were shoved home and the battle began. Above the pop, and sputter of the Mausers and Remingtons and the loud bang of the Krag-Jorgensens could be heard the shrill commands of the officers passed on down to the non-commissioned squad commanders. "Fire by volleys" brought the long even music of war which tells on the enemy. "Forward" brought the men struggling up off their bellies to rush ahead fifty yards to another vantage place and pour in the lead again. . . . Onward went the skirmish line, a little ragged perhaps, owing to the exhausted ones failing to keep up, but driving the Filipinos before it. Company F was ordered to take

the menacing hill from which the first shots rained, and dashed up its slope as one man. Surprising half a dozen insurrectos in a set of entrenchments, there was almost a hand to hand battle as every American got his man, and received not a scratch.[259]

The column then shifted direction down the ridge toward Parañaque, slowly moving as a skirmish line through the heavy vegetation. The insurrectos turned on the pursuing Americans, and so the First Colorado fought another action above Parañaque in the late afternoon.[260] One more private was wounded there.[261] Rather than try to force the town, the column bypassed Parañaque, and instead the monitor *Monadnock* shelled it for ten hours. At 6:00 A.M. on 11 June, the First Colorado occupied the coastal village of Los Piñas. The gunboat *Helena* had bombarded the vicinity the day before, and the town fell without resistance; Parañaque fell to other American troops in the same way, again because of naval gunfire.[262]

White flags fluttered, and the cinnamon faces of the inhabitants peered out from their huts. All Filipino warriors who had not escaped had buried their guns and become "amigos."[263] That afternoon, the First Colorado returned to Manila, then to Camp Alva the next day.[264] As had become the standard course of events, they had little substantive progress to show for their efforts. Arthur Johnson described their frustration.

> After putting up a nominal resistance the rebels invariably flee for safety. They have adopted the dodging warfare which is very exasperating to the Americans as they find it impossible to hold all the villages captured.[265]

By the summer of 1899, the Colorado troops were thoroughly tired of the Philippine Islands. They had served overseas for almost a year, against the Spanish and the Filipinos, assailed by bullets and disease, in torrential rains and baking heat. Carl Larsen wrote, "I will promise you the soldiers as well as their folks will be happy whenever we get back."[266] At the same time, the troops serving in the Philippines felt that they had begun a war that had to be completed. A reporter for the *Pittsburgh Post* interviewed 600 Pennsylvania volunteers in San Francisco as they returned to the United States in the summer of 1899. Sixty-two percent of the officers and ninety-three percent of the enlisted men denounced the conflict; they were unanimous in their conviction that the Americans had to beat the Filipinos. One corporal observed that "we should get out as soon as we can with honor" but not until "we've beaten them into submission."[267]

The men of the First Colorado echoed these sentiments. A soldier of the First wrote his parents to explain that the men couldn't come home "until the job of preaching Liberty, Union, and Religion to these poor ignorant heathen [was] accomplished."[268] In any event, the Coloradoans would be home well before the Filipinos were defeated. On 6 April 1899, Denver Health Commissioner William P. Munn wrote General Hale to warn him of three outbreaks of smallpox in Denver families receiving mail from the Philippines. In his reply of 21 June 1899, Hale suggested that "the most radical and pleasant remedy for any danger that may exist, as far as Colorado is concerned, would be the return of the Colorado Regiment,—and it now appears that this is liable to occur in the very near future."[269]

The First was pulled off the line and returned to its Manila barracks on 6 July 1899. They rested for over a week, and then, on the morning of 17 July, held their last dress parade on the Calle de Iris. As they marched down to the docks, their band played "When Johnny Comes Marching Home." It was the first time that the band played that particular tune; they never played it again. At the pier, the regiment found the *Isabel 2nd* waiting for them, the same little side-wheeler that had greeted them the year before. Four companies at a time, she ferried the men the eight miles out to the U.S.A[rmy] T[ransport] *Warren*, but with a typhoon blowing in, she had to dock before all had loaded. The remainder spent an uncomfortable night on the docks, and then, on 18 July 1899, after exactly one year on Philippine soil, the last of the First Colorado boarded the *Warren* and sailed for home.[270]

General Hale summarized the continuing American mission in the Philippines to a Loyal Legion Banquet by exclaiming, "we wouldn't quit if we could, because it would be a disgrace to our flag which was fired upon without provocation by the Filipinos.[271] An enlisted veteran was more succinct, when he noted that "the flag was left where it was planted."[272]

The First Colorado was well out of the fray. During November of 1899, General Otis pursued Aguinaldo with a pincer movement, one arm led by Brigadier General MacArthur, the other by Brigadier General Wheaton. Aguinaldo escaped to Bayambang, dissolved the Republican Army, and shifted to a program of guerrilla warfare.[273] The war, already brutal enough, immediately turned ugly, with atrocities committed on both sides. Just as the United States called the Filipinos' war of independence the "Philippine Insurrection," to suggest unlawful rebellion against legitimate authority, the rebels sometimes were called *ladrones*, meaning "bandits." The war would continue long after President Theodore Roosevelt declared victory in July of 1902, and would claim, by United States estimates, probably 200,000 Filipino dead.[274]

The First Colorado shared with the other American troops a popular marching song, sung to the tune of "Tramp, Tramp, Tramp." Its chorus somehow summed up their bitterness, contempt for the Filipinos, sense of mission, and homesickness, all in one verse.

> Damn, damn, damn the Filipinos!
> Cut-throat khakiac ladrones!
> Underneath the starry flag,
> Civilize them with a Krag,
> And return us to our beloved home.[275]

CHAPTER SIX

And Return Us to Our Own Beloved Home

The First Colorado enlisted to fight the Spanish. While they expected to serve in Cuba, the men willingly fought outside Manila, but with the Philippine capital city occupied and the war ended, the regiment looked toward home. They had responded to their nation's call, but most had no intention of staying in either the Army or the Philippines. Second Lt. James H. Gowdy complained to his mother, "I wish we could get some idea as to how long we have to stay in this country, for I am tired of it already and want to get home."[1] Spurred by their complaints, and those of soldiers' relatives back home, Governor Adams relayed the First Colorado's request to the War Department. H. C. Corbin, the adjutant general of the U.S. Army, responded by telegram that the government's policy was to bring the volunteers home as soon as other volunteers already en route reached the Philippines. By Governor Adams's estimate, that meant the First Colorado would arrive back in the state around mid-February 1899, at the latest.[2] The Philippine-American War intervened.

Of all the volunteer units in the Philippines, the Astor Battery enjoyed the best political connections. Recruited from New York City's high society, they quickly secured their discharge once hostilities with Spain ended. The Astor Battery left Manila Bay for home on 15 December 1898, and mustered out in New York City on 2 February 1899, two days before the outbreak of the fighting with the Filipinos. Left behind to fight the dirty war against the insurrectos, the western regiments rankled at what they saw as blatant favoritism.[3] Maj. Gen. Elwell Otis, commanding general of the Eighth Army Corps in the Philippines, explained in rejecting applications for individual discharges that

> applications of this character have been very numerous. . . . In all cases an invariable rule of action has been applied which is to disapprove unless sickness prevents performance of duty. The adoption of any other rule would result in more or less troop demoralization.[4]

The troops themselves had their own ideas on the subject. Pvt. Carl Larsen of Company C told a friend in Minnesota, "and I will promise you the soldiers as well as their folks will be happy whenever we get back."[5]

Despite General Otis's edict, well-connected officers, and sometimes even enlisted men, did secure individual discharges unrelated to physical disability. The first man of the First Colorado to obtain an early release was the band's slide trombone player, Ora Clarke. Friends in the United States brought their influence to bear on the Secretary of War, and on 25 November 1898, Clarke learned of his discharge.[6] Company B's Lt. Charles Hooper was allowed to resign his commission, in order to return to his position as a passenger agent for the Denver and Rio Grande Railroad.[7] By far the most famous of the western volunteers in the Philippines to use his political connections was California's Brig. Gen. Harrison Gray Otis. After Emilio Aguinaldo's capital at Malolos fell to the Americans on 31 March 1899, Otis anticipated a quick victory; he submitted his resignation, and landed in San Francisco on 30 April, on his way to resume his post as editor in chief and publisher of the *Los Angeles Times*.[8] The average soldier, unconnected to any powerful people, could only wait and hope. Company H's Cpl. Frank M. Dickey wrote home philosophically,

> I have nothing to regret in this business—I am glad I came for what I have seen and learned in the past year could never have

been learned anywhere else. So I may say in that respect I am glad
I enlisted but you know enough's enough of anything even war.[9]

In fact, Regular Army replacements for the volunteers began sailing
from the United States in January of 1899, even before the Philippine-
American War. First was the transport USS *Grant*, which sailed from
New York harbor on 19 January 1899 carrying the Fourth Infantry
and a battalion of the Seventeenth Infantry.[10] Other ships and units
followed, from New York and Newport News on the East Coast, and San
Francisco on the west. When news of the fighting with the Filipinos hit
Denver, Brig. Gen. Henry C. Merriam was able to reassure an audience
at the Brown Palace that 8,000 regulars were already on their way to the
Philippines.[11]

The First Colorado experienced numerous false rumors of returning
home. At 8:00 P.M. on 16 November 1898, Col. Henry McCoy read to his
officers a telegram from Governor Adams, stating "[Adjutant General]
Corbin writes troops en route to relieve volunteers at Manila." The
headquarters erupted in jubilation. Lt. Charles Hilton walked down the
center of the street on his hands. Maj. William Grove did the "Comanche
Indian quickstep" complete with yells. Noted martinet Capt. Ewing
Booth tried to climb a pillar at the former residence of Spanish General
Monet. The men of the regiment filled the streets, half-dressed and
shrieking, and bought out the Chinese stores' entire supply of fireworks.
Thirteen members of the band turned out to play "Hot Time in the Old
Town Tonight" as the soldiers waltzed, quadrilled, and jigged under the
arc lights. Maj. Cassius Moses concluded, "that settles it, we'll get drunk."
The band ended the impromptu celebration with a rendition of "Home,
Sweet Home," and the First Colorado retired for the night.[12] Their joy
was premature. In the crisis of the Philippine-American War, General
Otis used the new troops to augment, rather than replace, the volunteers,
giving him more troops with which to fight the insurrectos.

Five months later, Corporal Dickey complained,

every day since Aug 13–98 we have heard some report about going home—some fellow will say 'Oh I got this dead straight—Going home on the boat that is here now. She sails in two weeks with Colorado and Utah battery. No josh, two weeks and we will be on the way home.' Then in a day or two Mr. Boat sails to America with no one on but a few sick or discharged soldiers and mail.[13]

Back in Colorado, relatives and politicians shared their regiment's pessimism. They bombarded the War Department with demands and requests to release the troops. Arthur Johnson eventually concluded that "the amount of formal correspondence that ensues from each of these communications is amazing and it may be that the government could better afford to bring the boys home than hire an extra army of clerks."[14] Finally, in mid-summer of 1899, the War Department began shipping the state troops home, even then seeking to replace them in part with additional volunteers.[15]

With Cuba and Puerto Rico to be garrisoned, and the Philippines to be subdued, the nation needed additional troops. In the Army Bill of 2 March 1899, Congress approved the recruitment of additional regular soldiers, to bring the infantry and cavalry regiments up to their full wartime strength and create a 65,000-man army. In the same bill, Congress authorized the raising of volunteer forces of up to 35,000 men, to be enlisted for two years for service in the Philippines. The volunteers were to be assigned to twenty-five regiments of infantry and one cavalry troop, and would be commanded by "proven" regular and state officers.[16] The individual identities of state volunteer regiments, the source of so much pride to the states and so much political trouble for the regular army, would be subsumed within simple numbered regiments under this new system. State regiments had served the nation in every war, beginning in the American Revolution; the 1899 Army Bill ended that long tradition forever. President McKinley did not move immediately to recruit those volunteers, choosing instead to assign to the Philippines regular forces freed from garrisons in Cuba. On 5 July 1899, he authorized the organization of the first ten of the new volunteer regiments, to be numbered the Twenty-sixth through the Thirty-fifth Infantries. And on 18 July, he approved two more regiments, the Thirty-sixth and Thirty-seventh, with their complements to be recruited from Americans already in the Philippines.[17]

Surprisingly, not all of the First Colorado elected to return home. In the natural resources of the Philippines they saw economic opportunity. The islands were rich in hemp, and could clearly support tobacco and sugar. Large stands of mahogany and deposits of gold, silver, lead, copper, iron, and coal beckoned. Only a week after landing, Pvt. Fred K. Wollaston of Company K wrote his father to say "if I live I intend to see what there is in the mining question here."[18] Before the Philippine-American War, miners in the Idaho and Montana regiments had begun prospecting, and many in those two units hoped to muster out of the service in the Philippines in order to pursue their fortunes.[19] On 8 March 1899, Arthur Johnson reported that "a week ago" Private Bogan of Company I of the First Montana Volunteers had panned some gold in a Manila rivulet, the first gold strike of the campaign.[20] The Spanish were experienced miners, and Private Bogan's "strike" was as ephemeral as most reported in the American West, but hope springs eternal in the prospector's heart, and many of the Coloradoans hoped to find the mother lode in the Philippines.

Business represented as great a lure as gold. Pvt. Willis Miner of Company E requested a discharge on 10 December 1898, "as he wishes to go into business on these islands and make them his future home."[21] On 26 November 1898, Pvt. Harry Morgan was able to report to C. L. Stonaker of the State Board of Charities and Correction that "many are anxious to go home, but I think if a vote was taken the unanimous vote of company and regiment would be to stay."[22] Morgan may have overstated the sentiments of the regiment, especially considering that the men were still basking in the aftermath of their Thanksgiving Day feasts. But, at the end of January 1899 a group of the men prepared a petition asking to be discharged from the service in the Philippines, to take advantage of job opportunities there. Because of the outbreak of the Philippine-American War, they withheld their plea, but by 17 April 1899 they were ready to proceed. Arthur Johnson wrote approvingly of their request to be released from duty in the Philippines, but given travel pay to their place of enlistment, i.e., Denver. That pay represented for some an escape clause, to prevent their being stranded far from home if they did not fare as well as they hoped. For others, the travel allowance would provide a "stake" upon which to start their enterprise. In return, the men offered to enlist in some sort of a Philippine version of a national guard, to help the American government in the islands maintain order.[23] Nothing came of their offer at that time, but as the government began to prepare to bring the volunteers home, the Army did incorporate a form of the "escape clause." Soldiers were allowed to elect to receive their discharge in Manila. Volunteers accepting the option were guaranteed free passage by government transport back to the United States at any time within one year.[24]

With that promise, some men of the First Colorado began to apply for eventual discharge in the Philippines, one of the first being Private Morgan on 4 May 1899.[25] Upon reflection, some later withdrew their requests, choosing instead to accompany the regiment back to Colorado. Pvt. Harry L. Doxsee placed his signature on his request to "remain in Philippine Islands" on 10 May 1899. Tragically, he was killed in action on 23 May.[26] When it finally came time to board the USS *Warren* for home, 133 men elected to remain in the Philippines. Counting two more who later left the regiment in San Francisco and took ship to Honolulu, fully 10 percent of all the men who served in the First Colorado chose to remain overseas! Thirty-six joined the Thirty-sixth Infantry Veteran Volunteers, one of the new numbered volunteer regiments recruited in the Philippines, and three others joined the regulars, in either the engineer corps or the signal corps. First Colorado Maj. William G. Grove became the lieutenant colonel of the Thirty-sixth, while Capt. E. E. Booth, Lt.

Ben Lear Jr., and Lt. Cornelius O'Keefe all kept their old ranks in the new unit. Pvt. Charles Guidici of the First Colorado's Company I became the Thirty-sixth Infantry's sergeant major.[27]

The remaining ninety-four expatriates stayed in the Philippines, or in one case, Shanghai, as civilians. Some had already found jobs. Former hospital steward Alex McAllister took a position as a civilian clerk in the Army's Subsistence Department, while ex-quartermaster sergeant Grove Cunningham worked in a similar capacity for the quartermaster. Sgt. Ben Lear Jr. of Company C finished the war as a second lieutenant, and carried that rank with him into the Thirty-sixth Infantry, but his father, Ben Lear Sr., who had served under his son as a private, now worked in Manila's internal revenue office, along with two other Coloradoans. John Stanley became a custom house inspector. George Lynch, the British army veteran with the gift of many languages, was snapped up by the Department of Weights and Measures. Musician Fred Mendenhall settled in Shanghai, in charge of relations between the American Bible Society and Chinese book agents. Matthew Finnegan opened a "select rooming house" in the Plaza Santa Ana, and Walter H. Bell took a job as steward of the Bohemian Club. Luther Wiley transferred his prewar profession of teacher from Colorado to the Philippines, now instructing Spaniards and Filipinos in the conquerors' tongue. In like manner, former lawyer Addison Gibbs opened a law practice in Manila. Canadian Herbert G. Farris and Arkansas native William A. Ladner, fellows in Company E and both clerks before the war, combined to open the establishment of Farris and Ladner, purveyors of stationery. And Joseph B. Greer, a brakeman in Colorado before entering the First Colorado, took a promotion to conductor on the Manila and Dagupan Railroad, the same railway the First Colorado detachment had fought to keep in operating condition.[28]

The First Colorado was well represented in Manila's press, as well. Former printer Alexander Darley Jr. hired on as a reporter for the *Freedom*. William J. Matthews became the managing editor of the *American*.

Arthur Johnson, the man who in many ways had served as the "voice of the regiment," parlayed his experience as a correspondent for the *Rocky Mountain News* into a position as reporter for the *American*, augmenting that job by working as a stringer for other Manila publications and for eastern American newspapers.[29]

The other men who chose to remain in the islands apparently hoped to parlay their travel pay of slightly over $100 into some lucrative enterprise, or at least to subsist on it until they could find employment.[30] The number of Coloradoans who declined the chance to return home seems somewhat high; in the Second Oregon, by comparison, only seventy-five decided to remain in the Philippines.[31] On the other hand, many may have seen Manila as offering economic opportunities at least equal to, and perhaps greater than, those they had left in Colorado. Of the 133 who declined to return home, twenty-two were miners, ten worked in farming or livestock jobs, seventeen had left clerical positions, six were laborers, and five performed menial tasks on the railroads. Four of the expatriates were students, nine worked in the building trades, and six had service jobs such as hotel clerks or cooks. Fifteen were skilled artisans, another eight were printers, and ten were in retail sales. Even among the skilled workers, their abilities translated well to Manila, and for George Lynch, linguist and professional ship-rigger, the Philippines offered much more range for his talents than Denver.[32]

Muster rolls indicate ages for 121 of the expatriates, ranging from twenty to forty-three. The mean age for those who chose to stay was twenty-nine years, as opposed to the mean age at muster of twenty-five years, seven months, for the regiment as a whole (the entire regiment was now one year older than at time of muster). The median age of men remaining in the Philippines was twenty-eight, three years older than the regiment's median at that time of twenty-five. The regiment's youngest members returned to their families and studies; slightly older men, who had sampled independence in Colorado, and found prosperity wanting, were willing to give the Philippines a try. America's economic boundaries were expanding beyond the continental limits, with a gold rush in the Klondike and commercial opportunity in Hawaii; perhaps the Philippines could provide the United States with another new Eldorado.

Besides economic prospects, amorous attachments provide another potential incentive for members of the First Colorado to stay in the Philippines. In the years since the United States drew the Philippines into its orbit, legions of American servicemen have married Filipinas, and many have retired to the Islands. While there is no particular reason to think that the men of the First Colorado were any different, the total paucity of evidence, either one way or the other, reduces this possibility to mere conjecture.

The volunteer regiments began their return home in July of 1899. The U.S. Army Transport *Hancock* sailed from Manila on 1 July 1899, with the First Nebraska and the Utah batteries on board. Accompanying her, the USS *Senator* carried the Tenth Pennsylvania.[33] Finally, it was Colorado's turn, but those men eager to leave were frustrated by bad weather. On 17 July 1899, one year to the day after landing in the Philippines, the First Colorado boarded the U.S. Army Transport *Warren*. By nightfall, waves from a typhoon building in the South China Sea forced the port authorities to suspend operations. The last four companies boarded on the morning of 18 July after an uncomfortable night on the docks.[34] Some of the men, still recovering from wounds, remained behind, to follow when they were well enough to travel. The men suffering from illness accompanied the expedition.

The storm followed the *Warren* north to Japan. The men endured an uncomfortable passage as the ship plowed through heavy seas, and at one point the transport had to shelter on the lee side of Formosa to allow the pumps to catch up. Finally, 1,300 miles from Cavite, the *Warren* reached Nagasaki on 25 July 1899 where, during a twenty-four-hour coaling stop, the typhoon moved on. The men stayed on board, and for entertainment watched as a big ship was launched from the shipyard. The Sims brothers decided to remember her name, so that if they ever heard of her again, they could say they "knew her when." The name was so long, however, that they simply recorded her second name, "*Maru*," not realizing it meant "merchant vessel."[35] Leaving Nagasaki on 27 July, the transport steamed on for a brief stop at Kobe, and then anchored at Yokohama from 30 July until 2 August, during which time the men were allowed shore leave.[36] Leaving Japan for San Francisco, the *Warren* swung north near the Aleutian Islands, so that the voyage home was dominated by cold, foggy days. Unlike the *China*, the *Warren* stocked ample provisions, but the men had great difficulty in getting their rations properly cooked. Still, they agreed that conditions were better on their return voyage than on their trip over.[37] After rescuing a becalmed "windjammer" along the way, the transport passed the Faralone Islands, twenty-five miles from San Francisco, late on the afternoon of 16 August. The First Colorado passed through the Golden Gate at nightfall and anchored in the bay.[38]

On the morning of 17 August 1899, the *Warren* cleared quarantine and docked. At breakfast, the officers ordered the men to prepare to leave the ship at noon, an order they hardly needed to issue. The First Colorado hurriedly packed their gear in response.[39] Accompanied by various prominent citizens, Governor Charles Thomas had come from Colorado to welcome the troops home. The governor's party boarded the transport at the dock, shaking every hand in sight. Delivery wagons brought boxes of fruit and crates of melons, gifts from Colorado, for distribution to the men while still on board.[40]

Guy Sims, infested with internal parasites, was too ill to march with the regiment to the Presidio, and so he managed to get off the ship before the rest of the unit. On the dock, he sat on a box behind the welcoming crowd. In front of Sims stood an old civilian, wearing a Grand Army of the Republic badge, and accompanied by his wife and her sister. Each of the women had sons in the First California Infantry, not yet returned home. The Civil War veteran reassured them, "The boys are just having a little picnic over there. They don't know what real war is." Then, at

12:30 P.M. the regiment began walking down the gangplank. A port in the side of the ship opened, and out came the line of stretcher cases. Simultaneously, a steam winch at the forward hatch began lifting caskets from the hold and depositing them on the dock, six at a time.[41] Dead and living, the First Colorado were coming home together.

The regiment left the Philippines with 130 men on the sick list, suffering from such illnesses as malaria, pneumonia, bronchitis, dysentery, and "acute diarrhoea." Thirty more took ill while on the way home, and two of the 160, Privates Frank B. Lindsey and Ivan Tinnerholm, died at sea, the last casualties of the First Colorado. By arrival in San Francisco, only twenty-five men had to be transported to the hospital, including twenty-two-year-old musician Albert Hetherington, down with the mumps.[42] But, even the "fit for duty" looked like "scarecrows," shivering coatless in the cold, dark day, and dressed in a medley of each uniform they had been issued. With some understatement, the reporter for the *Denver Times* observed, "the men do not look to be in the best of health."[43] Poor rations, tropical diseases, and hard campaigning had sapped the strength of the First Colorado, and it showed in the men's appearance.

As the stretcher cases were loaded into ambulance wagons, the women standing in front of Sims began to cry. Color Sgt. Richard Holmes came down the gangplank bearing the remnants of the national colors, reduced by a year in the Philippines to little more than the starry field and five red stripes. The flag was so tattered that Holmes had to carry the staff horizontally, with the colors draped over it. The old veteran saw Holmes with the standard, and burst out, "Oh my God, that Flag!" He snatched off his hat, came to attention as the colors passed, and then turned so the women couldn't see his tears. Face to face with Sims and spying him for the first time, he gripped Sims's hand without a word, and hurried his companions away before they too spotted the emaciated young soldier.[44]

The regiment quickly formed up for the hike to the Presidio. Their march down Market Street turned into an impromptu parade, with steam whistles and cannon salutes calling crowds of San Franciscans to line the sidewalks and wave thousands of fluttering little American flags. First came a military band and four companies of the Third Artillery, brought down to escort the volunteers to the Presidio. Next came the field and staff officers of the regiment, along with Governor Thomas. As the crowd spotted Holmes marching with the colors, a cheer rolled along the street. The officers and officials were followed by the First Colorado's band, and then the men themselves, marching in a column of fours. The officers were dressed entirely in khaki, while most of the men wore their old battle dress of brown pants and blue wool shirts. After the troops, the ambulance wagons followed, and then the rented carriages of the Colorado civilians who had journeyed west to greet the regiment. A last company of the Third Artillery brought up the rear of the procession.[45] California had given the men a royal send-off the year before, and California provided a memorable return.

Given the condition of the men after a year of war and a month on shipboard, the march up over the top of San Francisco to the Presidio proved arduous. When they marched into the military reservation, the First Colorado found tents already set up for them, courtesy of their friends in the First Nebraska, who had arrived a "few days before." The regiment had eaten no dinner, and there were no commissary supplies in sight for supper. Again, the First Nebraska came to the rescue by inviting the Coloradoans to supper. The men were treated to "the best of everything and plenty of it." In fact, for three weeks the First Colorado remained at the Presidio, eating well and resting. Guy Sims believed the delay in returning home was intended to fatten the troops up, so that hometown opinion would not turn against the government officials that let the state's sons suffer so.[46]

In fact, the State of Colorado was trying to figure out how to get the regiment home. The men of the First Colorado were enormously impressed by California hospitality, both before and after the Philippines. They were less sure of their support from their native state. From Manila,

Lt. Charles Hooper wrote to his mother, "We feel that Denver owes us something in return for our services, and when we get back I hope that our reception will be no less cordial than our departure was cheerless."[47] Colorado citizens had already begun grappling with homecoming plans in the spring of 1899. Company I of the U.S. Engineers, a volunteer company drawn largely from Colorado, had spent the war stationed in Hawaii. They left Honolulu for home on 20 April 1899, and arrived in San Francisco on 27 April. At that time, Denver leaders decided to postpone the "reception" for all Colorado's sons until the First Colorado returned, rather than celebrate each unit's return separately.[48]

The Soldiers' Aid Society, organized on 21 June 1898, would have seemed like the logical agency to marshal the homecoming, but the group of 150 of the "best and most patriotic women of Denver" voted to end operations on 2 May 1899.[49] When they closed their books, they had only $200 remaining in their treasury.[50] The Aid Society had provided extensive relief to the Denver-area families of the Seventh Infantry, while the regulars served in Cuba.[51] But, its ten-month tenure had been marred by controversy. As the most visible agency through which to channel private funds to assist Colorado's soldiers, the Soldiers' Aid Society was seen by the public as the obvious organization to handle donations for the First Colorado. The Society instead chose to provide relief to the Denver-area families of the Seventh Infantry, off fighting in Cuba. The Society's standing suffered when a board member revealed to the press that 80 percent of all funds raised in Colorado were spent in Denver, rather than being forwarded to the First Colorado in the Philippines.[52] More damaging still was the January 1899 revelation that Mrs. M. A. Taft, chairman of the Aid Society's Relief Committee, had awarded herself a weekly salary of forty dollars for her efforts, an amount sufficient to sustain twenty soldiers' families.[53] Considering that the society at the same time was giving Dr. Rose Kidd Beere only a dollar a day to nurse the First Colorado in the Philippines, Mrs. Taft's self-indulgence seemed especially egregious.[54] Led by Mrs. Taft, the Society's Executive

Committee purged itself of some protesting board members; others chose to resign, and Executive Committee member Mrs. George Briggs quit to become the president of the competing South Side Soldiers' Aid Society.[55] Although the Soldiers' Aid Society's board intended to continue meeting to plan the homecoming reception, its credibility and energies were both expended. In the end, the Colorado Volunteers' Relatives' Union took responsibility for the affair.

As the First Colorado's train cars had left Denver for San Francisco on 17 May 1898, Mrs. Mary A. Ingersoll, mother of Company E's Sgt. Russell H. Ingersoll, turned to her daughter and said, "Vassie, it's up to us to do something for those boys." Two days later, in the First Baptist Church at Eighteenth and Stout Streets in Denver, she organized the Colorado Volunteers' Relatives' Union. During the war, they met troop trains, wrote letters to the soldiers in the Philippines, and tried to assist First Colorado families in financial difficulty.[56] With the First Colorado back on American soil, the Relatives' Union turned to plans to welcome their return to their hometowns. In preparation for that happy day, the Boulder "ladies" embroidered a big flag to present to the regiment upon their arrival.[57]

Whoever handled the homecoming had more to accomplish, however, than simply arranging a reception. On 2 June 1899 the Relatives' Union voted to request of Governor Charles Thomas that the First Colorado muster out of federal service in Denver, to add to the sense of ceremony.[58] On 13 June 1899, Governor Thomas received a cable from Col. Henry McCoy, notifying him that the regiment instead had voted to muster out when they got to San Francisco. By leaving federal service at a location other than their point of muster, the men would receive travel pay of fifty or sixty dollars from the War Department, money that would be useful in civilian life.[59] But, the men still felt that the state owed them transportation back to Colorado. The state government had exhausted its military fund, and so the burden fell to the citizens of Colorado.

Even after securing discounted rates from the railroads, $15,000 was needed to bring the First Colorado home. The Relatives' Union, in conjunction with state newspapers and business leaders, organized a "committee at large" chaired by Mrs. Marie E. Skillman, to solicit and administer a "free train fund."[60] The committee slowly raised the money, through donations and fund-raising events and by auctioning off old state-owned weapons used in 1864 at Sand Creek by Col. John Chivington's Third Colorado Cavalry.[61] A parallel fund-raising campaign sought to offset the $3,000 cost of commemorative bronze medals for each member of the First Colorado, with the decorations to be paid for by public subscription.[62] Dr. George Hartung, father of Company I's Cpl. Gus Hartung, served as chairman of the Relatives' Union's medal committee. On 23 July he could announce that contributions were flooding in, including twenty-five "pennies from a little girl." Governor Thomas drafted a certificate to accompany each medal, and pledged to personally sign each one.[63] The next day, the *Times* printed a powerful plea from "An Old Soldier," arguing eloquently that the circle of intended recipients for medals and certificates be enlarged, to include all Coloradoans who had volunteered to serve against the Spanish. Clearly in sympathy for those members of the prewar militia who had refused to accept demotions when the two regiments combined into one, he suggested that by wording the commemorative devices to include them, "some little atonement will have been made for the peculiar methods resorted to in the military organization in Colorado fifteen months ago."[64] His argument prevailed, and both medal and certificate dropped language specific to the Philippine campaigns.

The Relative's Union, by necessity, assumed some of the responsibilities formerly handled by the Soldiers' Aid Society. On 28 August 1899, the trains of the First Nebraska passed through Denver on their way to Omaha, and the Union organized a breakfast to repay the Nebraskans' hospitality to the Colorado regiment in San Francisco.[65] On 27 August, as the fund-raising effort neared its goal, Mary Ingersoll, Mrs. Briggs, and Free Train Fund Committee at Large chairman Marie Skillman made plans to travel to Grand Junction to meet the First Colorado as it entered the state, there to present a "handsome silk flag" made by Mrs. Briggs's South Side Soldiers' Aid Society.[66] Apparently, the regiment could not have too many flags.

Cooperative ventures between competing support groups still could falter. On the evening of 29 August 1899, 150 members of the Relatives' Union met at the State Capitol and voted to depose Mary Ingersoll from her position as president. The coup was led by Dr. Hartung and Mrs. America Anderson. Despite the vote of "no confidence," the reformers were thwarted when Ingersoll and Marie Skillman simply refused to acknowledge their standing. The founder of the Relatives' Union pointed out that her term of office had several months to run, and went on with her business.[67] Frustrated, the disaffected faction reluctantly continued to work through the union. The organization patched things up thoroughly enough that the local newspapers carried no hints on the origin of the dispute. The Relatives' Union needed to focus its energy, because it had taken on a very large project. On 7 September 1899, the Union's refreshments committee formally requested that the Daughters of the American Revolution and other societies of a "social, literary, or political nature" cooperate in arranging the First Colorado's reception.[68]

In San Francisco, the First Colorado officially mustered out of federal service on 8 September 1899.[69] That immediately ended the men's federal pay and subsistence allowances. Two of the First Colorado men recruited in Honolulu had sailed with the regiment back to San Francisco, and now used their travel money to sail back to Hawaii. It is 5,405 miles from Cavite to Hawaii, and only 2,095 miles from San Francisco to Honolulu; by returning to America with the regiment, the Honolulu men cut their travel costs considerably.[70] Pvt. Allen Walcott, a teacher before the war, returned to Honolulu to assume the assistant curatorship of the Bishop Museum.[71] Pvt. Bob White of Company K left San Francisco for Hawaii for other reasons. One day, an old couple entered the camp at the Presidio and, approaching a gaggle of the soldiers, asked to see Robert Kay of Company K. Guy Sims and the other men told the civilians that, while they had found Company K, there was no one in the regiment named Kay. They replied, "Well, now, that's strange. He wrote he was in the 1st Colo. Inft., Co. K." Edward Brady, a former law clerk and "smart as a whip," spoke up to ask where Kay was from. When the couple responded, "Brookline, Massachusetts," Brady asked them to wait in the tent he shared with Sims. He returned in a moment with Bob White, who didn't see the civilians until he was inside the tent. White jumped back and "turned as white as his name." The old woman asked, "Is this the Robert we used to know?" After shaking hands all around, White led them from the tent and straight out of camp. He explained to his fellows in Company K that he had left Brookline "just 2 jumps ahead of the sheriff." On the afternoon of 9 September 1899, as the First Colorado boarded a two-section train for their return home, "White" walked along the platform saying farewell to his friends, for he had determined to return to the relative safety of Honolulu.[72]

The train, considerably shorter than the one that had taken the Colorado regiment to San Francisco fifteen months before, reached Pueblo on 13 September. The community treated the men to a banquet, where the men cheered Dr. Rose Kidd Beere and snubbed Colonel McCoy. Then, the train proceeded to Denver, arriving at 10:00 A.M. on 14 September 1899, to be met by a throng on Seventeenth Street. At a banquet set up in the tramway company's power station, 900 soldiers and relatives dined on fried chicken and roast beef. The Solis Tobacco Company handed out 2,000 free cigars to the veterans. Led by the chief of police and sixteen mounted policemen, the soldiers then paraded down Sixteenth Street to the Capitol.[73] Afterward, the men greeted family members, if they had any in town, and went home. The two Sims brothers had been so changed by the privations they had endured that their family failed to recognize them in the crowd, and the soldiers ended up finding their own way home.[74] The final official observance came three days later, on 17 September. The Colorado Society of the Sons of the Revolution, the same group that had provided the First Colorado's national colors when the regiment left in 1898, presided over a somber memorial service on the lawn of the State Capitol. Twenty thousand citizens attended the commemoration. As the First Colorado band played "Nearer, My God, To Thee," Color Sgt. Richard Holmes unfurled the shredded colors and presented them to the governor. Gen. Irving Hale, Colonel McCoy, Senator Henry Teller, and Governor Thomas all spoke, but the memorial address was delivered by an Iowa member of the Sons of the Revolution, Reverend Thomas E. Green of Cedar Rapids. The men received their certificates and medals, and went on their way.[75]

In its time in service, the First Colorado lost thirty-five men: twelve killed in action or dying of wounds, and twenty-three dead by disease, drowning, or suicide. Another thirty-five had been wounded, according to official accounts.[76] If a man received a slight wound not requiring hospitalization, the regiment did not count it as an injury. One example was Capt. William Cornell. As Company K stormed Blockhouse No. 5, a Filipino soldier aimed his rifle at the American officer at point-blank range. Just as the insurrecto fired, one of the First Colorado shot him in the head; the impact of the heavy slug spoiled the Filipino's aim. Captain Cornell suffered only powder burns to his face, but he carried the blue freckles the rest of his life. Still, Guy Sims recalled, "we didn't count men as casualties if they were able to go on."[77]

Overall, compared to other volunteer regiments in the Philippines, the First Colorado had gotten off lightly. South Dakota lost sixty men dead. The Second Oregon and the First Nebraska each lost sixty-four men, and the Twentieth Kansas suffered sixty-five dead. Colorado's lower death toll was due in part to the care taken by the regiment to enlist only men who were completely healthy. The exacting physical examinations conducted at Camp Adams in April of 1898 had culled any men who were unlikely to stand up to long service. The Second Oregon's sixty-four dead included nineteen killed in combat, dying of wounds, or murdered by the Filipinos after capture, a combat loss 50 percent greater than that of the First Colorado. That difference is probably accounted for by simple luck. Oregon, however, lost forty-five men to disease or accident, double

TABLE 3: **Volunteer Regiment's Deaths in the Philippines**[78]

REGIMENT	DEATHS
20th Kansas	65
2nd Oregon	64
1st Nebraska	64
1st South Dakota	60
1st Washington	43
13th Minnesota	42
51st Iowa	40
1st California	36
1st Colorado	35
1st Montana	35
1st Tennessee	26
10th Pennsylvania	21
1st Idaho	21
1st North Dakota	18

the loss of the Coloradoans. Colorado's relative survival rate can be attributed, first, to the health of its men at time of enlistment, and second, to the regiment's efficient medical staff, military and civilian alike.[79]

Given those advantages, it is surprising how sick the men stayed after their return home. Before and during the war with Spain, the Army had given considerable attention to the dangers of both malaria and yellow fever, and precautions prescribed for Cuba and Puerto Rico applied as well in the Philippines. The year 1898 marked the first time that Americans had fought in the tropics, however, and the men came home with tropical diseases never before encountered by American medicine. Doctors in Colorado had trouble diagnosing, much less treating, the continuing malaise of the veterans. For seven months, the two Sims brothers teetered "on the brink." Finally, their desperate doctor surmised that they might be suffering from some sort of internal parasites. He fed them a worm remedy, and saved their lives. They had been infested with hookworms, and were not totally cured until March of 1900.[80] Their story, while dramatic, is also typical of the sort of health problems faced by the returning veterans. Fellow Coloradoan Damon Runyan was host to what he termed his "pet roundworm" for the remainder of his life.

Besides hookworms, the First Colorado returned with some more agreeable mementos of their wars. They were very conscious of having "seen the elephant," and anxious to commemorate what many believed would be the great adventure of their lives. Some of their souvenirs reflected their wonder at alien cultures, others were intended to demonstrate their prowess. A stand of captured arms surmounted by one of the regiment's many flags symbolically illustrated the First Colorado's victory over the Spanish or the Filipinos. The militiamen had grown up surrounded by such Grand Army of the Republic assemblages, and sought to emulate that sort of iconography for their own great struggle.

The individual men had gathered material for friends and family back home. Any sort of militaria was especially popular. Capt. Charles E. Locke sent home numerous "relics," including a "poison arrow blower" seven feet long and one inch in diameter.[81] Lt. Charles H. Hilton Jr. sent his wife a full suit of Filipino armor, which must have overwhelmed the salesman's parlor back in Colorado.[82] Other men bought more practical presents. Cpl. Roy Harris's 20 October 1898 diary entry recorded, "bought China tea set for mamma—$10.00."[83] Many souvenirs were simply looted from the Filipinos. Arthur Johnson described Company G as it re-entered Manila on 7 February, pockets bulging with "relics" from the villages.[84] Pvt. Carl J. Larsen of Company C wrote to a friend, that in one of the Mariquina forays, "I got a few trinkets myself. I got a d[r]esswaist as the ladies use them here. If you are a relic fiend I will keep it for you."[85] All of these items were intended for export, to impress and amaze the

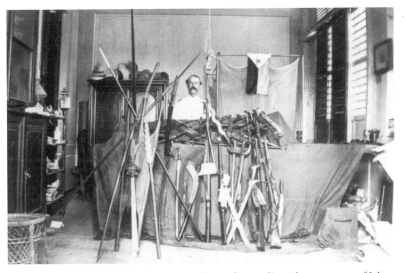

20. Captain Charles Locke with his assemblage of war relics. *Photo courtesy of John Stewart Post Number One, Veterans of Foreign Wars.*

folks back home. For themselves, the soldiers particularly liked to buy canes covered with snake skin.[86] And, they took photographs.

Unlike during the Civil War, photography was no longer the exclusive province of the professional. Kodak manufactured simple box cameras that used roll film, and war correspondents and privates alike snapped madly away. On 20 November 1898, Cpl. Roy Harris noted in his diary, "Stapleton and I went down to the trenches today and took all kinds of pictures."[87] They shot scenes of war, and fortifications, and also of the villages and streets and people of the islands. In the heat and humidity of the Philippines, the results could be spotty, literally. Carl Larsen complained,

Lewis [Hasseldahl] and I have bought a Kodak, and have taken quite a lot of pictures. We had one roll developed, but half of them are spoiled. The films are too old, and we can't get any here, but we will have some good ones.[88]

Purloined or purchased, photographic or physical, the artifacts and images gathered by the men and shipped to Colorado gave their friends and families back home a window into the new world the United States was acquiring. From a historical point of view, their "eye" was very good, and such of their photographs as have survived in public and private collections document many details of military and civilian life in Manila and its environs. The objects gathered by the individual men, by necessity, were portable trinkets or mementoes. Serious collecting for the historical record was the province of professional curators and the regimental staff, especially for anything large or "official."

Even before the regiment returned, Curator William C. Ferril of the State Historical Society was beginning to gather information on the First Colorado's service overseas. In what must have been a delicate negotiation, he wrote to Mrs. Jane Springstead of Antigo, Wisconsin, to request a "history" of her son Fred, Colorado's first man killed in action. At a 16 March 1899 ceremony in the Historical Society's rooms in the Capitol, the governor and Supreme Court judges dedicated a pastel portrait of young Fred, drawn by Mrs. J. B. Hicklin of Highlands.[89]

Besides the State Historical Society collections, the Capitol also housed the "War Relics Collection," founded in 1885 by donor and first curator Cecil Deane.[90] Transferred to the state in 1895, the medley of Civil War and "pioneer" artifacts offered a logical repository for militaria collected by the regiment itself. When Manila fell, the Spanish surrendered 23,000 Mauser rifles and 18 guns.[91] While the Utah artillerymen appropriated the most modern of those cannons for their own use, Colorado did secure two rifled guns from Fort San Antonio de Abad as trophies. Along with assorted stands of Mausers, bolos, machetes, and antique halberds, the two guns arrived at the Capitol and for a time were displayed there. After the 17 September Memorial Service, the regiment's tattered national colors were enshrined in the War Relics Room, in company with other Spanish-American War items.[92]

When the regiment returned from the Philippines, the national colors most symbolized their unit and their experience, and they treated the relic with a care approaching reverence. Colorado's great moment of the war, however, had been its raising of the flag at Fort San Antonio de Abad (and Malate, and the Waterworks, and . . .) The Colorado troops raised a lot of flags, but the flag on the fort was the first American flag raised over Manila, and the event caught the nation's attention. That particular flag had remained over the fort, and slowly became tattered by the weather. It was finally retired by Maj. Gen. Robert H. Allen, long after the First Colorado had sailed from the Philippines. In 1938, Maj. Gen. Ewing E. Booth of the United States Army, formerly a captain in the First Colorado, located Allen, and the flag, in Los Angeles. Forty-five members of what the *Rocky Mountain News* called the "Last Man's Club" of the First Colorado (after the groups actually formed by World War I veterans) met in Los Angeles on 29 June 1938 to receive the flag.[93] Fifty veterans assembled at Denver's Albany Hotel for a 13 August 1938 ceremony in which General Booth presented the flag to Colorado Adj. Gen. Alphonse P. Ardourel. The commander of the National Guard received the banner, acknowledging "when we receive this flag we realize we are accepting an emblem of patriotism. The state of Colorado is proud to have it returned to its home again."[94] Of course, the flag had never actually been in Colorado before, since Gen. Francis V. Greene first handed it to Adjutant Alexander Brooks on 13 August 1898, but the sentiment was real.[95] General Booth replied for the regiment.

> Recapturing the flag is more than recapturing memories of that day. No one can understand what it means to see it again unless he was there at the time it was raised over the fort. Tears came to the eyes of the veterans when I took the flag out of the box. It's almost like reliving the past.[96]

The flag, like its predecessor, went into the shrine at the War Relics Room, which by then was in the State Museum.

Such relics served to perpetuate and honor the experience and sacrifice of the First Colorado. Veterans' organizations, modeled on the Civil War's Grand Army of the Republic, offered another means to the same end. The Spanish-American War and the Philippine-American War together spawned at least twenty veterans' groups in Cuba, Puerto Rico, the Philippines, and the United States. Some of those groups were unit-specific, or restricted to officers only, or only regular army or navy officers, while others were open to the broadest possible number of veterans. Over time, most of the competing groups coalesced into one of two umbrella organizations, the United Spanish War Veterans, and the Veterans of Foreign Wars. The United Spanish War Veterans, or USWV, admitted only veterans of the 1898–1902 conflicts, and so doomed itself to eventual extinction. The Veterans of Foreign Wars, or VFW, by admitting veterans of subsequent overseas conflicts, has outlasted the last Spanish-American War soldier or sailor, and continues to serve its constituents. While many of the Colorado veterans were active in the USWV, the First Colorado was instrumental in establishing the VFW.

The men of the First Colorado created their first veterans' organization while on board the *China*. On 18 June 1898, Sgt. Harry Clotworthy presided as "Chief Whelp" over the first meeting of the "Ancient Order of Sea Dogs." The only membership qualification was that one be immune to seasickness. "The initiation dirge was the 'hoochee Coochee' and the neophyte was required to 'do a turn' of several minutes inside the mystic circle, which chanted and patted him inspiration."[97] The Ancient Order met each evening at 7:45, helping to alleviate the monotony of the passage.

In the Philippines, officers from various volunteer regiments organized the Eighth Corps Society in Manila in September of 1898. The Eighth Corps Society eventually opened membership to any man, officer or enlisted, volunteer or regular, who had served with the Eighth Corps during either the Spanish War or the Philippine-American War. The society endured, primarily in the Philippines where the Eighth

Corps was stationed, for a time after the return of the volunteers to the United States, but was defunct by 1913.[98] Membership does not seem to have caught on among the First Colorado.

The lull between Manila's fall and the Philippine-American War offered some time for such fraternal diversions, to remember fallen comrades and to honor their deaths. On 16 November 1898, men from Company D visited Maricaban, near the site of old Camp Dewey, and placed a white marble headstone on Fred Springstead's grave, located in a small enclosure near a convent. Company D paid for the stone with its own funds, and then erected an iron fence around the grave. In like manner, Company I bought a headstone for Charlie Phenix, buried in a cemetery closer to Manila, and placed it on 21 November. By then, Companies A and B had each lost one man to disease, and those companies also ordered stones for their two graves in Paco Cemetery.[99]

Grave tending was an important obligation of the Grand Army of the Republic. Most American communities, at least outside the South, had cemeteries containing a G.A.R. section, in which ranks of identical white stones ordered the Civil War veterans in death, as they had marched in life. As the veterans aged and their ranks thinned, they recognized their increasing difficulty in preserving and decorating the graves. To pass on their heritage, the G.A.R. formed a Corps of Cadets in 1878, which in turn became in 1881 the Sons of Veterans of the United States of America. Among other duties, the Sons of Veterans continued to preserve the G.A.R. cemeteries, and before the last G.A.R. member died, the G.A.R. officially designated the Sons, since 1904 called the Sons of Union Veterans of the Civil War, as its successor and heir, a trust they still uphold.[100] Between the G.A.R. and the Sons, Americans were accustomed to Memorial Day observances in plots dedicated to veterans of the War of the Rebellion. Spanish-American War and Philippine-American War veterans expected no less, and the G.A.R.-Sons pattern would be their model.

A week after the memorial service in Denver, the Colorado Relatives' Union appointed Major Suess to head a committee to determine where to bury men who died in the Spanish-American War, as their bodies were relocated from temporary graves in the Philippines.[101] Eventually, the committee selected a plot in Denver's Fairmount Cemetery where most of those who died in the Philippines now lie, although First Colorado veterans are buried in individual plots all over the state and country. That solved the real estate problem, but not the question of who would be responsible for ongoing commemoration. While the First Colorado was still in the Philippines, Parson Tom Uzell in Denver promoted the idea of a Denver reunion of volunteers from all the Western states that had sent men to the Philippines. Theodore Roosevelt's Rough Riders had held a reunion in Las Vegas, New Mexico, and scheduled a second for Denver in 1899. Uzell queried General Hale to see if a joint meeting might be possible. Hale cabled back the suggestion that non-Western Eighth Corps veterans, from the Tenth Pennsylvania, First Tennessee, and Astor Battery, should also be invited.[102]

In the summer of 1899, opinion was divided on the wisdom of organizing a formal veterans' group. Proponents surveyed a number of officers, among them Capt. George Borstadt of the First Colorado and Maj. S. K. Hooper, father of First Colorado Lt. Charles Hooper. Respondents varied in their enthusiasm, some feeling that with the regiment still overseas it was too soon, and others suggesting that perhaps a reunion could be held concurrent with the annual Mountain and Plain Festival. Once the regiment returned, momentum built, and by 15 October 1899 a loose veterans' organization committee had agreed to invite all Western regiments from the Spanish or Philippine Wars to a Denver Eighth Corps reunion, and then to organize along the patterns of the G.A.R.[103] On 19 November 1899, General Hale, who had mustered out of service in October, lent his prestige to the effort when he issued a call for a preliminary meeting to plan the Eighth Corps reunion. Over twenty-five veterans of the First Colorado showed up for the 23 November 1899 meeting at the Capitol, and there agreed to form a "Society of the Army of the Philippines."[104] To the organizing committee, Hale appointed Maj. Charles Anderson and

Lt. Charles Lewis of the First Colorado, and Lt. Col. Henry J. Lippincott of the Department of Colorado. On 1 December 1899, in Room 33 of the Capitol, the Colorado Society of the Army of the Philippines held its first meeting and elected Hale chairman. Former Company K Pvt. Frank Noble, described as "a soldier and the son of a soldier," was elected secretary; they elected no other officers, as the association still lacked a constitution. The group of twenty-nine men agreed on dues of one dollar per year, and each paid on the spot and signed the roster. Consistent with the egalitarian symbolism of the two elected officers being a general and a private, none of the signatures in the roster carried any rank designation. Finally, the little group determined to invite the entire Eighth Corps to a Denver reunion, to be held in the summer of 1900.[105]

As plans moved forward for the reunion, the committee set the date for 13–15 August 1900, to coincide with the second anniversary of the fall of Manila. They sent invitations to such dignitaries as President William McKinley, Secretary of State Elihu Root, Gen. Nelson Miles, Admiral Dewey, and, in a nonpartisan atmosphere, Colonels Theodore Roosevelt and William Jennings Bryan, both of whom had commanded regiments during the war. A parallel committee drafted the new organization's constitution, formally adopted on 3 February 1900. The constitution's preamble read:

> We, officers and enlisted men, and honorably discharged officers and enlisted men, hereby unite to establish this association, the chief aims of which shall be the perpetuation of the ties of friendship between the individuals and organizations of the Eighth Army Corps, honoring the memories of those who gave their lives for the flag and preserving the history and relics of the memorable campaign in the Philippine Islands.[106]

In electing its first officials, to serve until 1 February 1900, the Society turned to both officers and enlisted men. Hale was president, while

Colonel Lippincott became first vice-president. Hospital Steward Edgar Luce was elected second vice-president, Col. William Grove third vice-president, and Sgt. Ben F. Stapleton became the recording secretary. For corresponding secretary, the society turned to reporter and Cpl. Harry McCauley. Lt. Charles Lewis served as treasurer.[107]

Now officially launched, the Colorado Society of the Army of the Philippines performed the usual functions. In February, they attended the funeral of Pvt. Arthur Ramsey, whose body was finally shipped home from the Philippines. Recognizing the kindred nature of the new group, the G.A.R. invited the Army of the Philippines to march as a unit in the annual Decoration Day parade on 30 May 1900, and at the Memorial Exercise held that evening at Denver's Central Christian Church, General Hale gave the principal address. By the end of July, the Society of the Army of the Philippines opened its second branch, with fifty members in Colorado Springs. Above all, preparations for the reunion dominated the summer. The reception committee sent its printed invitations to the President, cabinet, Congress, and the governors of all Eighth Corps states. They secured reduced railroad rates for the delegates. They issued a formal request to employers to grant veterans leave to attend. And they braced themselves for over 1,000 delegates.[108]

The reunion was an enormous success. At the opening exercise, held on 12 August 1900 at Denver's Central Presbyterian Church, Governor Charles Thomas and Denver Mayor Henry V. Johnson welcomed the delegates to the state and city. Hale issued the welcome from the Colorado Society of the Army of the Philippines, and Brig. Gen. Owen Summers of the Second Oregon made the response. Harry Irvine led the band in "Hot Time." Gen. Francis Greene recounted the story of the flag raising over the fort. Then, as the opening exercise adjourned, grey-and blue-uniformed veterans of the Civil War, north and south, turned out to mingle with the brown-uniformed veterans of the Philippines. The Colorado Society had sold the concept of a national organization embracing the veterans of the entire Eighth Corps. While the mass of delegates spent the afternoon socializing, a committee met at the Brown Palace to hammer out a constitution for a national organization.

13 August 1900 began with a parade. In the afternoon, Hale called the reunion to order in the Brown Palace's eighth-floor assembly room. "We are here for a double purpose," he said, ". . . to renew acquaintances formed in the Philippines and to perfect a permanent organization of the Army of the Philippines." A committee composed of representatives from each state regiment and the regular army presented its draft constitution, and the delegates voted to become the National Association of the Army of the Philippines. The Colorado Society of the Army of the Philippines had successfully launched a national veterans' group. The body elected General Greene as its president, and General Hale as its first vice-president. The society further agreed to hold its annual meetings on 13 August, to admit any honorably discharged veteran, Army or Navy, from the Philippine conflicts, or (recognizing the perils of age) their sons. Like the G.A.R. and the Sons of Union Veterans, the new organization prohibited any political discussions at meetings.[109]

Subsequent meetings moved around the country. The second annual meeting, held in 1901 in Salt Lake City, elected Hale president, a position to which he was re-elected in 1902 at Council Bluffs, Iowa. In 1903, at St. Paul, Hale stepped down to be replaced by Gen. Charles King. The sixth annual meeting, held in Chicago in 1905, marked significant changes. The organization changed its name to the Army of the Philippines, dropping the "National Association" language. In a move of greater consequence, the Army of the Philippines modified its eligibility requirements to include any veteran who had completed honorable service in the Philippines, from 25 April 1898 until 4 July 1902, the date on which President Theodore Roosevelt declared the "Insurrection" at an end. While removing the provision allowing sons of veterans to join, the organization did provide for honorary memberships to be awarded by a majority vote of the members at any annual meeting. Following the G.A.R.-Sons pattern, local chapters or "camps" could be organized by any ten members.[110]

Soldiers make strong friendships during wartime. Being far from home, enduring hardships and sharing dangers all make for close bonds. The Army of the Philippines sought to preserve those bonds. As the conflict receded, however, the veterans got on with their lives. Some had returned to families, others married and began families. They pursued careers and hobbies, and many began to let their ties to other veterans, and their membership in the Army of the Philippines, slip. Some of the officers became active in the Military Order of the Carabao, an officers-only group organized in Manila in the fall of 1900. Both trends meant declining membership in the Army of the Philippines.[111] At the 1912 annual meeting of the Army of the Philippines in Lincoln, Nebraska, members of the American Veterans of Foreign Service suggested a merger between their group and the Philippine veterans. The American Veterans of Foreign Service had formed in Columbus, Ohio, in 1899, open to any man who had served outside the continental limits of the United States. They admitted not only veterans of the Philippine campaigns, but also participants in the Cuban and Puerto Rican segments of the Spanish-American War, members of the Boxer Rebellion relief expedition, occupation forces from Wake and Guam, the various Caribbean interventions, and even service in Hawaii. Their ranks were thinned by the same forces that afflicted the Philippine veterans. The Army of the Philippines suggested that the American Veterans of Foreign Service attend the 1913 annual meeting in Denver to further discuss a possible merger.[112]

Five hundred delegates, including members and officers of the American Veterans, assembled at Denver's Albany Hotel in August of 1913.[113] Recognizing the problem with declining membership, one motion proposed admitting anyone who had ever served in the Philippines, even after the Philippine-American War. In opposition, members pointed out that the Army of the Philippines existed to commemorate the Eighth Corps, and post-Philippine-American War veterans were not part of that Corps. Since the Eighth Corps Society had dissolved, the Army of the Philippines was the last keeper of the flame, they argued, and should not dilute its membership requirements. Debate was acrimonious, but the motion passed over the wishes of the national officers. If the Army of the Philippines could admit any Philippine veteran from any time, why should it limit its membership to just the Philippines? After addresses on 18 August 1913 by F. Warner Karling of Kansas City, Commander in Chief of the Army of the Philippines, and Robert G. Woodside of Pittsburgh, Commander in Chief of the American Veterans of Foreign Service, the delegates adjourned for the day. The debates continued, however, in hotel rooms and lobbies.[114]

On 19 August 1913, the Army of the Philippines and the American Veterans of Foreign Service voted to merge themselves into the new Army of the Philippines, Cuba, and Porto Rico [as it was then spelled]. Membership was open to Spanish-American War, Philippine-American War, and Boxer Rebellion veterans. Many of the Army of the Philippines members, led by Luzon Post No. 17 of Chicago, were vehemently opposed to losing their unique organization, and a number of delegates openly discussed secession. Again, those discussions continued through the evening, and by 20 August the meeting appeared largely reconciled to the merger. When the new Army of the Philippines, Cuba, and Porto Rico voted on its first national officers, the members bypassed the top leadership of each founding group and unanimously elected Rice W. Means, former lieutenant in the First Colorado and Entertainment Committee Chairman for the annual meeting, as its new commander in chief. As entertainment chairman, Means was very visible at the convention, and veterans enjoying the convention could easily feel grateful to the man who had provided the fun. Politically, Means's selection was a sop to the old Army of the Philippines veterans, while still allowing them to rebuke their national commanders by voting for a committee member instead of a former officer of the association.[115] As the convention broke up, many members left dissatisfied. That dissatisfaction was mirrored in the Army of the Philippines camps across the nation. A significant percentage seceded in protest and joined the rival United Spanish War Veterans.

The Army of the Philippines, Cuba, and Porto Rico met in Pittsburgh for its 1914 annual meeting, missing many of the Philippines veterans. Trying to move forward, the delegates changed their name one last time, to the Veterans of Foreign Wars of the United States, and elected Thomas Crago commander in chief. In Detroit the following year, still calming the waters, the VFW elected former First Colorado member Gus Hartung as commander in chief.[116] Since the VFW traces its lineage back to the Colorado Society of the Army of the Philippines, three members of the First Colorado served as VFW commanders in chief: Irving Hale, Rice Means, and Gus Hartung.

By 1921, Colorado had nine VFW posts, their membership boosted by veterans of World War I. At their May meeting that year, those posts combined to form the Department of Colorado. The next year, Wyoming joined to form a new Department of Colorado and Wyoming, a title and organizational structure that fit the far-flung West and matched exactly the solution previously adopted by both the G.A.R. and the Sons of Union Veterans of the Civil War. By 1939 Wyoming had enough VFW posts to form its own department. By 1988, the VFW worldwide had 2.5 million members. The Department of Colorado contained 171 posts with 25,370 members, a mixture of veterans from America's various twentieth-century conflicts.

The initial focus on the Philippine Wars has been largely overwhelmed, but Colorado's largest post, with 1,368 members in 1996, is Denver's John S. Stewart Post No. 1.[117] Named for the First Colorado's highest-ranking officer to be killed in the Philippines, Post No. 1 still proudly remembers its Spanish-American War heritage. Since VFW posts are numbered sequentially, in order of establishment, and the First Colorado volunteers founded the Colorado Society of the Army of the Philippines from which the VFW descends, the John Stewart Post is recognized as the first. After years in a building at Ninth and Speer, financial considerations prompted a 1996 trade with the neighbors next door at 955 Bannock Street. With the new quarters, the John S. Stewart Post No. 1 broke other new ground in 1996 when it elected Christine Downing-Hodges as its first female commander. An Army combat medic with service in Panama and Somalia, Downing-Hodges was the first female commander elected in the Department of Colorado.[118] Rose Kidd Beere would have been proud.

The largest organization for men who had served in the Spanish-American War was the United Spanish War Veterans. The USWV coalesced in 1904 by combining the National Army and Navy Spanish War Veterans, the National Association of Spanish-American War Veterans, and the Servicemen of the Spanish War. Almost immediately, the Society of the Hispano-American War joined as well, followed by the Society of the Veteran Army of the Philippines and the Legion of Spanish War Veterans (Massachusetts). Like the Army of the Philippines, the USWV followed the Grand Army of the Republic's model of local "camps" arranged into statewide "departments." Unlike the Army of the Philippines, the U.S.W.V. allowed Spanish-American War veterans from all theaters to join, as long as they served between 21 April 1898 and 4 July 1902. The organization was formed "to unite in fraternal bonds those men and those women nurses who served in the military or naval establishment of the United States of America at any time during the War with Spain, and at any time during the campaigns incidental to and growing out of that war."[119] The USWV had the advantage of numbers over the Army of the Philippines, even though it too lacked any provision for admitting sons of veterans. By refusing to admit any veterans of later conflicts, however, the USWV remained pure to its original purpose but consigned itself to a long, slow twilight, as its members died off.

After the acrimony of the 1913 Army of the Philippines meeting, many First Colorado veterans switched their allegiance to the United Spanish War Veterans. At one time, the Colorado Department of the USWV boasted 1,184 members in twenty camps.[120] Since the USWV included veterans who had not served in the Philippines, the First Colorado members also formed the First Colorado Infantry Association (FCIA), to preserve their particular identity. The FCIA membership was interwoven with Colorado's USWV camps. To be sure, there was nothing to prevent a First Colorado veteran from belonging to all three groups. In the FCIA-USWV symbiosis, the USWV handled the honor guards, and the FCIA periodically held reunion banquets and tried to keep track of members' addresses.

When the First Colorado Infantry Association held its twenty-seventh anniversary banquet in Denver on 13 August 1925, they could locate 245 men from the old First. Of that number, 113, or 46 percent, still lived in Colorado. Sgt. Ben Stapleton had risen to mayor of Denver. In fact, the First Colorado was well represented in the ranks of Colorado government, especially in law enforcement. Cpl. Ab Romans was district attorney in Loveland. In Pueblo, Lt. Samuel E. Thomas was sheriff, and Pvt. John Miller was with the police force. Wagoner Frank Lyons was a lieutenant on the Denver Fire Department, and Army deserter Pvt. Fred Reed was Denver's captain of detectives.[121] Reed, who carried a Filipino slug in his lung until he died, eventually rose to chief of police.[122] Lt. Rice Means had become an attorney, and after a brief stint as Denver's director of public safety, was serving a short term as United States senator.[123] Just across the border in Cheyenne, Pvt. Lon Davis was a federal prohibition officer.[124]

The war with Spain had been a war against Catholics, and the enlistment policies of the First Colorado in April of 1898, while not excluding Catholics, had drawn largely from lower- and middle-class Protestants. Recruited in part from the prewar militia, the First Colorado as a unit and as individuals held a strong bias against organized labor, and against the immigrants who mined Colorado's coal and minerals. It is not surprising that in 1925 some former soldiers of the First Colorado were prominent members of Colorado's Ku Klux Klan. Ben Stapleton achieved Denver's mayorship in 1923 because of Klan backing; within a month of his victory he had appointed Klan leader Rice Means as director of public safety. The Klan's power also elevated Means to the United States Senate. While the Klan dominated the Denver Police

Department and some other city bureaus for a time, it should not be assumed that Fred Reed and Frank Lyons were also Klan members. While high up in the police ranks, Reed was a lifetime policeman, and the fire department was a less-likely venue for furthering the Klan agenda than law enforcement. By the association's annual banquet in August of 1925, Klan power was rapidly waning. Mayor Stapleton had suspended a dozen Klansmen from the police department earlier in the year, and Reed was untouched in the purge. Still, the Klan offered the same sort of fellowship and sense of belonging as the regiment. Seventy percent of Denver had approved avowed Klan supporter Stapleton in a 1924 electoral contest against reformers, and it is likely that the Klan's emphasis on order and stability resonated with many of the First Colorado veterans.[125]

By 1925, at least 113 veterans of the First Colorado resided in Colorado, 46 percent of those with known addresses. Almost as many had ended up in California. The First Colorado had been enormously impressed by the hospitality they received in California, both on their way to the Philippines and on their return. Despite miserable weather during their stay at Camp Merritt, they enjoyed their time there. In 1925, ninety-three of the regiment, or 38 percent of those whose addresses were known, resided in California. Of those, eighty, or 86 percent, lived in Los Angeles or its suburbs, including a little colony of nine in the Soldiers Home in Sawtelle. In fact, the Los Angeles residents represented 33 percent of the First Colorado's known survivors. Fully 84 percent of the First Colorado were living in either Colorado or California in 1925. The rest were scattered fairly evenly through the western states. Only thirteen lived east of the Mississippi River; of those, two were serving officers in the United States Army, stationed in Washington, D.C. Color Sgt. Richard Holmes was living in Vancouver, British Columbia, and Lt. Frank De Votie was in Guanajuato, Mexico.[126]

Four members of the First Colorado had enjoyed military life enough to continue as officers in the United States Army. In 1925, Ralph Lister was a colonel, stationed in San Francisco.[127] Capt. Ewing E. Booth of Company C, famed as a stickler for details and a strict disciplinarian, rose to major general and was "one of the outstanding commanders" of the American Expeditionary Force in World War I.[128] After the First Colorado went home from the Philippines, Maj. William Grove became lieutenant colonel and later colonel of the Thirty-sixth Volunteer Infantry, earning the Medal of Honor while serving with that regiment. When the numbered volunteer regiments were disbanded, he entered the Regular Army as a captain, rising to colonel by World War I.[129] Pueblo printer Benjamin Lear Jr. may have had the most meteoric rise. When the regiment left for Manila, Lear was first sergeant of Company C, under Captain Ewing. While serving with the First Colorado in the Philippine-American War, he was promoted to second lieutenant. He took that rank with him into the Thirty-sixth Volunteers, but went into the regulars as a sergeant when the Thirty-sixth disbanded. Commissioned in the field in World War I, by 1941 he was a lieutenant general commanding a base near Memphis, Tennessee. "Old-fashioned, stern, and humorless," he was outraged when one of his convoys greeted female golfers with cries of "Yoo-hoo." After he forced the entire 235-man unit to march with full packs in the July sun, the men called him "Yoo-hoo Lear," by which sobriquet he was known forever after. During World War II, he commanded the Second Army and earned the Distinguished Service Medal; he died in Murfreesboro, Tennessee, in 1966.[130]

Each reunion brought fewer faces to the table. In 1952, the USWV mustered 150 men for a banquet. The First Colorado Infantry Association used the occasion to place a plaque at the site of Camp Adams, at Twenty-sixth Street and Colorado Boulevard in Denver.[131] Service in the Philippines had damaged the health of many of the men. In 1925, eleven of the 245 known First Colorado survivors were already living in Old Soldiers Homes.[132] Increasingly, the USWV camps met at Disabled American Veterans' Halls. In 1959, the Colorado Department represented 235 veterans, thirty of whom assembled for the state encampment.[133] By 1963, the number had dropped to 114 members; two years later, the

Colorado Department was down to eighty-four members in twelve active camps.[134] Each year, the survivors had more difficulty in getting together or even conducting their association business. Sgt. William S. Watson of Company E was a colorful character, long a fixture of Memorial Day parades. Active in the USWV, he was the last president of the First Colorado Infantry Association. He died on 7 December 1968. The remaining eight survivors of the First were scattered about the country, and let the association lapse.[135] On 3 June 1971, at the Disabled American Veterans' Hall at 1225 Broadway in Denver, Camp Henry W. Lawton No. 1, United Spanish War Veterans, closed its books forever. As Colorado's last USWV camp, its demise also closed the Department of Colorado.[136]

By then, the Spanish War and its veterans seemed almost quaint. The First Colorado had answered its country's call to fight the Spanish, although that fight came not in Cuba, as the men had expected, but in the Philippines. Less willingly, but still at the behest of their nation, the Colorado men had fought the Filipinos. Upon their return home, they tried to maintain their friendships and memorialize their war, through memorabilia and veterans' organizations. Participants in two World Wars, each far larger and involving far more Americans, overwhelmed the men who had fought in the Philippines in 1898 and 1899. Even the Korean and Vietnam conflicts were larger than the Luzon campaigns, and the Spanish-American War veterans, never that numerous in the first place, faded away as old age took its toll. The oldest survivors of the First Colorado lived long enough to witness the decidedly mixed welcome America gave to returning Vietnam veterans. Both the Vietnam and Philippine veterans fought in an ugly Asian war that few at home understood. Ultimately, one First Colorado veteran summed up his fellows' feelings to a newspaper reporter with an epigram.

> Remember the *Maine*,
> To Hell with Spain,
> But We Won't Volunteer Again![137]

21. The Starry Flag. *Photo courtesy of John Stewart Post Number One, Veterans of Foreign Wars.*

CHAPTER SEVEN

Underneath the Starry Flag

In his Manila quarters in October of 1898, Capt. Charles Eastman sat cross-legged on the floor, enveloped in red, white, and blue cloth, hand-sewing a United States flag out of silk he had ordered from Hong Kong. Although the Women's Relief Corps, Sons of the American Revolution, Colorado College Students, and Brig. Gen. Francis V. Greene himself all had given flags to the First Colorado, the one given to Eastman's Company H had gone to some other purpose, and the company had none. Unable to buy an American flag in the Philippines, Captain Eastman was making his own.[1]

The First Colorado was a long way from home. The only thing familiar in the Philippine Islands was the regiment itself. Strangers to each other when the various companies assembled in Denver in April of 1898, the First Colorado had become a sort of extended family for its members, a portable community built on military discipline, shared laughter and privations and tensions and frictions, and very real danger and sacrifice. A letter from home took six weeks to arrive, and any reply another six weeks to return. In a strange land, America seemed very far away. For Captain Eastman, sewing himself an American flag was the closest he could get to his loved ones back in Colorado. Unable to return to America, he sought to bring America to him.

If the regiment was an extended family, the company was the nuclear family.[2] In nineteenth-century families, women embodied virtue and order. But, in the all-male society of an infantry regiment, what happened when there were no women to moderate the behavior of the "boys," as the men in the ranks called each other?[3] Captain Eastman may not have been Company H's "mother," but as its commanding officer he was most certainly its "father," and he took very seriously his duty of providing his "boys" an ordered community bounded by laws and order and expectations. One symbol of that community was the flag.

The regiment's progress from Colorado to the Philippines was a process of steadily expanding horizons: from city and town and farm to Camp Adams in Denver, from Colorado across the Rocky Mountains and Sierra Nevada to San Francisco, from the Presidio to Hawaii, from Honolulu to Wake, and on to Manila. Flags marked every stage of that journey. Hometown citizens gave flags to their companies as the men boarded trains for the muster in Denver. In the capital city, the people of Colorado presented the First Colorado with regimental and national colors, as the men prepared to leave the state. At Camp Merritt in San Francisco, each day's drill began with the men forming up on the color line, falling in behind the regiment's flags, and each day of the long Pacific passage ended with the national anthem and a formal retreat ceremony, as the flag came down. When the First Colorado's expedition took Wake Island, they raised a flag on the old Spanish flagpole there. At 7:45 A.M. on 5 July 1898, Walter Wise, the band's snare drummer, died of either "typhoid pneumonia" or spinal meningitis; three hours later, as a squad fired a salute over his remains, the young private's body slid out from under an American flag and into the waters of the Pacific.[4] Landing in the Philippines, the regiment set up another flag in front of their headquarters in the trenches outside Manila.

In their fight against the Spanish, the First Colorado raised one flag over Fort San Antonio de Abad, the first American flag erected over Manila's defenses, and then displayed another in the Malate district of the city. In Gerald Linderman's analysis, volunteer regiments only supported the efforts of the regulars in the campaigns in Cuba and Puerto Rico.[5] Fighting the Spanish in the Philippines, however, the volunteers were in the van. Years later, Colorado veterans cited the vision of the flag rising over the fort as their defining memory of the war, for it represented the accomplishment of an identifiable goal in a conflict that lacked clear outcomes. Sgt. William "Billy" Watson recalled in 1963, "that was the biggest kick I got out of the war."[6] At the start of the Philippine-American War, the volunteer regiments again fought in the thick of it; a Nebraska man sparked the conflict and the First Colorado came on line alongside the Nebraskans in the first night's battle. Fighting the Filipinos, the regiment mounted the national colors above captured Blockhouse No. 5, and even raised a pocket-sized flag at the Santolan waterworks. The men of the First Colorado enlisted under the American flag, they assembled into formation behind it, and they followed it into battle. It flew over their headquarters, and their conquests, and their graves.

The flag was at once a practical tool to guide the men's movements, and a symbolic device, representing the soldiers' homes and customs and nation and system of government, all rolled up in one powerful banner. The First Colorado left Denver with a brand new set of silk regimental colors, one national flag, and one regimental device. The regimental banner symbolized Colorado, and the pride the people of the state felt for their soldiers, and reminded the men of home while they served in distant lands. The national flag, given to the unit by a patriotic organization, stood for the nation and the constitutional system of government the United States presumably was attempting to export to Spain's Caribbean colonies. Even the national flag, lettered with the legend "1ST. REGT. INF. COLORADO VOLUNTEERS," linked the men to their home state.[7] The two crisp new banners, presented to the First Colorado in a public ceremony reminiscent of Civil War leave-takings, reflected the men's exuberant confidence in their society and their mission. Neither the flags, nor that confidence, survived the Philippine Wars intact.

The First Colorado Regiment enlisted in the nineteenth century, and returned home in the twentieth. Their experience in the Spanish-American War and the Philippine-American War transformed their vision of themselves, their society, and their nation. As the United States exchanged its traditional focus on continental affairs for an expanded vision of empire and a place on the world stage, the men of the First Colorado adapted their prewar values and attitudes to place themselves in the new century.

The men left Colorado secure in their belief in the superiority of their race and institutions. Gerald Linderman has pointed out that Americans of the late nineteenth century possessed far fewer categories into which to place people and concepts, than do modern Americans. People, and issues, were black and white, with no possibility of intermediate shades.[8] As the men of the First Colorado traveled from the United States to first, Hawaii, and then the Philippines, they moved from a society in which non-White peoples were a minority into foreign lands where they themselves were a minority. Their concept of "foreigners" was challenged by encountering those foreigners in their own lands. Of course, for some of the First Colorado, racism served as a defensive mechanism in a strange place, and meeting different peoples on their home ground only reinforced their racist preconceptions.

Others remarked in surprise as their attitudes changed. Observing the Chinese crew members of the *China* on the voyage to the Philippines, Pvt. Al Silverstein reported to his mother that "one's ideas of Chinamen change at seeing these neat little fellows running the ship."[9] Lt. Rice Means could tell his parents that the Filipinos were "a filthy set of people" who "rob you of everything they can," and in the same letter praise a Filipino youth as "the gamest lad I ever saw."[10] Even in Means's racial hierarchy, a Filipino could be praised in what Richard Drinnon calls "paternalistic or accommodationist racism," as long as that Filipino "lad" was in a subordinate position, in this case literally under the lieutenant's knife, in the midst of a field operation for which the American had no training whatsoever.[11]

When they left Colorado, the soldiers of the regiment perceived their flag as a sort of crusader's banner, under which they would liberate island peoples from Spain's oppressive rule. The outbreak of the Philippine-American War necessitated some re-evaluation of that interpretation. Pvt. Carl Larsen wrote, "I fight these people with a very difference [*sic*] feeling from what I had toward the Spainiards [*sic*]. Then we was fighting for a good cause, and now? The fact is, I don't know what we are fighting for now."[12] Pvt. Guy Sims described his insurrecto opponents as "*brave stubborn* fighters" [his emphasis], and concluded "they were brave and patriotic. We respected their courage and favored their independence."[13] The First Colorado stormed across the bridge into Manila singing the Civil War tune "Marching through Georgia," complete with the line in its chorus about "The Flag that makes you free." By the Philippine-American War, the American flag, instead of standing for liberation, had become at best a symbol of American authority, and at worst the ensign of oppression.

Flags are potent symbols, and those men of the First Colorado who questioned the American role in the Philippines were not alone in their concern. In a speech on 4 January 1901, Mark Twain noted, "I knew enough about the Philippines to have a strong aversion to sending our bright boys out there to fight with a disgraced musket under a polluted flag."[14] Later in the year, he "apologized" for his remark.

> I was not properly reared, and had the illusion that a flag was a thing which must be sacredly guarded against shameful uses and unclean contacts, lest it suffer pollution; and so when it was sent out to the Philippines to float over a wanton war and a robbing expedition I supposed it was polluted, and in an ignorant moment I said so. But I stand corrected. I concede and acknowledge that it was only the government that sent it on such an errand that was polluted. Let us compromise on that. I am glad to have it that way. For our flag could not well stand pollution, never having been used to it, but it is different with the administration.[15]

At a Loyal Legion banquet back in Denver on 4 October 1899, Gen. Irving Hale was asked why the United States simply didn't leave the Filipinos to their own devices. No one laughed when Hale explained, "we wouldn't quit if we could, because it would be a disgrace to our flag which was fired upon without provocation by the Filipinos."[16] That flag had taken a long journey in order to be fired upon by Filipino patriots, but the irony was lost on both Hale and his audience.

By 1901, the American public was increasingly concerned about reports of Army brutality in the Philippines, and many assumed that any troops who had served there had committed atrocities against either civilians, or insurrectos, or both.[17] Guy Sims complained that, when he returned home, "everybody seemed to hate us."[18] In contrast to the stereotype, however, the First Colorado fought their war within boundaries that met at least their definition of honorable. So long as enemy soldiers were in the field, even if fleeing, they were fair game, but if they attempted to surrender, the First Colorado accepted. To shoot fleeing soldiers at extreme range can seem somehow "unsporting," but not in the context of nineteenth-century warfare (modern warfare accomplishes the same effect from 40,000 feet). That practice was rooted in the custom of the Indian Wars, but just as deeply in the temperament of males, especially young males, in the late Victorian era.

The "boys" in the regiment were often little more than that, with over 33 percent of the regiment less than twenty-three years old. E. Anthony Rotundo has profiled American "boy culture" in the last half of the nineteenth century. "Home" was a domestic sphere, dominated by the mother. Outdoors was a boy's realm, uncivilized and unregulated, at least by women. There, Victorian boys hunted and fished, flew kites, built forts, swam, and fought each other. "The experience of boy culture encouraged a male child to become the master, the conqueror, the owner of what was outside him."[19] Besides such impromptu sporting encounters, boys engaged in vigorous physical sports as part of club and school activities. Civil War veterans favored sports for young men as a way to encourage virility and resist what they saw as the debilitating effects of urbanization. Further, they saw in team sports a reflection of their wartime subordination of individual will to the greater good.[20] That emphasis on sports, along with an educational philosophy that emphasized for boys "suppression of feeling, action over thought," suggests that the young men of the First Colorado brought less than reflective attitudes to the regiment.[21]

Without citing any particular evidence, Michael C. C. Adams explains that "for some men who were divorced from their emotions, aggressive physical encounters with other men and animals became a primary form of communication."[22] Seen in that light, the First Colorado's "kangarooing" and football games make more sense, as does General Hale's prewar year of hunting and trapping. On a more ominous note, Adams warns that "a society divided on gender lines encourages male violence," and suggests that sexual repression led late nineteenth-century men to kill things.[23] If people are the highest animals, then killing them becomes the highest form of sport.

In the Indian Wars, the regular Army on campaign often regarded any armed male Indian as a legitimate target; those on reservations usually were not. In the Philippine-American War, the First Colorado saw armed insurrectos, at whatever distance, as equally legitimate targets, and Arthur Johnson could boast that "to shoot down human beings like pigeons as they are hurled from the trap has surely been the dream of every warrior."[24] Adams explains:

> What makes this unfeeling possible is a blurring between sport and war, so that the killing of men can be sloughed off as tribute to athletic prowess. The enemy, reduced to a hunting quarry, is stripped of humanity, leaving the killer free to destroy without guilt.[25]

Despite such rationalizations, "civilized" nations were supposed to wage war in a "civilized" manner.

Drinnon cites Frederick Jackson Turner's characterization of the frontier as "the meeting place between savagery and civilization" as a clear color line, with race deciding the respective positions.[26] "Civilized" people are supposed to fight by "civilized" means, but if the opponent fails to conform to accepted standards, that failure justifies extreme brutality. While the First Colorado fought the Filipinos, the British fought the Boers in South Africa. Adams quotes British officer J. F. C. Fuller's rationalization that "an uncivilized or semi-civilized people do not understand kindness and consideration and one has to leave one's mark on them before they will recognize one."[27] The Boers and the British are of the same "race," demonstrating that conventional troops could still respond to unconventional warfare on the part of their opponents with brutality.

For the First Colorado, that brutality was evidenced in destruction of property, rather than by killing noncombatants. During the Civil War, "foraging" or appropriation of foodstuffs from enemy civilians was common practice, and the men of the First Colorado had grown up with veterans' tales of such activities.[28] In *Embattled Courage: The Experience of Combat in the American Civil War*, Gerald Linderman has traced an ethical journey traveled by many Civil War soldiers, from respecting civilian property to foraging ("we need what they have"), to looting ("we want what they have"), to burning ("we will destroy what you have, as punishment").[29] The First Colorado reached the first two stages in one day, 5 February 1899. At first, the huts and villages they burned, including those torched on 5 February, were destroyed for tactical reasons, to remove cover used by Filipino snipers. After repeated fights through supposedly friendly Mariquina, however, the Colorado men resorted to the third level, burning as punishment, when they torched Mariquina on 15 April 1899. Even so, in contrast to other volunteer regiments, they did not execute surrendered insurrectos, and they continued to provide medical care for Filipino wounded. There were limits, beyond which they would not go.

As the First Colorado prepared to return to the United States, their regimental colors and idealism both in tatters, the Philippine-American War continued. Despite their hard service and the turmoil in the islands, 10 percent of the regiment elected to remain in the Philippines, most of them to seek their fortunes. Their suspicion of and contempt for non-Whites and "foreigners" had abated to the degree that they could envision a life in Manila, at least a life in which they held dominant positions over the Filipinos. For the remainder of the men, home beckoned, and they eagerly boarded their transport and turned their backs on the Philippines. While many questioned the wisdom of the United States in deciding to retain the islands, they regarded their war against the Filipinos with a sort of fatalistic sense of inevitability. One member of the First wryly observed, "It looks to me very much . . . like our grand 'War for Down trodden Humanity' will end up in a war of conquest, and here, conquest means extermination."[30] The men of the First Colorado felt that they had dared much, and risked much, and suffered much in their year of Philippine service. They had fought the Spanish and raised the first American flags over Manila, and then held their own in the campaigns against the insurrectos. They debated their government's policies, but the men did their duty as they understood it. Half a century later, asked to sum up the overall meaning of the First Colorado's Philippine Wars, Sgt. Walter Weber of Company D concluded simply, "The flag was left where it was planted."[31]

Notes

Introduction

1. Linderman, *Mirror of War*, 60.
2. Drinnon, *Facing West*, 464.
3. Williams, "United States Indian Policy," 810–31.
4. Harper, "Fighting Far from Home," 6.
5. Cosmas, *An Army for Empire*; Jamieson, *Crossing the Deadly Ground*.
6. Anderson, *A People's Army*, 251–53.
7. Linderman, *Mirror of War*, 71–72.
8. Johnson, *Operations of the First Colorado*.
9. Weber, *Golden Anniversary*.
10. Linderman, *Mirror of War*, 74–75.
11. Harper, *Just Outside Manila*, viii.
12. Garraty, *The American Nation*, 621–23.
13. Harper, *Just Outside Manila*, ix. In 1976 Rear Admiral Hyman G. Rickover's research team concluded, through study of maintenance reports, ship's plans, and submarine analysis of the wreckage, that the *Maine* was destroyed by spontaneous combustion in a coal bunker next to a reserve magazine loaded with ammunition. See Karnow, *In Our Image*, 97.
14. Jamieson, *Deadly Ground*, 132.
15. *Rocky Mountain News*, 16 April 1898, 1.
16. Ibid., 17 April 1898, 3.
17. Garraty, *The American Nation*, 623.
18. *Rocky Mountain News*, 20 April 1898, 1.
19. Ibid., 21 April 1898, 2.
20. Ibid., 22 April 1898, 10; Stonaker I:180.
21. *Rocky Mountain News*, 24 April 1898, 5, 12.
22. Garraty, *The American Nation*, 623; Overstreet, *History of the Veterans of Foreign Wars*, 11.
23. Harper, *Just Outside Manila*, xi–xii.
24. Karnow, *In Our Image*, 11.
25. Gantenbein, *Official Records*, 1.
26. Keenan, *The Conflict with Spain*, 126.
27. Linn, *Counterinsurgency*, 1–2.
28. Ibid., 3.
29. Karnow, *In Our Image*, 14, 20–21.
30. Ibid., 62.

31. Linn, *Counterinsurgency*, 3.
32. Karnow, *In Our Image*, 59–60.
33. Ibid., 63; Linn, *Counterinsurgency*, 4.
34. Linn, *Counterinsurgency*, 4–5.
35. Ibid., 5–6.
36. Ibid., 6–7.
37. Keenan, *The Conflict with Spain*, 147.
38. Johnson to the *Rocky Mountain News*, 23 August 1898, Stonaker II:15, 17.
39. *New York Sun*, 16 July 1898, Stonaker I:234.
40. Baker, *The Colorado Volunteers*, 46.
41. Harper, "Fighting Far from Home," 5.
42. Karnow, *In Our Image*, 115.
43. Keenan, *The Conflict with Spain*, 429.
44. Linn, *Counterinsurgency*, 6–7.

Chapter One

1. *Rocky Mountain News*, 18 April 1898, 2.
2. Long, *The Civil War Day by Day*, 705.
3. Jamieson, *Deadly Ground*, 38.
4. Utley, *Frontier Regulars*, 144.
5. Utley, *Frontier Regulars*, 315.
6. Jamieson, *Deadly Ground*, 42–43; Utley, *Frontier Regulars*, 255.
7. General John Gibbon, "Arms to Fight Indians," *United Service* I (April 1879): 240, as cited in Jamieson, *Deadly Ground*, 44.
8. "Line Officer: A Tactical Necessity," *Army Navy Journal* 23 (16 January 1886): 488, as quoted in Jamieson, *Deadly Ground*, 10, 158.
9. Utley, *Frontier Regulars*, 407.
10. Williams, "United States Indian Policy," 810–31.
11. Jamieson, *Deadly Ground*, 100.
12. Ibid., 63–64, 101.
13. *Infantry Drill Regulations, United States Army* (Washington, D.C.: Government Printing Office, 1891), 195–96.
14. Jamieson, *Deadly Ground*, 108.
15. Kagan, Ozment, and Turner, *The Western Heritage*, 857.
16. Brecher, "The 1877 Railroad Strike," 30, 46.
17. Ibid., 30, 41; Nash, *The American People*, 629.
18. Cosmas, *An Army for Empire*, 10–11.
19. Brecher, "The 1877 Railroad Strike," 30.
20. Cosmas, *An Army for Empire*, 11–12.
21. Nankivell, *Military Organizations*, 94–97, 107–8.
22. Cosmas, *An Army for Empire*, 13.
23. Nankivell, *Military Organizations*, 91.
24. Cosmas, *An Army for Empire*, 6–7.

25. Jamieson, *Deadly Ground*, 100–101.

26. Smiley, ed., *History of Denver*, 921–22.

27. Nankivell, *Military Organizations*, 96.

28. Smiley, ed., *History of Denver*, 923; Lamb and Smith, *Pioneers and Politicians*, 47.

29. Tarsney, *Biennial Report*, 31–33.

30. Nankivell, *Military Organizations*, 96–97.

31. *Rocky Mountain News*, 16 March 1894, 1.

32. Nankivell, *Military Organizations*, 97–98.

33. Jamieson, *Deadly Ground*, 102.

34. Nankivell, *Military Organizations*, 111.

35. *The National Standard*, 21 August 1897, 1.

36. *Rocky Mountain News*, 23 April 1898, 3.

37. Ibid., 15 April 1898, 10.

38. Ibid., 18 April 1898, 2.

39. Nankivell, *Military Organizations*, 111.

40. *Rocky Mountain News*, 18 April 1898, 2.

41. Ibid.

42. Ibid., 20 April 1898, 1, 10; Keenan, *The Conflict with Spain*, 24.

43. *Rocky Mountain News*, 24 April 1898, 5.

44. Ibid., 25 April 1898, 2.

45. Keenan, *The Conflict with Spain*, 25.

46. Nankivell, *Military Organizations*, 90–91.

47. Ibid., 92–93.

48. Ibid., 108–9.

49. L. 1897, Ch. 63, Colorado State Archives.

50. Cosmas, *An Army for Empire*, 11.

51. *Rocky Mountain News*, 17 April 1898, 2.

52. *Rocky Mountain News*, 26 April 1898, 5.

53. *Rocky Mountain News*, 26 April 1898, 1.

54. Nankivell, *Military Organizations*, 112.

55. *Rocky Mountain News*, 26 April 1898, 5.

56. Ibid., 28 April 1898, 8, 10.

57. Ibid., 27 April 1898, 10.

58. Ibid., 28 April 1898, 8.

59. Ibid.

60. Ibid., 18 April 1898, 2.

61. Sims, untitled TMs, 2.

62. Stonaker I:190–91.

63. *Rocky Mountain News*, 27 April 1898, 5.

64. Ibid., 28 April 1898, 8.

65. Nankivell, *Military Organizations*, 104.

66. Capt. Charles E. Locke from Manila to his wife, 21 July 1898, Stonaker I:193.

67. Arthur C. Johnson from Manila to the *Rocky Mountain News*, 25 August 1898, Stonaker II:7.

68. Al Silverstein on *China* to his mother, Mrs. E. Silverstein of Denver, 17 June 1898, Stonaker I:83; Arthur C. Johnson from Manila to the *Rocky Mountain News*, 17 November 1898, Stonaker II:93.

69. *The National Standard*, 21 August 1897, 1.

70. *Rocky Mountain News*, 29 April 1898, 10.

71. Lt. George Borstadt from Manila to Dr. Henry Borstadt, 31 August 1898, Stonaker II:35.

72. *Rocky Mountain News*, 15 May 1898, 13.

73. Baker, *The Colorado Volunteers*, 7.

74. *Rocky Mountain News*, 29 April 1898, 3.

75. Ibid., 7.

76. Ibid., 26 April 1898, 5.

77. Sims, untitled TMs, 2–3.

78. Ibid., 3.

79. Baker, *The Colorado Volunteers*, 6.

80. *Rocky Mountain News*, 26 April 1898, 5; 17 August 1969, 26; Baker, *The Colorado Volunteers*, 7.

81. Baker, *The Colorado Volunteers*, 6.

82. *Rocky Mountain News*, 27 April 1898, 8.

83. Frances Melrose, *Rocky Mountain News*, 14 June 1992.

84. Ibid.

85. *Rocky Mountain News*, 23 April 1898, 10.

86. Ibid., 28 April 1898, 4; Nankivell, *Military Organizations*, 111.

87. *Rocky Mountain News*, 28 April 1898, 3.

88. Baker, *The Colorado Volunteers*, 7.

89. Moses, *Report of the Adjutant General*, 13–14.

90. *Rocky Mountain News*, 29 April 1898, 7.

91. Weber, *Golden Anniversary*, 14.

92. Baker, *The Colorado Volunteers*, 15.

93. Source: Moses, *Report of the Adjutant General*, 13–14; Johnson, *Official History*, 2.

94. Johnson, *Official History of the Operations of the First*, 2.

95. Ibid., 116.

96. *Rocky Mountain News*, 29 April 1898, 10.

97. Anderson, *A People's Army*, 67–68.

98. Nankivell, *Military Organizations*, 113, 115.

99. Baker, *The Colorado Volunteers*, 7.

100. Sims, untitled TMs, 4.

101. *Rocky Mountain News*, 26 April 1898, 1; Baker, *The Colorado Volunteers*, 7.

102. *Book D 1st Infantry*, 1.

103. Sims, untitled TMs, 4.

104. *Rocky Mountain News*, 31 August 1941, 4.

105. Ibid., 24 April 1898, 12.

106. Ibid., 28 April 1898, 8.

107. Nankivell, *Military Organizations*, 115; Baker, *The Colorado Volunteers*, 7–8.

108. *Rocky Mountain News*, 31 August 1941, 4.

109. Baker, *The Colorado Volunteers*, 9.

110. Nankivell, *Military Organizations*, 115; Arthur C. Johnson from Manila to the *Rocky Mountain News*, 3 September 1898, Stonaker II:31–32; ibid., 1 December 1898, Stonaker II:116; *Book D 1st Infantry*.

111. Arthur C. Johnson from Manila to the *Rocky Mountain News*, 1 December 1898, Stonaker II:116; ibid., 18 March 1899, Stonaker II:222.

112. *Book D 1st Infantry*.

113. Nankivell, *Military Organizations*, 116.

114. Moses, *Report of the Adjutant General*, 10; Earl, *Sagebrush Volunteers*, 137–38, 147.

115. Stonaker I:191; Mabey, *The Utah Batteries*, 16.

116. *The Denver Republican*, 8 May 1898, 18.

117. *Rocky Mountain News*, 11 May 1898, 10.

118. Cosmas, *An Army for Empire*, 8; Karnow, *In Our Image*, 119.

119. Jamieson, *Deadly Ground*, 110.

120. *Rocky Mountain News*, 29 April 1898, 7.

121. Ibid., 31 August 1941, 4.

122. Ibid., 23 March 1898, 3.

123. Overmeyer, *Biennial Report of the Adjutant General*, 6, 10–11.

124. Arthur C. Johnson from Manila to the *Rocky Mountain News*, 11 May 1898, 10; Nankivell, *Military Organizations*, 115.

125. Irving Hale from Manila to his father, Stonaker II:142.

126 Nankivell, *Military Organizations*, 116.

127. Ibid., 118.

128. Sims, untitled TMs, 4–5.

129. Weber, *Golden Anniversary*, 17–18.

130. *Rocky Mountain News*, 28 April 1898, 7.

131. Nankivell, *Military Organizations*, 118.

132. Ibid.; Baker, *The Colorado Volunteers*, 10–11.

133. Nankivell, *Military Organizations*, 118.

134. Sims, untitled TMs, 5.

135. Baker, *The Colorado Volunteers*, 10–11.

136. *Army Overseas Operations*, 102.

137. Linn, *Counterinsurgency*, 2.

138. *Army Overseas Operations*, 102.

139. *Eighth Army Corps, Letters Received Register*, No. 57, entry 361.

140. *Army Overseas Operations*, 102.

141. *Army Overseas Operations*, 102; Baker, *The Colorado Volunteers*, 25.
142. Earl, *Sagebrush Volunteers*, 153; Baker, *The Colorado Volunteers*, 11–12.
143. Baker, *The Colorado Volunteers*, 11–12.
144. Nankivell, *Military Organizations*, 118.
145. Sims, untitled TMs, 5.
146. *The Wave*, Military Life-Spanish American War-Clippings [Vertical File], Western History Collections, Denver Public Library, Denver, Colorado; Rutledge, *Campaign Clothing*, 10, 26, 45; Poyer and Riesch, *The .45–70 Springfield*, 104–5.
147. *Rocky Mountain News*, 31 August 1941, 4.
148. Sims, untitled TMs, 5.
149. Rutledge, *Field Uniforms*, 13, 45.
150. Stonaker I:88.
151. Baker, *The Colorado Volunteers*, 14.
152. Ibid., 118.
153. Jamieson, *Deadly Ground*, 146.
154. Sims, untitled TMs, 16.
155. *Eighth Army Corps, Letters Received Register*, No. 217, p. 34.
156. Ibid., No. 453, p. 70.
157. Capt. Jonathan Stewart, 30 September 1898, in *Colorado: Company Letters Sent*, 3.
158. Earl, *Sagebrush Volunteers*, 155.
159. Eugene F. Bert letter to Commander, Eighth Army Corps, 28 May 1898, *Eighth Army Corps, Letters Received Register*, No. 206, p. 31.
160. Baker, *The Colorado Volunteers*, 13–14.
161. *Rocky Mountain News*, 23 June 1959, 22.
162. Earl, *Sagebrush Volunteers*, 155.
163. Ibid., 153, 155.
164. Nankivell, *Military Organizations*, 118.
165. Maj. Louis H. Kemble report to Eighth Army Corps, 12 June 1898, *Eighth Army Corps, Letters Received Register*, No. 389, p. 60.
166. *Book D 1st Infantry*.
167. Baker, *The Colorado Volunteers*, 15; Nankivell, *Military Organizations*, 118.
168. Adjutant General's Office to Eighth Army Corps, 1 June 1898, *Eighth Army Corps, Letters Received Register*, No. 50, p. 2; 2nd Lt. Charles E. Hooper to Eighth Army Corps, 4 June 1898, *Eighth Army Corps, Letters Received Register*, No. 207, p. 32.
169. Gantenbein, *Official Records*, 1.
170. Baker, *The Colorado Volunteers*, 15–16; Nankivell, *Military Organizations*, 118.
171. Sims, untitled TMs, 7.

Chapter Two

1. Weber, *Golden Anniversary*, 17.
2. Gantenbein, *Official Records*, 1.
3. Stonaker I:58.

4. Keenan, *The Conflict with Spain*, 450.

5. St. Louis *Globe-Democrat*, 16 March 1899, Stonaker II:203.

6. Weber, *Golden Anniversary*, 18.

7. Sims, Untitled TMs, 7.

8. 1st Lt. Charles Henry Hilton from San Francisco to his wife Mamie, 14 June 1898, in Harper, *Just Outside Manila*, 4.

9. Stonaker I:86.

10. Arthur C. Johnson from Manila to the *Rocky Mountain News*, 18 January 1899, Stonaker II:179; ibid., I:83.

11. Arthur C. Johnson to *Rocky Mountain News*, Stonaker I:85.

12. Stonaker I:82.

13. Gantenbein, *Official Records*, 1.

14. 1st Lt. William Sweeney to the *Pueblo Chieftan*, Stonaker I:82.

15. Weber, *Golden Anniversary*, 18.

16. Sims, Untitled TMs, 7.

17. Ibid.

18. Stonaker I:83.

19. Arthur C. Johnson to *Rocky Mountain News*, Stonaker I:86.

20. Stonaker I:86.

21. Harris, unpublished diary, 18 June 1898.

22. Stonaker I:82–83.

23. 1st Lt. Charles H. Hilton from *China* to his wife Mamie, 22 June 1898, in Harper, *Just Outside Manila*, 7.

24. Stonaker I:85.

25. Ibid., I:83.

26. Harris, unpublished diary, 18 June 1898.

27. Stonaker I:83.

28. Brig. Gen. Francis V. Greene from *China* to Maj. Gen. Wesley Merritt in San Francisco, 21 June 1898, *Eighth Army Corps, Letters Received Register*, No. 605, p. 874.

29. John Bass from Manila to the *New York Herald*, as printed in the *Denver Republican*, Stonaker II:232.

30. Irving Hale Papers, Box 12/File 739.

31. Sims, Questionnaire, 2.

32. Arthur Johnson to the *Rocky Mountain News*, Stonaker I:86.

33. Harris, Diary, 1 July 1898, 5 July 1898.

34. Lamar, *The Reader's Encyclopedia* (1977), s.v. "Hawaii."

35. Stonaker I:88.

36. Sims, Untitled TMs, 7.

37. Baker, *The Colorado Volunteers*, 20; Stonaker I:88.

38. Sims, Untitled TMs, 7–8.

39. Stonaker I:88.

40. Sims, Untitled TMs, 7.

41. Ibid.; Lamar, *The Reader's Encyclopedia* (1977), s.v. "Hawaii."

42. Stonaker I:88; Baker, *The Colorado Volunteers*, 21.
43. Stonaker I:88.
44. Baker, *The Colorado Volunteers*, 21.
45. Mabey, *The Utah Batteries*, 20.
46. Sims, Untitled TMs, 8.
47. Baker, *The Colorado Volunteers*, 21.
48. Stonaker I:88.
49. Baker, *The Colorado Volunteers*, 22.
50. Sims, Untitled TMs, 8.
51. Karnow, *In Our Image*, 119.
52. Sims, Untitled TMs, 8.
53. *General Orders No. 5*, on *China*, 3 July 1898, Box 13/File 823, Irving Hale Papers.
54. Stonaker I:83.
55. Sims, Untitled TMs, 8.
56. Ibid., 8–9.
57. Harris, unpublished diary, 4 July 1898.
58. Keenan, *The Conflict with Spain*, 450. (Keenan says only "A Western Volunteer On *China*;" internal evidence establishes the rank and First Colorado connection.)
59. Stonaker I:83.
60. Ibid., 85.
61. Ibid., 83.
62. Weber, *Golden Anniversary*, 18.
63. Stonaker I:221; Keenan, *The Conflict with Spain*, 450; 1st Lt. Charles H. Hilton from *China* to his wife Mamie, 14 July 1898, in Harper, *Just Outside Manila*, 13.
64. Keenan, *The Conflict with Spain*, 450–51.
65. Harris, unpublished diary, 8 July 1898.
66. *Rocky Mountain News*, 29 June 1965, 5.
67. 1st Lt. Charles H. Hilton from *China* to his wife Mamie, 14 July 1898, in Harper, *Just Outside Manila*, 13.
68. Harris, unpublished diary, 11 July 1898.
69. Stonaker I:83.
70. Arthur C. Johnson from *China* to the *Rocky Mountain News*, 17 July 1898, Stonaker I:222.
71. Stonaker I:87.
72. Ibid., I:83.
73. Ibid., I:87.
74. Ibid., I:83.
75. Al Silverstein on *China* to his mother, Mrs. E. Silverstein of Denver, 17 June 1898, Stonaker I:83.
76. Arthur C. Johnson from Manila to the *Rocky Mountain News*, 17 November 1898, Stonaker II:98; anonymous First Colorado officer from *China*, Keenan, *The Conflict with Spain*, 451.

77. *Rocky Mountain News*, 29 June 1965, 5.

78. Anonymous First Colorado officer on *China*, Keenan, *The Conflict with Spain*, 451.

79. Pvt. Al Silverstein from *China* to his mother, 19 June 1898, Stonaker I:83.

80. Stonaker I:85–86, 88.

81. Keenan, *The Conflict with Spain*, 451.

82. Cpl. Harry McCauley from *China*, Stonaker I:83.

83. Pvt. Al Silverstein from *China* to his mother, 19 June 1898, Stonaker I:83; anonymous First Colorado officer from *China*, Keenan, *The Conflict with Spain*, 451.

84. Lt. William Sweeney from *China* to the Pueblo *Chieftan*, Stonaker I:82.

85. Stonaker I:86; Sims, untitled TMs, 7.

86. Arthur C. Johnson from Manila to the *Rocky Mountain News*, 18 January 1898, Stonaker II:179.

87. Irving Hale Papers, Box 13/File 824.

88. Sims, Untitled TMs, 9; Mabey, *The Utah Batteries*, 20.

89. Stonaker I:86–87.

90. Sims, Untitled TMs, 9.

91. Keenan, *The Conflict with Spain*, 441, 448.

92. Sims, Untitled TMs, 9.

93. Keenan, *The Conflict with Spain*, 220, 550–51.

94. Ibid., 195, 215.

95. *Chicago Record*, Stonaker I:106.

96. Gantenbein, *Official Records*, 2.

97. Baker, *The Colorado Volunteers*, 24.

98. Mabey, *The Utah Batteries*, 20.

99. Arthur Sims, Unpublished novel, 45; United States Army Military History Research Collection, No. 1898-142.

100. Sims, Untitled TMs, 10; Sims, Unpublished novel, 46.

101. Sims, Untitled TMs, 10; Stonaker I:184.

102. Sims, Untitled TMs, 10; Pvt. Edward Lazell, Hospital Corps, from Manila to *Denver Post*, received 17 August 1898, Stonaker I:181.

103. Sims, Unpublished novel, 46.

104. Private Edward Lazell, Hospital Corps, from Manila to *Denver Post*, received 17 August 1898, Stonaker I:181.

105. Arthur C. Johnson from Manila to the *Rocky Mountain News*, 21 July 1898, Stonaker I:183.

106. Sims, Unpublished novel, 45.

107. Henry J. Youngs Jr. from Manila to his father, 20 July 1898, Stonaker I:182.

108. Sims, Unpublished novel, 45.

109. Mabey, *The Utah Batteries*, 20.

110. Sims, Unpublished novel, 45.

111. Ibid., 46.

112. Sims, Unpublished novel, 46.

113. Sims, Untitled TMs, 11; Sims, Unpublished novel, 45.

114. Arthur C. Johnson from Camp Dewey to *Rocky Mountain News*, 20 July 1898, Stonaker I:237–38.

115. 2nd Lt. Rice Means from Camp Dewey to his parents, 27 July 1898, Stonaker I:208.

116. Sims, Questionnaire, 7; Linn, *Counterinsurgency*, 3.

117. Keenan, *The Conflict with Spain*, 452.

118. Ibid., 453.

119. Ibid., 452.

120. Linn, *Counterinsurgency*, 3.

121. "News from Manila," 26 October 1898, Stonaker II:76.

122. Arthur C. Johnson from Manila to the *Rocky Mountain News*, 17 July 1898, Stonaker I:222.

123. Sims, Untitled TMs, 46.

124. Sims, Unpublished novel, 46.

125. Ibid., 10–11; Sims, Unpublished novel, 46.

126. Arthur C. Johnson from Camp Dewey to *Rocky Mountain News*, 20 July 1898, Stonaker I:237–38.

127. Ibid.; Linn, *Counterinsurgency*, 8.

128. Cody, *Lists of Officers*, 65.

129. Weber, *Golden Anniversary*, 20.

130. Linn, *Counterinsurgency*, 2.

131. Ibid., 8.

132. Capt. William Grove from Manila to his wife, 21 July 1898, Stonaker I:191.

133. Karnow, *In Our Image*, 122–23.

134. Sims, Untitled TMs, 11. Sims mistakenly identifies 24 July 1898 for the night movement; other sources clearly place the action on 29 July: Mabey, *The Utah Batteries*, 21; *Record of Events*, 14.

135. Nankivell, Military Organizations, 129.

136. Sims, Untitled TMs, 11–12; *Record of Events*, 14.

137. Johnson, *Operations of the First Colorado*, 6.

138. Ibid., 46–47.

139. Mabey, *The Utah Batteries*, 21–22.

140. Thomas, *Autobiography*, , 6.

141. Prentiss, *History of the Utah Volunteers*, 695.

142. Sims, Untitled TMs, 12.

143. Weber, *Golden Anniversary*, 13; Mabey, *The Utah Batteries*, 22.

144. Mabey, *The Utah Batteries*, 22.

145. George Fisher diary, 31 July 1898 entry. Fisher did not specify Colorado troops, but he was in Battery A according to the *Official Roster of the Utah Volunteers*, 5; and Battery A was posted in the Colorado lines on 31 July 1898, according to Mabey, *The Utah Batteries*, 21–22.

146. Sims, Untitled TMs, 12; Mabey, *The Utah Batteries*, 23.

147. Mabey, *The Utah Batteries*, 23.

148. Karnow, *In Our Image*, 123.

149. Johnson, *Operations of the First Colorado*, 7.

150. Arthur C. Johnson from Manila to the *Rocky Mountain News*, 3 August 1898, Stonaker I:230.

151. Weber, *Golden Anniversary*, 20.

152. Baker, *The Colorado Volunteers*, 30–32.

153. Sims, Unpublished novel, 45.

154. Captain William R. Grove from Manila to his wife, 21 July 1898, Stonaker I:191.

155. Lt. Rice Means from Camp Dewey to his parents, 27 July 1898, Stonaker I:208.

156. Lt. Charles Hooper, from Camp Dewey, Stonaker I:181.

157. Pvt. Harry J. Collins from Camp Dewey to his father, Stonaker I:190.

158. *New York Sun*, 16 July 1898, Stonaker I:237.

159. Arthur C. Johnson from Camp Dewey to *Rocky Mountain News*, 3 August 1898, Stonaker I:229.

160. Col. Irving Hale to Asst. Adjutant General, Second Brigade, Second Division, Eight Army Corps, 25 August 1898, *Eighth Army Corps, Letters Received Register*, as cited in Jamieson, *Deadly Ground*, 138–39.

161. Sims, Untitled TMs, 2.

162. Arthur C. Johnson from Camp Dewey to *Rocky Mountain News*, 3 August 1898, Stonaker I:229, 233.

163. Pvt. Harry J. Collins from Camp Dewey to his father, Stonaker I:190.

164. Sims, Untitled TMs, 45–46.

165. 2nd Lt. Rice Means from Camp Dewey to his parents, 27 July 1898, Stonaker I:208.

166. Harry McCauley from Manila to *Denver Republican*, 16 August 1898, Stonaker II:1.

167. Gantenbein, *Official Records*, 3.

168. Ibid.

169. Harris, "Unpublished diary," 12 August 1898.

170. Arthur C. Johnson from Manila to the *Rocky Mountain News*, 13 August 1898, Stonaker I:230; *Rocky Mountain News*, 31 August 1941, 4.

171. Sims, Untitled TMs, 13.

172. Arthur C. Johnson from Manila to the *Rocky Mountain News*, 13 August 1898, Stonaker I:230.

173. Arthur C. Johnson from Manila to the *Rocky Mountain News*, 28 August 1898, Stonaker II:12.

174. Sims, Untitled TMs, 13.

175. Arthur C. Johnson from Manila to the *Rocky Mountain News*, 28 August 1898, Stonaker II:12; Sims, Untitled TMs, 13.

176. Arthur C. Johnson from Manila to the *Rocky Mountain News*, 28 August 1898, Stonaker II:12.

177. Lt. Charles E. Hooper from Manila to his father, Maj. S. K. Hooper, 21 August 1898, Stonaker II:13.

178. Johnson, *Operations of the First Colorado*, 8.

179. Keenan, *The Conflict with Spain*, 455.

180. Arthur C. Johnson from Manila to the *Rocky Mountain News*, 28 August 1898, Stonaker II:13.

181. Keenan, *The Conflict with Spain*, 455; Johnson, *Operations of the First Colorado*, 8.

182. Johnson, *Operations of the First Colorado*, 8.

183. *Harper's Weekly*, 15 October 1898, cover.

184. Col. Hale from Manila to Governor Adams, 5 October 1898, Stonaker II:42.

185. Johnson, *Operations of the First Colorado*, 8; Keenan, *The Conflict with Spain*, 455.

186. Johnson, *Operations of the First Colorado*, 8.

187. Sims, Untitled TMs, 13.

188. Karnow, *In Our Image*, 124.

189. Sims, Untitled TMs, 14.

190. Arthur C. Johnson from Camp Dewey to *Rocky Mountain News*, 28 August 1898, Stonaker II:14; Johnson, *Operations of the First Colorado*, 8–9.

191. Stonaker II:164.

192. *Rocky Mountain News*, 31 August 1941, 4; Lt. Charles Hooper from Manila to his father, 21 August 1898, Stonaker I:14.

193. Baker, *The Colorado Volunteers*, 36.

194. Arthur C. Johnson from Manila to *Rocky Mountain News*, 28 August 1898, Stonaker II:14.

195. Lt. Col. Moses from Manila to friend, 1 October 1898, Stonaker I:65; Harry McCauley from Manila to *Denver Republican*, 16 August 1898, Stonaker II:2.

196. Harry McCauley from Manila to *Denver Republican*, 16 August 1898, Stonaker II:2; Arthur C. Johnson from Manila to *Rocky Mountain News*, 28 August 1898, Stonaker II:14.

197. Harry McCauley from Manila to *Denver Republican*, 16 August 1898, Stonaker II:2; Johnson, *Operations of the First Colorado*, 9.

198. Pvt. Carl Larsen from Manila to "Dear Friend," 25 February 1899.

199. 1st Lt. George Borstadt from Manila to Dr. Henry, 31 August 1898, Stonaker II:35.

200. Johnson, *Operations of the First Colorado*, 9; Arthur C. Johnson from Manila to the *Rocky Mountain News*, 28 August 1898, Stonaker II:14.

201. Harper, "Fighting Far from Home," 5.

202. Johnson, *Operations of the First Colorado*, 9.

203. *Record of Events*, 1.

204. Johnson, *Operations of the First Colorado*, 9.

205. Ibid.; *Record of Events*, 1.

206. *Denver Times*, 19 August 1898, 1.

207. Denver morning newspaper, 16 March 1899, Stonaker II:188.

208. Gantenbein, *Official Records*, 3.

209. Irving Hale letter from Manila to his father, reprinted in newspaper article, Stonaker II:142.

210. *Army Overseas Operations*, 102.

211. Cody, *Lists of Officers*, General Order No. 4, 67.

212. Karnow, *In Our Image*, 132.

213. Linn, *Counterinsurgency*, 8.

214. *Army Overseas Operations*, General Order No. 9, General Order No. 10, 102.

215. Gantenbein, *Official Records*, 4.

216. Cody, *Lists of Officers*, General Order No. 13, 67, 69.

217. Arthur C. Johnson from Manila to the *Rocky Mountain News*, 21 September 1898, Stonaker I:37.

218. 2nd Lt. Ralph Lister from Camp Dewey, 21 July 1898, Stonaker I:191.

Chapter Three

1. Anderson, *A People's Army*, 251–53.

2. Marshall, *Men Against Fire*, 162.

3. Denver newspaper article, 3 May 1899, Stonaker I:237.

4. Ibid.; Stonaker I:96; William M. Phillips letter from Denver to Col. Henry McCoy, 28 October 1898, Stonaker II:115.

5. Col. Henry McCoy letter from Manila to William M. Phillips, 16 October 1898, Stonaker II:75–76.

6. *Rocky Mountain News*, 26 April 1898, 5.

7. Ibid., 29 April 1898, 2.

8. Nankivell, *Military Organizations*, 118.

9. Melrose, "A 'Rose' as American as Old Glory," *Rocky Mountain News*, 16 August 1981, 13.

10. Meredith, "Dr. Rose Kidd Beere," 162.

11. Dr. Rose Kidd Beere letter from San Francisco to the Soldiers' Aid Society, 17 August 1898, Stonaker I:143.

12. Stonaker I:143.

13. Dr. Rose Kidd Beere letter from Manila to Emma H. Eldredge in Colorado Springs, 30 September 1898, Stonaker II:80.

14. Ibid.; Arthur C. Johnson from Manila to the *Rocky Mountain News*, 1 October 1898, Stonaker I:62.

15. Adjutant William H. Sweeney Jr. to Colorado Legislative inquiry, Stonaker II:216.

16. Arthur C. Johnson from Manila to *Rocky Mountain News*, 1 October 1898, Stonaker I:62.

17. Dr. Rose Kidd Beere letter from Manila to Denver Soldiers' Aid Society, 8 October 1898, Stonaker I:44.

18. Pvt. W. T. Byrne letter from Manila to his brother, 9 October 1898, Stonaker I:54.

19. Dr. Rose Kidd Beere letter from Manila to Denver Soldiers' Aid Society, 8 October 1898, Stonaker I:44.

20. Brig. Gen. Irving Hale letter from Manila to the Soldiers' Aid Society, 13 November 1898, Stonaker II:96.

21. Dr. Rose Kidd Beere letter from Manila to the Soldiers' Aid Society, 22 November 1898, Stonaker II:111.

22. Col. Henry McCoy letter from Manila to the Soldiers' Aid Society, 16 October 1898, Stonaker II:75–76.

23. Dr. Rose Kidd Beere letter from Manila to the Soldiers' Aid Society, 22 November 1898, Stonaker II:111.

24. Ibid.

25. Frank M. Dickey letter from Manila to his parents, 4 January 1899.

26. Capt. John S. Stewart letter from Manila to Governor Alva Adams, 30 September 1898, in Stonaker I:66.

27. Pvt. W. T. Byrne letter from Manila to his brother, 9 October 1898, in Stonaker I:54.

28. Dr. Rose Kidd Beere letter from Manila to the Soldiers' Aid Society, 22 November 1898, Stonaker II:111.

29. Ibid.

30. Anonymous letter from the Philippines to the *Denver Post*, 6 December 1898, Stonaker II:127.

31. Dr. Rose Kidd Beere letter from Manila to the Soldiers' Aid Society, 22 November 1898, Stonaker II:111.

32. Ibid.

33. Anonymous letter from the Philippines to the *Denver Post*, 6 December 1898, Stonaker II:127.

34. Dr. Rose Kidd Beere letter from Manila to the Soldiers' Aid Society, 22 November 1898, Stonaker II:112.

35. Dr. Rose Kidd Beere letter from Manila to Henry Van Kleeck in Denver, 11 November 1898, Stonaker I:97.

36. Karnow, *In Our Image*, 148.

37. Harris diary, 25 October 1898.

38. Guyot cable from Hong Kong to Governor Alva Adams, 31 October 1898, Stonaker II:127.

39. Melrose, "A 'Rose,'" 15.

40. Dr. Rose Kidd Beere letter from Manila to the Soldiers' Aid Society, 22 November 1898, Stonaker II:112.

41. General Hale cable from Manila to Governor Alva Adams, 11 November 1898, Stonaker II:54.

42. Colonel McCoy cable from Manila to Governor Adams in Denver, 22 November 1898, Stonaker II:105.

43. Stonaker I:40.

44. Arthur C. Johnson from Manila to the *Rocky Mountain News*, 11 November 1898, Stonaker II:100.

45. Arthur C. Johnson from Manila to the *Rocky Mountain News*, 25 November 1898, Stonaker II:102.

46. Lieutenant Hooper from Manila to his father, S. K. Hooper in Denver, 22 November 1898, Stonaker II:104.

47. Arthur C. Johnson from Manila to the *Rocky Mountain News*, 6 December 1898, Stonaker II:123.

48. Arthur C. Johnson from Manila to the *Rocky Mountain News*, 1 December 1898, Stonaker II:116.

49. Arthur C. Johnson from Manila to the *Rocky Mountain News*, 26 December 1898, Stonaker II:131–32; Stonaker II:164.

50. *Rocky Mountain News*, Pueblo byline, 10 November 1898, 49.

51. *Pueblo Chieftan*, 25 February 1899, Stonaker II:175.

52. Ibid., Stonaker II:176.

53. "Alf Alfa" letter from Manila, 18 January 1899, Stonaker II:171.

54. *Pueblo Chieftan*, 25 February 1899, Stonaker II:176.

55. *Denver Post*, 31 January 1899, Stonaker II:182.

56. Dr. Rose Kidd Beere letter from Manila to the Soldiers' Aid Society, 22 November 1898, Stonaker II:112.

57. Ibid.

58. Stonaker II:115.

59. *Denver Times*, Stonaker II:118.

60. *Denver Republican*, Stonaker II:117.

61. Henry Van Kleeck to *Denver Times*, Stonaker II:118.

62. Arthur C. Johnson from Manila to the *Rocky Mountain News*, 13 February 1899, Stonaker II:197.

63. *Denver Times*, 29 June 1899.

64. Melrose, "A 'Rose,'" 15.

65. *Denver Times*, 13 September 1899.

66. *Denver Republican*, 15 September 1899.

67. Dr. Rose Kidd Beere letter from Manila to the Soldiers' Aid Society, 22 November 1898, Stonaker II:112.

Chapter Four

1. Sims, untitled TMs, 1.

2. Harper, "Fighting Far from Home," 4.

3. Harry McCauley, from Manila to *Denver Republican*, 21 July 1898, Stonaker I:184.

4. Arthur C. Johnson, from Manila to the *Rocky Mountain News*, 27 July 1898, Stonaker I:227.

5. Stonaker I:191–92.

6. Ibid., I:227.

7. Lt. Charles B. Lewis, from Manila, 21 July 1898, Stonaker I:193.

8. Karnow, *In Our Image*, 106.

9. Brig. Gen. Thomas M. Anderson to Adjutant General, U.S. Army, 18 and 21 July 1898, *Correspondence Relating to the War with Spain* 2:809, as quoted in Linn, *Counterinsurgency*, 7.

10. Lt. Charles B. Lewis from Manila, 21 July 1898, Stonaker I:193.

11. Harper, "Fighting Far from Home," 7.

12. Capt. William Grove letter to his wife, from Manila, 21 July 1898, Stonaker I:191.

13. Arthur C. Johnson from Manila to the *Rocky Mountain News*, 6 August 1898, Stonaker II:25.

14. Harper, "Fighting Far from Home," 7; Karnow, *In Our Image*, 131.

15. Arthur C. Johnson from Manila to the *Rocky Mountain News*, 28 October 1898, Stonaker II:84.

16. 2nd Lt. Rice W. Means letter from Manila to his parents, 27 July 1898, Stonaker I:208.

17. Harris, diary, 20 July 1898.

18. Arthur C. Johnson from Manila to the *Rocky Mountain News*, 27 July 1898, Stonaker I:229.

19. *New York Sun*, 16 July 1898, Stonaker I:234.

20. Maj. Cassius Moses letter to wife, from Manila, Stonaker I:181.

21. Arthur C. Johnson from Manila to the *Rocky Mountain News*, 27 July 1898, Stonaker I:229.

22. Arthur C. Johnson from Manila to the *Rocky Mountain News*, 26 October 1898, Stonaker II:82.

23. Sims, untitled TMs, 11.

24. *New York Sun*, 16 July 1898, Stonaker I:236.

25. 2nd Lt. Rice W. Means letter to parents, from Manila, 27 July 1898, Stonaker I:208.

26. 2nd Lt. Charles O. Zollars, letter from Manila, 21 July 1898, Stonaker I:194.

27. Karnow, *In Our Image*, 107.

28. Arthur C. Johnson from Manila to the *Rocky Mountain News*, 6 August 1898, Stonaker II:25.

29. Arthur C. Johnson from Manila to the *Rocky Mountain News*, 27 July 1898, Stonaker I:228.

30. Arthur C. Johnson from Manila to the *Rocky Mountain News*, 6 August 1898, Stonaker II:25.

31. Sgt. G. A. Thurber letter from Manila, 21 July 1898, Stonaker I:192.

32. Mabey, *The Utah Batteries*, 26.

33. Arthur C. Johnson from Manila to the *Rocky Mountain News*, 6 August 1898, Stonaker II:25.

34. Ibid.

35. Ibid.

36. Brig. Gen. Irving Hale letter to Maj. Gen. Francis V. Greene, 28 February 1900, Irving Hale Papers, Box 12/File 692.

37. Keenan, *The Conflict with Spain*, 428–30.

38. Stonaker I:5.

39. Harry McCauley, from Manila to *Denver Republican*, 16 August 1898, Stonaker II:2.

40. Maj. Gen. Francis V. Greene order to Brig. Gen. Irving Hale, 13 August 1898, Irving Hale Papers, Box 14/File 830.

41. Arthur C. Johnson from Manila to the *Rocky Mountain News*, 28 August 1898, Stonaker II:15.

42. Ibid., II:16.

43. Mabey, *The Utah Batteries*, 37.

44. Harry McCauley to *Denver Republican*, 16 August 1898, Stonaker II:2; Gen. Irving Hale, *Denver Times*, 28 September 1898, 8.

45. Arthur C. Johnson from Manila to the *Rocky Mountain News*, 28 August 1898, Stonaker II:16; Johnson, *Operations of the First Colorado*, 8–9.

46. Mabey, *The Utah Batteries*, 37–38.

47. Ibid., 37.

48. Martin Egan, *New York Sun*, Stonaker II:136.

49. Johnson, *Operations of the First Colorado*, 10.

50. Arthur C. Johnson from Manila to the *Rocky Mountain News*, 12 December 1898, Stonaker II:153.

51. Lt. Charles Hooper to his wife, from Manila, 24 August 1898, Stonaker II:15.

52. Arthur C. Johnson from Manila to the *Rocky Mountain News*, 21 September 1898, Stonaker II:38.

53. Arthur C. Johnson from Manila to the *Rocky Mountain News*, 26 October 1898, Stonaker II:82–83.

54. Sims, Questionnaire, 2 February 1969.

55. Arthur C. Johnson from Manila to the *Rocky Mountain News*, 26 October 1898, Stonaker II:83.

56. Arthur C. Johnson from Manila to the *Rocky Mountain News*, 23 August 1898, Stonaker II:17.

57. Arthur C. Johnson from Manila to the *Rocky Mountain News*, 1 November 1898, Stonaker II:97–98.

58. Arthur C. Johnson from Manila to the *Rocky Mountain News*, 21 September 1898, Stonaker II:38.

59. Harry McCauley from Manila to the *Denver Republican*, 9 March 1899, Stonaker II:216.

60. Lt. Charles Hooper to his father, from Manila, 21 August 1898, Stonaker II:14.

61. Capt. William A. Cornell to his father, L. S. Cornell, from Manila, 22 August 1898, Stonaker II:21.

62. Irving Hale Papers, Box 14/File 826.

63. *New York Sun*, 16 July 1898, Stonaker I:235.

64. Arthur C. Johnson from Manila to the *Rocky Mountain News*, 1 December 1898, Stonaker II:119.

65. Arthur C. Johnson from Manila to the *Rocky Mountain News*, 28 October 1898, Stonaker II:84.

66. Arthur C. Johnson from Manila to the *Rocky Mountain News*, 6 December 1898, Stonaker II:124.

67. Karnow, *In Our Image*, 131.

68. Arthur C. Johnson from Manila to the *Rocky Mountain News*, 14 December 1898, Stonaker II:128.

69. Arthur C. Johnson from Manila to the *Rocky Mountain News*, 3 October 1898, Stonaker II:72.

70. Arthur C. Johnson from Manila to the *Rocky Mountain News*, 3 August 1898, Stonaker I:231.

71. Arthur C. Johnson from Manila to the *Rocky Mountain News*, 22 August 1898, Stonaker II:10.

72. *Regimental Letters Received*, , 106.

73. Ibid., 107.

74. Ibid., 103.

75. Ibid., 127.

76. Ibid., 91–92.

77. Ibid., 94.

78. Capt. C. E. Locke to his wife, from Manila, 21 July 1898, Stonaker I:193.

79. Arthur C. Johnson from Manila to the *Rocky Mountain News*, 25 August 1898, Stonaker II:7.

80. Harry W. McCauley, *Denver Republican*, 7 February 1899, Stonaker II:188.

81. Arthur C. Johnson from Manila to the *Rocky Mountain News*, 25 August 1898, Stonaker II:7.

82. Lt. Charles Hooper from Manila to his wife, 24 August 1898, Stonaker II:15.

83. Rudyard Kipling, Irving Howe, ed., *The Portable Kipling* (New York: Penguin Books, 1982), 602.

84. Arthur C. Johnson from Manila to the *Rocky Mountain News*, 17 November 1898, Stonaker II:93.

85. Ibid.

86. Ibid.

87. Arthur C. Johnson from Manila to the *Rocky Mountain News*, 21 September 1898, Stonaker II:38; 13 November 1898, Stonaker II:96.

88. Arthur C. Johnson from Manila to the *Rocky Mountain News*, 13 November 1898, Stonaker II:96.

89. Arthur C. Johnson from Manila to the *Rocky Mountain News*, 21 September 1898, Stonaker II:38.

90. Stonaker II:84.

91. Capt. E. E. Booth to Adjutant, 1 November 1898, *Colorado: Company Letters Sent*, 4–5.

92. Captain Hilton to Adjutant, 6 July 1899, Company I #29, *Colorado: Company Letters Sent*, 10.

93. *Rocky Mountain News*, 29 June 1965, 5.

94. Chief Surgeon from Manila, 27 July 1898, *Letters Received Register*, Letter #718.

95. Arthur C. Johnson from Manila to the *Rocky Mountain News*, 22 September 1898, Stonaker II:39.

96. Arthur C. Johnson from Manila to the *Rocky Mountain News*, 1 November 1898, Stonaker II:97.

97. Arthur C. Johnson from Manila to the *Rocky Mountain News*, 29 December 1898, Stonaker II:153.

98. Lieutenant Gowdy from Manila to his mother, 4 October 1898 newspaper dateline, Stonaker II:49.

99. Captain Booth from Manila to Colorado Adj. Gen. Lewis Barnum, 1 October 1898, Stonaker II:70.

100. Arthur C. Johnson from Manila to the *Rocky Mountain News*, 26 November 1898, Stonaker II:110.

101. *The Herald Democrat*, 12 November 1898 (Leadville, Colo.), 7.

102. Pvt. W. G. Lumbard from Manila, 17 July 1898, Stonaker I:181.

103. Clipping from *The Denver Post* (n.d., n.a.), titled "Colo Soldiers DELF."

104. Sims, Questionnaire, 7.

105. Bowe, *With the Thirteenth Minnesota*, 71–72.

106. Arthur C. Johnson from Manila to the *Rocky Mountain News*, 25 August 1898, Stonaker II:8–9.

107. Arthur C. Johnson from Manila to the *Rocky Mountain News*, 18 January 1899, Stonaker II:179.

108. Arthur C. Johnson from Manila to the *Rocky Mountain News*, 25 August 1898, Stonaker II:8.

109. Arthur C. Johnson from Manila to the *Rocky Mountain News*, 25 October 1898, Stonaker II:78.

110. Arthur C. Johnson from Manila to the *Rocky Mountain News*, 18 January 1899, Stonaker II:179.

111. Arthur C. Johnson from Manila to the *Rocky Mountain News*, 30 October 1898, Stonaker II:101.

112. Harper, "Fighting Far from Home," 7.

113. Ibid.

114. *Denver Republican*, 11 November 1898.

115. William Currier from Manila to parents, 27 December 1898, Stonaker II:157.

116. Oliver Lomax from Manila to his brother, 1 October 1898, Stonaker I:48.

117. Baker, *The Colorado Volunteers*, 51–52.

118. Lamar, *The Reader's Encyclopedia*, s.v. "Kearney, Denis."

119. Ibid., s.v. "Chinese immigration."

120. Arthur C. Johnson from Manila to the *Rocky Mountain News*, 8 September 1898, Stonaker II:33.

121. Ibid.

122. John M. Bass, dispatch filed 30 August 1898, *Harper's Weekly* Vol. 42 (15 October 1898), 1008.

123. W. T. Byrne from Manila to his brother, 9 October 1898, Stonaker I:54.

124. Karnow, *In Our Image*, 131.

125. Ibid., 131–132.

126. *Literary Digest* XVII (10 September 1898), 307–8, as quoted in Dulles, *America's Rise*, 49.

127. Linn, *Counterinsurgency*, 9.

128. Dulles, *America's Rise*, 50.

129. Linn, *Counterinsurgency*, 9.

130. Karnow, *In Our Image*, 128.

131. Baker, *The Colorado Volunteers*, 52.

132. Dulles, *America's Rise*, 51.

133. Linn, *Counterinsurgency*, 9–10.

134. Hale to Adjutant General, 2d Division, 8th Army Corps, 12 December 1898, Irving Hale Papers, Box 14/File 831.

135. Harris, Diary, 14 December 1898.

136. Linn, *Counterinsurgency*, 129–30.

137. O. K. Davis, Manila representative of the *New York Sun*, interviewed in Chicago by the *Interocean*, Stonaker II:149.

138. Harry W. McCauley from Manila to *Denver Republican*, 3 October 1899.

139. Arthur C. Johnson from Manila to the *Rocky Mountain News*, 14 December 1898, Stonaker II:120.

140. Ibid.

141. Kipling, "The White Man's Burden," 291.

142. Dulles, *America's Rise*, 48.

143. Ibid., 52–53.

144. Arthur C. Johnson from Manila to the *Rocky Mountain News*, 1 January 1899, Stonaker II:134.

145. Linn, *Counterinsurgency*, 8.

146. Frank M. Dickey from Manila to parents, 4 January 1899, Frank M. Dickey File.

147. Stonaker II:160–61.

148. Hale, Papers, Box 14/File 826.

149. Arthur C. Johnson from Manila to the *Rocky Mountain News*, 12 January 1898, Stonaker II:162.

150. Ibid.

151. Col. Juan Cailles, 10 January 1899, Exhibit 374, Taylor, *Philippine Insurrection*, 10 KU.

152. Frank M. Dickey from Manila to parents, 11 January 1899, Frank M. Dickey File.

153. Arthur C. Johnson from Manila to the *Rocky Mountain News*, 1 January 1899, Stonaker II:134.

154. "Alf Alfa" from Manila, 18 January 1899, newspaper clipping, Stonaker II:171.

155. Arthur C. Johnson from Manila to the *Rocky Mountain News*, 25 January 1899, Stonaker II:172.

156. Arthur C. Johnson from Manila to the *Rocky Mountain News*, 1 January 1899, Stonaker II:134.

157. Arthur C. Johnson from Manila to the *Rocky Mountain News*, 12 January 1899, Stonaker II:162.

158. Linn, *Counterinsurgency*, 11.

159. Brig. Gen. Irving Hale letter to Adjutant General, Second Division, Eighth Army Corps, 30 January 1899, Irving Hale Papers, Box 14/File 832.

160. Ibid., Box 14/File 828.

161. Col. McCoy to Governor Thomas, 1 February 1899, Stonaker II:182.

162. Arthur C. Johnson from Manila to the *Rocky Mountain News*, 1 February 1899, Stonaker II:180.

163. Arthur C. Johnson from Manila to the *Rocky Mountain News*, 2 February 1899, Stonaker II:180.

164. Harry W. McCauley from Manila to the *Denver Republican*, 13 January 1899, Stonaker II:162.

165. Harry W. McCauley from Manila to the *Denver Republican*, 2 February 1899, Stonaker II:180.

Chapter Five

1. Harry McCauley from Manila to *Denver Republican*, 13 January 1899, Stonaker II:162.

2. *Plan*, Wedgewood Collection, Box 5.

3. Wedgwood Collection, Box 5.

4. Ibid.; Harry McCauley from Manila to *Denver Republican*, 13 January 1899, Stonaker II:162; Arthur C. Johnson from Manila to the *Rocky Mountain News*, 6 February 1899, Stonaker II:183.

5. Ibid.

6. Harry McCauley from Manila to *Denver Republican*, 7 February 1899, Stonaker II:187.

7. Muriel Bailey from Manila to *San Francisco Examiner*, Stonaker II:225; Sgt. Will L. Rule from Manila to Prof. W. L. Rule, Stonaker II:198.

8. Johnson, *Operations of the First Colorado*, 12–13; Arthur C. Johnson from Manila to the *Rocky Mountain News*, 6 February 1899, Stonaker II:183.

9. Karnow, *In Our Image*, 139–40; Harry McCauley from Manila to *Denver Republican*, 7 February 1899, Stonaker II:187.

10. Arthur C. Johnson from Manila to the *Rocky Mountain News*, 6 February 1899, Stonaker II:183.

11. 5 February 1899 cable from Manila to the *New York Sun*, Stonaker II:135.

12. Arthur C. Johnson from Manila to the *Rocky Mountain News*, 6 February 1899, Stonaker II:183–84.

13. Ibid., 183.

14. Ibid.

15. Harry McCauley from Manila to *Denver Republican*, 7 February 1899, Stonaker II:187.

16. Arthur C. Johnson from Manila to the *Rocky Mountain News*, 6 February 1899, Stonaker II:183.

17. Ibid.; Harry McCauley from Manila to *Denver Republican*, 7 February 1899, Stonaker II:187.

18. Harry McCauley from Manila to *Denver Republican*, 7 February 1899, Stonaker II:187.

19. Ibid.

20. Ibid.; Johnson, *Official History*, 12.

21. Gantenbein, *Official Records* 7.

22. Muriel Bailey from Manila to *San Francisco Examiner*, Stonaker II:225.

23. Harry McCauley from Manila to *Denver Republican*, 7 February 1899, Stonaker II:187.

24. Arthur C. Johnson from Manila to the *Rocky Mountain News*, 6 February 1899, Stonaker II:184–85.

25. Sgt. Will L. Rule from Manila to Professor W. L. Rule, Stonaker II:198.

26. Arthur C. Johnson from Manila to the *Rocky Mountain News*, 6 February 1899, Stonaker II:182.

27. Harry McCauley from Manila to *Denver Republican*, 7 February 1899, Stonaker II:187.

28. Ibid.

29. Ibid.

30. Arthur C. Johnson from Manila to the *Rocky Mountain News*, 6 February 1899, Stonaker II:183.

31. Ibid.

32. Canney, *The Old Steam Navy*, 145.

33. Keenan, *The Conflict with Spain*, 211.

34. Ibid., 211.

35. Webber, *Monitors*, 42.

36. Ibid., 5.

37. Ibid., 39, 42.

38. Moore, *Jane's Fighting Ships*, 153.

39. Herbert, "Attack on the Outpost," 2.

40. *Denver Times*, n.d.

41. Harry W. McCauley from Manila to the *Denver Republican*, 7 February 1899, Stonaker II:187; Lieutenant Kelly to Colonel Thompson, 5 February 1899, Irving Hale Papers, Box 14/File 828.

42. Keenan, *The Conflict with Spain*, 211; *Manila Times*, 4 February 1899.

43. Muriel Bailey from Manila to the *San Francisco Examiner*, Stonaker II:226.

44. Barth, *Instant Cities*, 210.

45. *Manila Times* [1899].

46. 5 February 1899 cable from Manila to the *New York Sun*, Stonaker II:135; Moore, *Jane's Fighting Ships*, 143.

47. 6 February 1899 from Manila to the *New York Sun*, Stonaker II:144.

48. Mabey, *The Utah Batteries*, 39, 42; Johnson, *Official History*, 12–13.

49. Mabey, *The Utah Batteries*, 42–43.

50. Harry McCauley from Manila to *Denver Republican*, 7 February 1899, Stonaker II:187; Arthur C. Johnson from Manila to the *Rocky Mountain News*, 6 February 1899, Stonaker II:182.

51. Arthur C. Johnson from Manila to the *Rocky Mountain News*, 6 February 1899, Stonaker II:185.

52. Arthur C. Johnson from Manila to the *Rocky Mountain News*, 6 February 1899, Stonaker II:182; Harry McCauley from Manila to *Denver Republican*, 7 February 1899, Stonaker II:187. Johnson suggests that a platoon of H, rather than E, participated (Johnson, *Official History*, 13), but company records confirm McCauley's account (*Record of Events*, 9, 12).

53. Unidentified newspaper dispatch, from Manila 8 February 1899, Stonaker II:201.

54. Mabey, *The Utah Batteries*, 42.

55. Unidentified newspaper dispatch, from Manila 8 February 1899, Stonaker II:201.

56. Arthur C. Johnson from Manila to the *Rocky Mountain News*, 6 February 1899, Stonaker II:183.

57. Ibid., 184.

58. Harry McCauley from Manila to *Denver Republican*, 7 February 1899, Stonaker II:187.

59. *Record of Events*, 15; Arthur C. Johnson from Manila to the *Rocky Mountain News*, 6 February 1899, Stonaker II:182–85.

60. Arthur C. Johnson from Manila to the *Rocky Mountain News*, 6 February 1899, Stonaker II:182.

61. *Record of Events*, 6.

62. Harry McCauley from Manila to *Denver Republican*, 7 February 1899, Stonaker II:187; Mabey, *The Utah Batteries*, 43.

63. Mabey, *The Utah Batteries*, 43.

64. Arthur C. Johnson from Manila to the *Rocky Mountain News*, 6 February 1899, Stonaker II:184.

65. *Record of Events*, 13.

66. Arthur C. Johnson from Manila to the *Rocky Mountain News*, 6 February 1899, Stonaker II:182, 184.

67. Ibid.

68. Arthur C. Johnson from Manila to the *Rocky Mountain News*, 6 February 1899, Stonaker II:183.

69. Ibid.

70. Ibid., II:184.

71. Cable from Manila to *San Francisco Sun*, 6 February 1899, Stonaker II:144.

72. Arthur C. Johnson from Manila to the *Rocky Mountain News*, 6 February 1899, Stonaker II:184.

73. Wedgwood Collection, Box 5.

74. Harry McCauley from Manila to *Denver Republican*, 7 February 1899, Stonaker II:188.

75. *Plan*, Wedgewood Collection, Box 5; Arthur C. Johnson from Manila to the *Rocky Mountain News*, 6 February 1899, Stonaker II:184; ibid., 8 February 1899, Stonaker II:185; ibid., 13 February 1899, Stonaker II:196.

76. Brady Diary, 7 February 1899.

77. Arthur C. Johnson from Manila to the *Rocky Mountain News*, 13 February 1899, Stonaker II:196; Harry McCauley from Manila to *Denver Republican*, 7 February 1899, Stonaker II:187.

78. Cpl. Arthur Davenport, Company I, from Manila to his father J. J. Davenport, 11 February 1899, Stonaker II:204; Mabey, *The Utah Batteries*, 41.

79. Arthur C. Johnson from Manila to the *Rocky Mountain News*, 6 February 1899, Stonaker II:184.

80. Ibid., 8 February 1899, Stonaker II:185.

81. Harry McCauley from Manila to *Denver Republican*, 7 February 1899, Stonaker II:187.

82. Arthur C. Johnson from Manila to the *Rocky Mountain News*, 6 February 1899, Stonaker II:182.

83. Harry McCauley from Manila to *Denver Republican*, 7 February 1899, Stonaker II:188.

84. Ibid.

85. Karnow, *In Our Image*, 144; Arthur C. Johnson from Manila to the *Rocky Mountain News*, 9 February 1899, Stonaker II:192.

86. Mabey, *The Utah Batteries*, 43; *Plan*, Wedgewood Collection, Box 5, 14.

87. Harry McCauley from Manila to *Denver Republican*, 7 February 1899, Stonaker II:187.

88. Arthur C. Johnson from Manila to the *Rocky Mountain News*, 6 February 1899, Stonaker II:183–85; *Record of Events*, 2, 6, 8, 13, 15.

89. Frank Harper, "Fighting Far from Home," 6.

90. Harry W. McCauley, *Denver Republican*, 7 February 1899, Stonaker II:187.

91. Unidentified newspaper dispatch, from Manila, 8 February 1899, Stonaker II:202.

92. Arthur C. Johnson from Manila to the *Rocky Mountain News*, 6 February 1899, Stonaker II:184; Harry McCauley from Manila to *Denver Republican*, 7 February 1899, Stonaker II:187.

93. Arthur C. Johnson from Manila to the *Rocky Mountain News*, 6 February 1899, Stonaker II:184.

94. Sims, Questionnaire, 2 February 1969, 7.

95. Ibid.

96. Ibid., Stonaker II:183–84.

97. Ibid., Stonaker II:184.

98. Arthur C. Johnson from Manila to the *Rocky Mountain News*, 9 February 1899, Stonaker II:193.

99. Arthur C. Johnson from Manila to the *Rocky Mountain News*, 6 February 1899, Stonaker II:184.

100. Arthur C. Johnson from Manila to the *Rocky Mountain News*, 9 February 1899, Stonaker II:192.

101. Harry McCauley from Manila to *Denver Republican*, 7 February 1899, Stonaker II:188.

102. Arthur C. Johnson from Manila to the *Rocky Mountain News*, 6 February 1899, Stonaker II:184.

103. Newspaper article, 8 February 1899, Stonaker II:202.

104. Arthur C. Johnson from Manila to the *Rocky Mountain News*, 8 February 1899, Stonaker II:185; Mabey, *The Utah Batteries*, 41.

105. Mabey, *The Utah Batteries*, 41.

106. Ibid., 42; Hale to Adjutant General, Second Division, Eighth Army Corps, 10 February 1899, Irving Hale Papers, Box 14/File 832.

107. Mabey, *The Utah Batteries*, 42; Hale to Adjutant General, Second Division, Eighth Army Corps, 10 February 1899, Irving Hale Papers, Box 14/File 832; Arthur C. Johnson from Manila to the *Rocky Mountain News*, 13 February 1899, Stonaker II:196.

108. Mabey, *The Utah Batteries*, 42.

109. Dave Burnett from Manila to the *San Francisco Chronicle*, 11 February 1899, Stonaker II:237.

110. Arthur C. Johnson from Manila to the *Rocky Mountain News*, 8 February 1899, Stonaker II:185.

111. Ibid.; 1st Lt. Charles Hilton from Manila to Adjutant, *Colorado, Company Letters Sent*, 9.

112. Harry McCauley from Manila to *Denver Republican*, 7 February 1899, Stonaker II:188.

113. Newspaper article, 8 February 1899, Stonaker II:203; *Recommendations*, Irving Hale Papers, Box 13/File 810.

114. 1st Lt. Charles Hilton from Manila to Adjutant, *Colorado, Company Letters Sent*, 9; Arthur C. Johnson from Manila to the *Rocky Mountain News*, 8 February 1899, Stonaker II:185.

115. Newspaper article, 8 February 1899, Stonaker II:203; Harry McCauley from Manila to *Denver Republican*, 7 February 1899, Stonaker II:188.

116. Arthur C. Johnson from Manila to the *Rocky Mountain News*, 8 February 1899, Stonaker II:185.

117. Newspaper article, 8 February 1899, Stonaker II:202.

118. Faust, *Campaigning in the Philippines*, 302; Arthur C. Johnson from Manila to the *Rocky Mountain News*, 19 February 1899, Stonaker II:204.

119. *New York Sun*, 5 February 1899, Stonaker II:138.

120. Keenan, *The Conflict with Spain*, 600.

121. Ibid., 605–6.

122. *London Morning Post* from London to *New York Sun*, 6 February 1899, Stonaker II:136.

123. Cable from Manila to *New York Sun*, 5 February 1899, Stonaker II:135.

124. Harper, "Fighting Far from Home," 6.

125. Carl Larsen letter to "Dear Friend," 25 February 1899.

126. Sims, Questionnaire, 2 February 1969, 8–9.

127. General Hale letter from Manila to Van Kleeck in Denver, 2 March 1899, Irving Hale Papers, Box 13/File 820.

128. Harry McCauley from Manila to *Denver Republican*, 7 February 1899, Stonaker II:187.

129. *Rocky Mountain News*, 23 June 1959, 22.

130. Arthur C. Johnson from Manila to the *Rocky Mountain News*, 6 and 7 February 1899, Stonaker II:185.

131. Harry McCauley from Manila to *Denver Republican*, 7 February 1899, Stonaker II:188.

132. Pvt. Carl J. Larsen from Manila to "Dear Friend" in Minnesota, 25 February 1899.

133. Memorandum from Colonel Stotsenburg to Maj. William Grove, 7 February 1899, Irving Hale Papers, Box 14/File 832.

134. *Manila Times*, 8 February 1899.

135. Johnson, *Operations of the First Colorado*, 14–15.

136. Arthur C. Johnson from Manila to the *Rocky Mountain News*, 8 February 1899, Stonaker II:185.

137. Arthur C. Johnson from Manila to the *Rocky Mountain News*, 11 February 1899, Stonaker II:193.

138. Ibid.

139. Ibid.; Arthur C. Johnson from Manila to the *Rocky Mountain News*, 13 February 1899, Stonaker II:196.

140. Arthur C. Johnson from Manila to the *Rocky Mountain News*, 11 February 1899, Stonaker II:193.

141. Harry McCauley from Manila to *Denver Republican*, 15 February 1899, Stonaker II:200.

142. Johnson, *Official History*, 15.

143. Sims, untitled TMs, 15–16.

144. Gantenbein, *Official Records*, 8.

145. Arthur C. Johnson from Manila to the *Rocky Mountain News*, 21 February 1899, Stonaker II:197.

146. Ibid.

147. Codman and Storey, *Secretary Root's Record*, 11–15.

148. Mabey, *The Utah Batteries*, 48.

149. Muriel Bailey from Manila to the *San Francisco Examiner*, Stonaker II:225; Cable from Manila to the *New York Sun*, 23 February 1899, Stonaker II:171; Arthur C. Johnson from Manila to the *Rocky Mountain News*, 23 February 1899, Stonaker II:213.

150. Mabey, *The Utah Batteries*, 48; Arthur C. Johnson from Manila to the *Rocky Mountain News*, 23 February 1899, Stonaker II:213.

151. *Record of Events*, 2.

152. Cable to the *New York Sun*, 24 February 1899, Stonaker II:170; Mabey, *The Utah Batteries*, 48.

153. Gantenbein, *Official Records*, 8.

154. Arthur C. Johnson from Manila to the *Rocky Mountain News*, 11 March 1899, Stonaker II:219.

155. Harry McCauley from Manila to *Denver Republican*, 17 March 1899, Stonaker II:221.

156. Arthur C. Johnson from Manila to the *Rocky Mountain News*, 18 March 1899, Stonaker II:222.

157. Harry McCauley from Manila to *Denver Republican*, 17 March 1899, Stonaker II:221; *Record of Events*, 3.

158. Weber, *Golden Anniversary*, 23.

159. *Plan*, Wedgewood Collection, Box 5.

160. Gantenbein, *Official Records*, 9.

161. *Record of Events*, 2.

162. Johnson, *Operations of the First Colorado*, 16; Weber, *Golden Anniversary*, 23; Mabey, *The Utah Batteries*, 53.

163. Arthur C. Johnson from Manila to the *Rocky Mountain News*, 18 March 1899, Stonaker II:222.

164. Ibid.

165. Johnson, *Operations of the First Colorado*, 16.

166. *Record of Events*, 2.

167. Harry McCauley from Manila to *Denver Republican*, 23 March 1899, Stonaker II:238.

168. Arthur C. Johnson from Manila to the *Rocky Mountain News*, 18 March 1899, Stonaker II:222.

169. *Record of Events*, 3.

170. Arthur C. Johnson from Manila to the *Rocky Mountain News*, 18 March 1899, Stonaker II:222; Mabey, *The Utah Batteries*, 54.

171. Brig. Gen. Irving Hale, "General Orders No. 4," 24 March 1899, as cited in Jamieson, *Deadly Ground*, 144–48.

172. Harry W. McCauley, *Denver Republican*, 27 March 1899, Stonaker II:224, 233.

173. Harry McCauley from Manila to *Denver Republican*, 27 March 1899, Stonaker II:233.

174. Arthur C. Johnson from Manila to the *Rocky Mountain News*, 18 March 1899, Stonaker II:222; Arthur C. Johnson from Manila to the *Rocky Mountain News*, 27 March 1899, Stonaker II:235.

175. Mabey, *The Utah Batteries*, 54.

176. James Creelman cable from Manila to the *New York Journal*, 25 March 1899, Stonaker II:206.

177. Harry McCauley from Manila to *Denver Republican*, 27 March 1899, Stonaker II:224.

178. *Record of Events*, 2; Harry McCauley from Manila to *Denver Republican*, 27 March 1899, Stonaker II:224.

179. Ibid.

180. Sims, untitled TMs, 11.

181. Harry McCauley from Manila to *Denver Republican*, 27 March 1899, Stonaker II:224, 233.

182. Ibid., Stonaker II:224.

183. Arthur C. Johnson from Manila to the *Rocky Mountain News*, 27 March 1899, Stonaker II:235.

184. Harry McCauley from Manila to *Denver Republican*, 27 March 1899, Stonaker II:224, 233.

185. Ibid., Stonaker II:224, 233; *Record of Events*, 2, 4.

186. Harper, "Fighting Far from Home," 8.

187. Mabey, *The Utah Batteries*, 59.

188. Harry W. McCauley from Manila to *Denver Republican*, 27 March 1899, Stonaker II:224.

189. Ibid., 235.

190. Harry McCauley from Manila to *Denver Republican*, 27 March 1899, Stonaker II:224.

191. Ibid.; Stonaker II:233.

192. Harry McCauley from Manila to *Denver Republican*, 27 March 1899, Stonaker II:224.

193. Ibid.

194. *Roster of First Regiment Colorado*.

195. Harry McCauley from Manila to *Denver Republican*, 27 March 1899, Stonaker II:224.

196. Arthur C. Johnson from Manila to the *Rocky Mountain News*, 27 March 1899, Stonaker II:236.

197. Sims, Questionnaire, 5.

198. Arthur C. Johnson from Manila to the *Rocky Mountain News*, 3 August 1898, Stonaker I:231; Lt. Maury Nichols, Stonaker I:117.

199. Harry W. McCauley, *Denver Republican*, 7 February 1899, Stonaker II:187.

200. Harry W. McCauley from Manila on 15 February 1899 to the *Denver Republican*, 28 March 1899, Stonaker II:201.

201. Kimball, Questionnaire, 13 December 1968, 5.

202. Sims, Questionnaire, 11.

203. Harry W. McCauley to *Denver Republican*, 9 March 1899, Stonaker II:216; Harry W. McCauley, *Denver Republican*, 10 April 1899; Arthur C. Johnson from Manila to the *Rocky Mountain News*, 8 March 1899, Stonaker II:217.

204. Harper, "Fighting Far from Home," 5.

205. Harry W. McCauley, *Denver Republican*, 13 January 1899, Stonaker II:162.

206. Arthur C. Johnson from Manila to the *Rocky Mountain News*, 13 February 1899, Stonaker II:197.

207. Arthur C. Johnson from Manila to the *Rocky Mountain News*, 6 February 1899, Stonaker II:184.

208. Webber, *Monitors*, 39; 6 February 1898 cable from Manila to the *New York Sun*, Stonaker II:145.

209. Johnson, *Operations of the First Colorado*, 16.

210. Arthur C. Johnson from Manila to the *Rocky Mountain News*, 27 March 1899, Stonaker II:236; Harry W. McCauley, *Denver Republican*, 23 March 1899, Stonaker II:238; Nankivell, *Military Organizations*, 140.

211. Arthur C. Johnson from Manila to the *Rocky Mountain News*, 27 March 1899, Stonaker II:236; Harry W. McCauley, *Denver Republican*, 23 March 1899.

212. Johnson, *Operations of the First Colorado*, 16; Harry W. McCauley, *Denver Republican*, 23 March 1899, Stonaker II:238.

213. Kimball, Questionnaire, 2.

214. Johnson, *Operations of the First Colorado*, 16.

215. Arthur C. Johnson from Manila to the *Rocky Mountain News*, 1 April 1899, Stonaker II:238.

216. Sims, untitled TMs, 16–19.

217. Harry W. McCauley, *Denver Republican*, 2 April 1899, Stonaker II:238; Arthur C. Johnson from Manila to the *Rocky Mountain News*, 1 April 1899, Stonaker II:238.

218. Maj. Gen. Elwell Otis cable from Manila to U.S. War Department, 31 March 1899, Stonaker II:213.

219. Harry McCauley from Manila to *Denver Republican*, 2 April 1899, Stonaker II:238.

220. Arthur C. Johnson from Manila to the *Rocky Mountain News*, 1 April 1899, Stonaker II:238; Mabey, *The Utah Batteries*, 60; *Record of Events*, 2.

221. Harry McCauley from Manila to *Denver Republican*, 2 April 1899, Stonaker II:238; Mabey, *The Utah Batteries*, 60; *Record of Events*, 2.

222. Harry McCauley from Manila to *Denver Republican*, 2 April 1899, Stonaker II:238.

223. Arthur C. Johnson from Manila to the *Rocky Mountain News*, 1 April 1899, Stonaker II:239.

224. Harry McCauley from Manila to *Denver Republican*, 2 April 1899, Stonaker II:238.

225. Arthur C. Johnson from Manila to the *Rocky Mountain News*, 1 April 1899, Stonaker II:239.

226. *Record of Events*, 2; Arthur C. Johnson from Manila to the *Rocky Mountain News*, 1 April 1899, Stonaker II:238; Mabey, *The Utah Batteries*, 60.

227. Mabey, *The Utah Batteries*, 60.

228. *Colorado: Company Letters Sent*, 26.

229. Nankivell, *Military Organizations*, 144.

230. Capt. E. E. Booth to Charles H. Anderson, 22 June 1899, *Colorado: Company Letters Sent*, 62.

231. *Record of Events*, 2.

232. Johnson, *Operations of the First Colorado*, 21.

233. Ibid.; Arthur C. Johnson from Manila to the *Rocky Mountain News*, 17 April 1899, Stonaker II:245.

234. Arthur C. Johnson from Manila to the *Rocky Mountain News*, 17 April 1899, Stonaker II:245.

235. Mabey, *The Utah Batteries*, 49.

236. Cable from Manila to the *New York Sun*, 23 April 1899, Stonaker II:229; Mabey, *The Utah Batteries*, 66–67.

237. Sims, Questionnaire, 2 February 1969, 11.

238. Chin, *Artillery at the Golden Gate*, 3.

239. *Morning Reports, Co[mpanie]s G-K, Col[orado] 1st Inf[antry], Adjutant General's Office, War With Spain* (Washington, D.C.: National Archives, 949W3), Company K, May 1, 1899.

240. *Record of Events*, 14.

241. Sims, untitled TMs, 19.

242. *Record of Events*, 14.

243. Karnow, *In Our Image*, 185.

244. Utley, *Frontier Regulars*, 268–69, 272–73.

245. Arthur C. Johnson from Manila to the *Rocky Mountain News*, 1 April 1899, Stonaker II:239.

246. *Record of Events*, 3.

247. Colonel McCoy from Camp Alva to Asst. Adjutant General, 1st Brigade, 1st Division, 8th Army Corps in Manila, 16 June 1899, in Lawton, *Expedition to Morong*.

248. Brig. Gen. Robert Hall from *Depósito* to Adjutant General, 1st Division, 8th Army Corps in Manila, 9 June 1899, in Lawton, *Expedition to Morong*, 34, 39.

249. Col. McCoy from Camp Alva to Asst. Adjutant General, 1st Brigade, 1st Division, 8th Army Corps in Manila, 16 June 1899, in Lawton, *Expedition to Morong*.

250. Johnson, *Operations of the First Colorado*, 23, 25–26.

251. Ibid., 18, 24.

252. *Record of Events*, 15; Col. McCoy from Camp Alva to Asst. Adjutant General, 1st Brigade, 1st Division, 8th Army Corps in Manila, 16 June 1899, in Lawton, *Expedition to Morong.*

253. Brig. Gen. Robert Hall from *Depósito* to Adjutant General, 1st Division, 8th Army Corps in Manila, 9 June 1899, in Lawton, *Expedition to Morong*, 32, 37.

254. *Record of Events*, 4.

255. Sims, untitled TMs, 20.

256. Wedgwood Collection, Box 5.

257. Earl, *Sagebrush Volunteers*, 216.

258. *Record of Events*, 3; Sims, untitled TMs, 25.

259. Nankivell, *Military Organizations*, 150.

260. Earl, *Sagebrush Volunteers*, 216.

261. *Record of Events*, 3.

262. Earl, *Sagebrush Volunteers*, 217.

263. Johnson, *Operations of the First Colorado*, 29.

264. *Record of Events*, 3.

265. Arthur C. Johnson from Manila to the *Rocky Mountain News*, 17 April 1899, Stonaker II:245.

266. Carl Larsen letter to "Dear Friend," 25 February 1899.

267. Karnow, *In Our Image*, 155.

268. Harper, "Fighting Far from Home," 7.

269. William P. Munn letter to Brig. Gen. Irving Hale, 6 April 1899; Brig. Gen. Irving Hale letter to William P. Munn, 21 June 1899, Irving Hale Papers, Box 12/File 688.

270. Sims, untitled TMs, 20–22.

271. *Denver Times*, 5 October 1899.

272. Weber, *Golden Anniversary*, 31.

273. Karnow, *In Our Image*, 157.

274. Ibid., 140.

275. Ibid., 155.

Chapter Six

1. Lt. James H. Gowdy from Manila to his mother, 4 October 1898, Stonaker I:49.

2. Newspaper clipping, Stonaker I:67–68.

3. Gantenbein, *Official Records*, 6–7, 50.

4. Maj. Gen. Elwell Otis, through Asst. Adj. Gen. Thomas Barry, 27 December 1898, *Regimental Letters Received*, 132–33.

5. Pvt. Carl J. Larsen letter from Manila to "Dear Friend" in Minnesota, 25 February 1899.

6. Arthur C. Johnson from Manila to the *Rocky Mountain News*, 25 November 1898, Stonaker II:103.

7. Arthur C. Johnson from Manila to the *Rocky Mountain News*, 14 December 1898, Stonaker II:120; *Book D, 1st Infantry.*

8. San Francisco byline, newspaper clipping, 30 April 1899, Stonaker II:233.

9. Cpl. Frank M. Dickey letter "In Camp" to "Ma" in Boulder, 26 April 1899.

10. Gantenbein, *Official Records*, 7.

11. Stonaker II:139.

12. Arthur C. Johnson from Manila to the *Rocky Mountain News*, 17 November 1898, Stonaker II:89; *Rocky Mountain News*, 31 August 1941.

13. Cpl. Frank M. Dickey letter "In Camp" to "Ma" in Boulder, 26 April 1899.

14. Arthur C. Johnson from Manila to the *Rocky Mountain News*, Stonaker II:68.

15. Gantenbein, *Official Records*, 13.

16. Linn, *Counterinsurgency*, 14.

17. Gantenbein, *Official Records*, 13.

18. Pvt. Fred K. Wollaston from Malate to his father in Denver, 21 July 1898, Stonaker I:193.

19. O. K. Davis, Manila representative of the *New York Sun*, interviewed in Chicago by the *Interocean*, Stonaker II:150.

20. Arthur C. Johnson from Manila to the *Rocky Mountain News*, 8 March 1899, Stonaker II:217.

21. Pvt. Willis P. Miner from Manila, 10 December 1898, *Regimental Letters Received, Courts Martial, and Miscellaneous: Col[orado] 1st Inf[antry]*, Adjutant General's Office, War With Spain (Washington, D.C.: National Archives, 949W3), 67.

22. Pvt. Harry Morgan from Manila to Mr. C. L. Stonaker, 26 November 1898, Stonaker II:108.

23. Arthur C. Johnson from Manila to the *Rocky Mountain News*, 17 April 1899, Stonaker II:245–46.

24. Gantenbein, *Official Records*, 96.

25. Pvt. Harry Morgan to Adjutant General, 4 May 1899, *Colorado: Company Letters Sent—*, 31–32.

26. *Colorado: Company Letters Sent—*, 33–50.

27. *Rocky Mountain News*, 18 August 1899, 8.

28. *The Denver Times*, 17 August 1899, 1.

29. Ibid.

30. Ibid.

31. Gantenbein, *Official Records*, 96.

32. *The Denver Times*, 17 August 1899, 1; *Book D, 1st Infantry*.

33. Gantenbein, *Official Records*, 12.

34. Sims, untitled TMs, 21.

35. Ibid., 22; Moore, *Jane's Fighting*, 128; *Record of*, 15.

36. *Record of Events*, 15.

37. *The Denver Times*, 17 August 1899, 1; Sims, untitled TMs, 22.

38. Sims, untitled TMs, 22–23.

39. *The Denver Times*, 17 August 1899, 1.

40. *Rocky Mountain News*, 13 August 1899, 9; *The Denver Times*, 17 August 1899, 1.

41. Sims, untitled TMs, 23.

42. *The Denver Times*, 17 August 1899, 1.

43. Ibid.; Sims, untitled TMs, 21, 23.

44. Sims, untitled TMs, 23.

45. *The Denver Times*, 17 August 1899, 1; "Company F, 1st Colo. Inf." photograph, Spanish-American War Collections.

46. Sims, untitled TMs, 24.

47. Lt. Charles Hooper to his mother from Manila, 17 August 1898, Stonaker II:15.

48. *The Denver Times*, 26 April 1899, 1.

49. Ibid., 3 May 1899, 1.

50. Ibid., 23 April 1899, 1.

51. Ibid., 3 May 1899, 1.

52. Mr. H. Van Kleek to *The Denver Times*, Stonaker II:118.

53. Mrs. George Briggs to the *Denver Times*, Stonaker II:118.

54. Arthur C. Johnson from Manila to the *Rocky Mountain News*, 1 October 1898, Stonaker I:62.

55. *The Denver Times*, Stonaker II:118.

56. *Rocky Mountain News*, 16 August 1959, 46.

57. *The Denver Times*, 27 June 1899, 1.

58. Ibid., 2 June 1899, 1.

59. Ibid., 13 June 1899, 1.

60. Ibid., 18 August 1899, 1; 27 August 1899, 1.

61. Military Life-Spanish American War-Clippings.

62. *The Denver Times*, 9 July 1899, 1.

63. Ibid., 23 July 1899, 1.

64. Ibid., 24 July 1899, 1.

65. Ibid., 27 August 1899, 1.

66. Ibid.

67. Ibid., 30 August 1899, 1.

68. Overstreet, *History of the Veterans of Foreign Wars*, 12.

69. *Record of Events*, 3.

70. Moore, *Jane's Fighting Ships*, 128.

71. *The Denver Times*, 17 August 1899, 1.

72. Sims, untitled TMs, 24–25.

73. Harper, "Fighting Far from Home," 10.

74. Sims, untitled TMs, 26.

75. *Chicago Times-Herald*, 18 September 1899; Memorial Service Program, Military Life-Spanish American War-Clippings.

76. Harper, *Just Outside Manila*, 98.

77. Sims, untitled TMs, 25.

78. 1899 Adjutant General's Office Reports, as cited in Gantenbein, *Official Records*, xiii.

79. Gantenbein, *Official Records*, xii–xiii.

80. Sims, untitled TMs, 26.

81. Arthur C. Johnson from Manila to the *Rocky Mountain News*, 21 February 1899, Stonaker II:197.

82. Arthur C. Johnson from Manila to the *Rocky Mountain News*, 25 October 1898, Stonaker II:79.

83. Harris, Diary, 20 October 1898.

84. Arthur C. Johnson from Manila to the *Rocky Mountain News*, 6 and 7 February 1899, Stonaker II:185.

85. Pvt. Carl J. Larsen from Manila to "Dear Friend" in Minnesota, 25 February 1899.

86. Stonaker II:84.

87. Harris, Diary, 20 November 1898.

88. Pvt. Carl J. Larsen from Manila to "Dear Friend" in Minnesota, 25 February 1899.

89. *Rocky Mountain News*, 16 March 1899, Stonaker II:188.

90. Smiley, *History of Denver*, 769.

91. Harper, "Fighting Far from Home," 5.

92. Stonaker II:10; *Chicago Times-Herald*, 18 September 1899.

93. *Rocky Mountain News*, 30 June 1938.

94. Ibid., 14 August 1938, 7.

95. Arthur C. Johnson from Manila to the *Rocky Mountain News*, 28 August 1898, Stonaker II:13.

96. *Rocky Mountain News*, 14 August 1938, 7.

97. Stonaker I:87.

98. Eisenberg, "Societies of the Spanish-American War," 13, 18.

99. Arthur C. Johnson from Manila to the *Rocky Mountain News*, 25 November 1898, Stonaker II:103.

100. *The Sons of Union Veterans of the Civil War*, 1.

101. *The Denver Times*, 21 September 1899.

102. Ibid., 28 June August 1899, 11–12.

103. Overstreet, *History of the Veterans of Foreign Wars*, 12–13.

104. Ibid., 13; Harper, *Just Outside Manila*, 7.

105. Overstreet, *History of the Veterans of Foreign Wars*, 13–15, 21.

106. Ibid., 15–16.

107. Ibid., 16.

108. Ibid., 17–18.

109. Ibid., 18–20.

110. Ibid., 21–22.

111. Eisenberg, "Societies of the Spanish-American War," 18.

112. Ibid., 24; Overstreet, *History of the Veterans of Foreign Wars*, 22.

113. Overstreet, *History of the Veterans of Foreign Wars*, 22–24.

114. Eisenberg, "Societies of the Spanish-American War," 18; Overstreet, *History of the Veterans of Foreign Wars*, 22–23.

115. Overstreet, *History of the Veterans of Foreign Wars*, 23–24.

116. Ibid., 24–25; Eisenberg, "Societies of the Spanish-American War," 18.

117. Overstreet, *History of the Veterans of Foreign Wars*, 25–26, 29, 33; Connor, "Woman To Command VFW Post," B:1.

118. Connor, "Woman To Command VFW Post," B:1.

119. de Queseda, "Officer and Membership Badges," 14–15.

120. *Rocky Mountain News*, 29 June 1965, 5.

121. First Colorado Infantry Association, *Reunion and Dinner, First Colorado Infantry U.S.V., August 13, 1925* (Denver, Colorado: The Service Printing Company, 1925).

122. Sims, untitled TMs, 12.

123. Abbott, Leonard, and McComb, *Colorado*, 269–70.

124. First Colorado Infantry Association, *Reunion and Dinner*.

125. Abbott, Leonard, and McComb, *Colorado*, 269–71.

126. First Colorado Infantry Association, *Reunion and Dinner*.

127. Ibid.

128. *Rocky Mountain News*, 31 August 1941, 4.

129. Weber, *Golden Anniversary*, 29–30.

130. *Rocky Mountain News*, 31 August 1941, 4; 5 November 1966, 39.

131. *The Denver Post*, 13 August 1952, 42.

132. First Colorado Infantry Association, *Reunion and Dinner*.

133. *Rocky Mountain News*, 23 June 1959, 22.

134. Ibid., 25 June 1963, 11; 29 June 1965, 5.

135. Ibid., 17 August 1969, 26.

136. Ibid., 3 June 1971, 8.

137. Ibid., 29 June 1965, 5.

Chapter Seven

1. Arthur C. Johnson from Manila to the *Rocky Mountain News*, 18 October 1898, Stonaker II:74.

2. Mitchell, *The Vacant Chair*, 158.

3. Ibid., 74.

4. Col. Henry McCoy to Governor Charles Thomas, 31 January 1899, Stonaker II:182; Pvt. Albert Silverstein on *China* to his mother, 6 July 1898, Stonaker I:246; Harris, unpublished diary, 5 July 1898.

5. Linderman, *The Mirror of War*, 60.

6. *Rocky Mountain News*, 25 June 1963, 11.

7. Ibid., 11 May 1898, 10.

8. Linderman, *The Mirror of War*, 1.

9. Pvt. Al Silverstein on *China* to his mother, Mrs. E. Silverstein of Denver, 17 June 1898, Stonaker I:83.

10. 2nd Lt. Rice Means from Manila to his parents, 27 July 1898, Stonaker I:208.

11. Drinnon, *Facing West*, 261.

12. Pvt. Carl Larsen to "Dear Friend," 25 February 1899 letter.

13. Sims, Questionnaire, 2 February 1969, 7–9.

14. Zwick, *Mark Twain's Weapons of Satire*, 16.

15. Ibid., 17.

16. *Denver Times*, 5 October 1899.

17. Codman and Storey, *Secretary Root's Record*.

18. Sims, Questionnaire, 2 February 1969, 4.

19. Rotundo, "Boy Culture," 23, 28.

20. Adams, *The Great Adventure*, 37–38.

21. Ibid., 44.

22. Ibid., 37.

23. Ibid., 7, 135.

24. Arthur C. Johnson from Manila to the *Rocky Mountain News*, 6 February 1899, Stonaker II:183.

25. Adams, *The Great Adventure*, 43.

26. Drinnon, *Facing West*, 551.

27. Adams, *The Great Adventure*, 71.

28. Mitchell, *The Vacant Chair*, 10; Linderman, *Embattled Courage*, 185–87.

29. Linderman, *Embattled Courage*, 213–14.

30. Harper, "Fighting Far from Home," 6.

31. Weber, *Golden Anniversary*, 31.

Selected Bibliography

Primary Sources

Newspapers
Chicago Record.
Chicago Times-Herald, 18 September 1899.
Denver Post.
Denver Republican.
Denver Times.
Harper's Weekly, 15 October 1898.
The Herald Democrat, (Leadville, Colorado).
Literary Digest. XVII (10 September 1898), 307–8.
Manila Times, 8 February 1899. Military Life-Spanish American War-Clippings [Vertical File], Western History Collections, Denver Public Library, Denver, Colorado.
The Wave [1899?]. Military Life-Spanish American War-Clippings [Vertical File], Western History Collections, Denver Public Library, Denver, Colorado.
The National Standard. Colorado Springs, Colorado: Camp Adams Publication, 21 August 1897.
New York Journal, 25 March 1899.
New York Sun.
Pueblo Chieftain.
Rocky Mountain News (Denver, Colorado).
San Francisco Chronicle, 11 February 1899.
San Francisco Examiner.
St. Louis Globe-Democrat, 16 March 1899.

Government Records and Regulations
A[djutant] G[eneral's] O[ffice], Nat[iona]l Guards Colo[rado], Book D, 1st Inf[antry], [Rosters 1893–1903]. Microfilm Roll GR608. Colorado State Archives, Denver, Colorado.
Cody, William H. (Return Clerk). *Lists of Officers 1898–1900 of the Second Division Eight Army Corps Phillippine [sic] Islands.* Washington, D.C.: National Archives, 395–4W3, E862.
Colorado: Company Letters Sent—1st Inf[antry], Adjutant General's Office, War With Spain. Washington, D.C.: National Archives, 94–8W3.

Colorado State Statutes, L. 1897, Ch. 63, Colorado State Archives.

Infantry Drill Regulations, United States Army. Washington, D.C.: Government Printing Office, 1891.

Lawton, Henry W. *Report of an Expedition to the Province of Morong with Objectives, Antipolo, Cainta, Taytay and Morong, with Appendix Containing Copies of All Records Pertaining Thereto.* 8 October 1899, Adjutant General's Office, War With Spain. Washington, D.C.: National Archives.

Letters Received and Endorsements Sent by the Second Brigade, Second Division, Eighth Army Corps: Adjutant General's Office, War with Spain. Washington, D.C.: National Archives.

Morning Reports, Co[mpanie]s G-K, Col[orado] 1st Inf[antry], Adjutant General's Office, War With Spain. Washington, D.C.: National Archives, 949W3.

Moses, Cassius M. *Report of the Adjutant General of the State of Colorado from December 1, 1896, to May 5, 1898.* Microfilm Roll 1, GR 600, Military Affairs, National Guard, Annual/Biennial Reports. Colorado State Archives, Denver, Colorado.

Official Roster of the Utah Volunteers. General Edgar A. Wedgwood Collection, MSS B399. Utah Historical Society, Salt Lake City, Utah.

Overmeyer, J. C. *The Biennial Report of the Adjutant General of Colorado from December 1, 1898 to November 30, 1900, Inclusive.* Denver, Colorado: Smith-Brooks Printing Company, State Printer, 1901.

Plan of Cavite, Manila, Morong, Bulacan and Pampanga Provinces, Covering Entire Scope of American Operations in the Island of Luzon to May 1, 1898. Edgar A. Wedgewood Collection, MSS, B399, Box 5, Utah Historical Society, Salt Lake City, Utah, 1899.

Preliminary Inventory of the Records of United States Army Overseas Operations and Commands, 1898–1942, Volume I. Washington, D.C.: National Archives, Record Group 395, 1971.

Quartermaster General of the Army. *U.S. Army Uniforms and Equipment, 1889: Specifications for Clothing, Camp and Garrison Equipage, and Clothing and Equipage Materials.* Philadelphia: Philadelphia Depot of Quartermaster's Department, 1889; University of Nebraska Press Edition with a foreword by Jerome A Greene, 1986.

Recommendations for Rewards for Distinguished Services, Filipino Insurgent War, February 4th to May 5th, 1899, Second Brigade, Second Division, Eighth Army Corps. Irving Hale Papers, Western History Collections, Denver Public Library, Denver, Colorado.

Record of Events of 1st Colorado Volunteer Infantry, May, 1898, to September, 1899, Col[orado] 1st Inf[antry], Adjutant General's Office, War with Spain. Washington, D.C.: National Archives.

Regimental Letters Received, Courts Martial, and Miscellaneous: Col[orado] 1st Inf[antry], Adjutant General's Office, War with Spain. Washington, D.C.: National Archives, 949W3.

Roster of First Regiment Colorado U.S.V. Inf. United States Army Military History Research Collection, Carlisle Barracks, Carlisle, Pennsylvania, [1899].

Tarsney, Thomas Jefferson. *Biennial Report of the Adjutant General of the State of Colorado for the Years 1893–1894.* Denver: The Smith-Brooks Printing Company, State Printers, 1894.

Taylor, John R. M. *History of the Philippine Insurrection Against the United States, 1898–1903: A Compilation of Documents and Introduction.* Micro-copy 254, Philippine Insurgent Records. Washington, DC: National Archives, 1906.

Diaries and Correspondence

Bass, John M. Dispatch filed 30 August 1898. *Harper's Weekly* 42 (15 October 1898): 1008.

Brady, John D. Diary. Collection No. SAWS-W-1831, Nebraska Infantry First Regiment, Spanish-American War Surveys. United States Army Military History Research Collection, Carlisle Barracks, Carlisle, Pennsylvania.

Dickey, Frank M. Papers. Spanish American War Survey, 1898-W-268, United States Army Military History Research Collection, Carlisle Barracks, Carlisle, Pennsylvania.

Fisher, George. Diary. George Fisher Papers, Spanish-American War Survey, United States Army Military History Research Collection, Carlisle Barracks, Carlisle, Pennsylvania.

Hale, Irving. Papers. Western History Collections, Denver Public Library, Denver, Colorado.

Harper, Frank, ed. *Just Outside Manila: Letters from Members of the First Colorado Regiment in the Spanish-American and Philippine-American Wars.* Denver: Colorado Historical Society, Essays and Monographs, Monograph No. 7, 1991.

Harris, Roy E. Unpublished diary. [catalogued as "Edward A. Wilson Diary"], M917, M88–1830, Western History Collections, Denver Public Library, Denver, Colorado.

Herbert, Edres. "Attack on the Outpost." *Leadville Herald Democrat*, 26 September 1898, 2.

Larsen, Carl J. Papers. Subject Collections: Military Affairs: Spanish-American War/ Letters, Colorado Historical Society, Denver.

Stonaker, C. L. Scrapbook, *War of 1898: War with Spain.* Subject Collections: Military Affairs: Spanish-American War, Colorado Historical Society, Denver.

Participants' Memoirs

Baker, A[rthur] G. *The Colorado Volunteers.* Denver, Colo.: Privately printed, [1898].

Bowe, John. *With the Thirteenth Minnesota in the Philippines.* Minneapolis: A. B. Farnham Printing & Stationery Company, 1905.

Gantenbein, C. U. *The Official Records of the Oregon Volunteers in the Spanish War and Philippine Insurrection.* Salem, Ore.: W. H. Leeds, State Printer, 1902.

Johnson, Arthur C. *Official History of the Operations of the First Colorado Infantry, U.S.V. in the Campaigning in the Philippine Islands* [published in the back of Colorado editions of Karl Irving Faust, *Campaigning in the Philippines*. San Francisco: The Hicks-Judd Company, 1899.]

Keenan, Henry F. *The Conflict with Spain: A History of the War, Based upon Official Reports and Descriptions of Eye-Witnesses, Illustrated with Original Drawings from Photographs and Sketches Made on the Scene of Action*. Philadelphia: P. W. Ziegler and Company, 1898.

Kimball, Jay. Questionnaire, 13 December 1968. Colo.Inf.1st Regt.: Spanish-American War Questionnaires. United States Army Military History Research Collection, Carlisle Barracks, Carlisle, Pennsylvania.

Mabey, Charles R. *The Utah Batteries: A History*. Salt Lake City: Daily Reporter Company, 1900.

Sims, Arthur. Unpublished novel. Spanish-American War Survey Collection No. 1898-142, United States Army Military History Research Collection, Carlisle Barracks, Carlisle, Pennsylvania.

Sims, Guy R. Untitled TMs, Wauneta, Nebraska, 1941, Collection No. 1898–142. United States Army Military History Research Collection, Carlisle Barracks, Carlisle, Pennsylvania.

———. Questionnaire, 2 February 1969. Colo.Inf.1st Regt.: Spanish-American War Questionnaires, United States Army Military History Research Collection, Carlisle Barracks, Carlisle, Pennsylvania.

Thomas, Elmer Gwyn. *Autobiography*. Mss A 2245, Utah Historical Society, Salt Lake City, Utah.

Weber, Walter W. *Golden Anniversary: The First Colorado Infantry, U.S.V., Spanish-American War, 1898, Philippine Insurrection, 1899*. Denver, Colo.: n.p., 1948.

Other Primary Materials

"Company F, 1st Colo. Inf." photograph. Spanish-American War Collections, Golden Gate National Recreation Area, National Park Service, San Francisco, California.

Connor, Chance. "Woman to Command VFW Post." *The Denver Post*, 27 May 1996, B:1.

First Colorado Infantry Association. *Reunion and Dinner, First Colorado Infantry U.S.V., August 13, 1925*. Denver, Colo.: The Service Printing Company, 1925.

Kipling, Rudyard. "The White Man's Burden." *McClure's Magazine XXI* (February 1899): 291.

Memorial Service Program. Military Life-Spanish American War-Clippings [Vertical File], Western History Collections, Denver Public Library, Denver, Colorado.

Military Life-Spanish American War-Clippings [Vertical File], Western History Collections, Denver Public Library, Denver, Colorado.

Subject Collections: Military Affairs: Spanish-American War, Colorado Historical Society, Denver, Colorado.

United States Army Military History Research Collection, Carlisle Barracks, Carlisle, Pennsylvania.

Secondary Sources

Abbott, Carl; Leonard, Stephen J., and David McComb. *Colorado: A History of the Centennial State.* Niwot: University Press of Colorado, 1982.

Adams, Michael C. C. *The Great Adventure: Male Desire and the Coming of World War I.* Bloomington: Indiana University Press, 1990.

Agoncillo, Teodore A. *Malolos: The Crisis of the Republic.* Quezon City, Republic of the Philippines: n.p., 1960.

Anderson, Fred. *A People's Army: Massachusetts Soldiers and Society in the Seven Years' War.* New York: W. W. Norton and Company, 1985, by arrangement with University of North Carolina Press, 1984.

Bain, David Howard. *Sitting in Darkness: Americans in the Philippines.* Boston: Houghton Mifflin Co., 1984.

Barth, Gunther. *Instant Cities: Urbanization and the Rise of San Francisco and Denver.* New York: Oxford University Press, 1975.

Brand, H. W. *Bound to Empire: The United States and the Philippines.* Cambridge: Oxford University Press, 1992.

Brecher, Jeremy. "The 1877 Railroad Strike," in William Graebner and Leonard Richards, eds., *The American Record: Images of the Nation's Past, Volume II, Since 1865.* New York: McGraw-Hill Publishing Company, 1982, Second Edition 1988: 29–47.

Canney, Donald L. *The Old Steam Navy, Volume I: Frigates, Sloops, and Gunboats, 1815–1885.* Annapolis, Md.: Naval Institute Press, 1990.

Carnes, Mark C. "Middle Class Men and the Solace of Fraternal Ritual." In Mark C. Carnes and Clyde Griffen, ed., *Meanings for Manhood: Constructions of Masculinity in Victorian America.* Chicago: University of Chicago Press, 1990, 37–66.

Chin, Brian B. *Artillery at the Golden Gate: The Harbor Defenses of San Francisco in World War II.* Missoula, Mt.: Pictorial Histories Publishing Company, Inc., 1994.

Codman, Julian, and Moorfield Storey. *Secretary Root's Record: "Marked Severity" in Philippine Warfare: An Analysis on the Law and Facts Bearing on the Action and Utterances of President Roosevelt and Secretary Root.* Boston: George H. Ellis Company, 1902.

Cosmas, Graham A. *An Army for Empire: The United States Army in the Spanish-American War.* Columbia: University of Missouri Press, 1971.

de Queseda, Alejandro M., Jr. "Officer and Membership Badges of the United Spanish War Veterans." *The Medal Collector* 47, 4 (May 1996): 14–19.

Drinnon, Richard. *Facing West: The Metaphysics of Indian-Hating and Empire-Building.* New York: Schocken Books, 1980, 1990.

Dulles, Foster Rhea. *America's Rise to World Power, 1898–1954.* New American Nation Series. New York: Harper and Row, 1954; Harper Torchbook 1963.

Earl, Phillip Irving. *Sagebrush Volunteers: Nevadans in the Spanish-American War and the Philippine Insurrection, 1898–1900.* Ann Arbor, Mich.: University Microfilm, 1978.

Eisenberg, Harvey S. "Societies of the Spanish-American War, Philippine Insurrection and Boxer Rebellion." *The Medal Collector* 24, 11 (November 1973): 3–24; 24, 12 (December 1973): 9–17.

Faust, Karl Irving. *Campaigning in the Philippines.* San Francisco: The Hicks Judd Company, 1899.

Garraty, John A. *The American Nation: A History of the United States Since 1865,* Volume II. New York: HarperCollins Publishers, Seventh Edition 1991.

Gates, John Morgan. *Schoolbooks and Krags: The United States Army in the Philippines 1898–1902.* Westport, Ct.: Greenwood Press, 1973.

Harper, Frank. "Fighting Far from Home." *Colorado Heritage* 1988/I Denver: Colorado Historical Society, 1988: 2–11.

Jamieson, Perry D. *Crossing the Deadly Ground: United States Army Tactics, 1865–1899.* Tuscaloosa: University of Alabama Press, 1994.

Kagan, Donald, Steven Ozment, and Frank Turner. *The Western Heritage, Volume II: Since 1648.* Upper Saddle River, N.J.: Prentice-Hall, Inc., 1979, Fifth Edition 1995.

Karnow, Stanley. *In Our Image: America's Empire in the Philippines.* New York: Random House, 1989.

Lamar, Howard R., ed. *The Reader's Encyclopedia of the American West.* New York: Harper and Row Publishers, 1977. s.v.v. "Chinese immigration," "Hawaii," "Kearney, Denis."

Lamb, Richard D., and Duane A. Smith. *Pioneers and Politicians: 10 Colorado Governors in Profile.* Boulder, Colo.: Pruett Publishing Company, 1984.

Linderman, Gerald. *The Mirror of War: American Society and the Spanish-American War.* Ann Arbor: University of Michigan Press, 1974.

———. *Embattled Courage: The Experience of Combat in the American Civil War.* New York: The Free Press, 1987.

Linn, Brian McAllister. *The U.S. Army and Counterinsurgency in the Philippine War, 1899–1902.* Chapel Hill: University of North Carolina Press, 1989.

Long, E. B., with Barbara Long. *The Civil War Day by Day: An Almanac, 1861–1865.* Garden City, N.Y.: Doubleday and Company, 1971.

Marshall, S[amuel] L. A. *Men Against Fire: The Problem of Battle Command in Future War.* New York: William Morrow and Company, 1947.

May, Ernest R. *Imperial Democracy: The Emergence of America as a Great Power.* New York: Harcourt, Brace & World, 1961.

Melrose, Frances. *Rocky Mountain News,* 14 June 1992.

Meredith, Ellis. "Dr. Rose Kidd Beere, First Colorado Nurse in the Philippines." *The Colorado Magazine* (Denver, Colorado: State Historical Society of Colorado, XXVI/3, July 1949), 162.

Mitchell, Reid. *The Vacant Chair: The Northern Soldier Leaves Home.* New York: Oxford University Press, 1993.

Moore, John, compiler. *Jane's Fighting Ships of World War I.* London, Jane's Publishing Company, 1919; reprinted in New York by Military Press in 1990.

Nankivell, John N. *History of the Military Organizations of the State of Colorado, 1860–1935.* Denver, Colo.: W. H. Kistler Stationery Company, 1935.

Nash, Gary, Julie Roy Jeffrey, John Howe, Peter Frederick, Allen Davis, and Allan Winkler. *The American People: Creating a Nation and a Society, Volume II, Since 1865.* New York: HarperCollins College Publishers, Third Edition 1994.

Overstreet, George H. *History of the Veterans of Foreign Wars of the United States in Colorado, 1898–1988.* Denver, Colo.: John S. Stewart VFW Post No. 1, 1950; reprinted and updated 1988.

Preliminary Inventory of the Records of United States Army Overseas Operations and Commands, 1898–1942, Volume I. Record Group 395. Washington, D.C.: National Archives, 1971.

Prentiss, A., ed. *The History of the Utah Volunteers in the Spanish-American War and in the Philippine Insurrection.* Salt Lake City: Tribune Job Printing Company-William F. Ford, Publisher, 1900.

Poyer, Joe, and Craig Reisch. *The .45–70 Springfield.* Tustin, Calif.: North Cape Publications, 1991; 3rd Edition 1999.

Record of Events of 1st Colorado Volunteer Infantry, May 1898, to September 1899. Washington, D.C.: National Archives.

Rotundo, E. Anthony. "Boy Culture: Middle-Class Boyhood in Nineteenth-Century America," in Mark C. Carnes and Clyde Griffen, eds., *Meanings for Manhood: Constructions of Masculinity in Victorian America.* Chicago: University of Chicago Press, 1990, 15–36.

Rutledge, Lee A. *Campaign Clothing: Field Uniforms of the Indian War Army, 1872–1886.* Tustin, Calif.: North Cape Publications, 1997.

Smiley, Jerome C. ed. *History of Denver.* Denver: Times-Sun Publishing Company, 1901.

The Sons of Union Veterans of the Civil War. Chillicothe, Ohio: Sons of Union Veterans, 1993.

Utley, Robert M. *Frontier Regulars: The United States Army and the Indian, 1866–1890.* New York: Macmillan Publishing Company, 1973.

———. *Frontiersmen in Blue: The United States Army and the Indian, 1848–1865.* Lincoln: University of Nebraska Press, 1967; Bison Book Printing, 1986.

Webber, Richard H. *Monitors of the U.S. Navy, 1861–1937.* Washington, D.C.: U.S. Government Printing Office, 1969.

Williams, Walter L. "United States Indian Policy and the Debate over Philippine Annexation: Implications for the Origins of American Imperialism." *Journal of American History* 66, 4 (1980): 810–831.

Zwick, Jim, ed. *Mark Twain's Weapons of Satire: Anti-Imperialist Writings on the Philippine-American War.* Syracuse, N.Y.: Syracuse University Press, 1992.

Index

Twentieth Kansas Infantry, 168, 175
Twenty-Third Infantry, 176, 187

Union Iron Works, 155
United Service (Gibbon), 19
United Spanish War Veterans (USWV), 222,
    229, 231, 232, 234, 235
U.S. Engineers Company 1, 211
Utah Light Artillery, 155, 168, 176, 177, 180,
    187, 207
Utah volunteers, 172
Uzell, Tom, 224

Van Kleeck, Henry, 99
Vannice, William, 178
veterans' groups, 222
Veterans of Foreign Wars (VFW), 4, 222, 230
Vietnam conflict, 235

Waite, Davis H., 24
Wake Island, 1, 68, 228, 238
Walcott, Allen, 214
War Relics Room, 221
Watson, William S., 132, 235, 239
weapons: B. L. (breech loading) rifles (3.2-
    inch), 85, 155; field gun (3.2-inch), 187;
    Gatling guns, 28, 70, 85, 172; Hotchkiss
    mountain guns (1.65-inch), 76, 85; Krag-
    Jörgensen rifles, 4, 46–48, 184, 188, 195;
    Krupp-pattern mountain guns, 89; losses
    blamed on inferior, 183; Martini-Henry
    rifle, 184; Mauser rifles, 15, 86, 95, 115,
    116–17, 144, 177, 181, 183, 184, 185, 195, 220;
    Maxim machine guns, 28; Mountain
    Guns, 85; muzzle-loading musket, 17;
    Nordenfeldt guns, 89, 161, 187; Ordnance
    Rifle (3-inch), 85; Remington rifles, 161,
    195; Savage rifles, 47; Springfield rifles,
    3, 46–48, 55, 86, 150, 183, 184, 185, 186, 187,
    188; Winchester rifles, 47–48
Weaver, Orton, 156
Weber, Walter W., 5, 245
Wedgewood (captain), 155
West, Adelbert, 142
West, Cecil, 163
West, Claude, 95
Westfall, Harry, 138

Weyler, Valeriano, 9
Wheaton (general), 180, 198
Wheaton, Lloyd, 195
Wheeler, Harry "Joe", 156
Wheeler, W. G., 31
Whipple, C. W., 55
White, Bob, 214, 215
White, Cass, 160, 164
The White Man's Burden (Kipling), 130
Wiley, Luther, 205
Willcox, E. F., 42
Williams, Casper "Billy", 55
Williams, Oscar, 114
Williams, Walter L., 2, 20
Wise, Walter, 238
Wolcott, Edward O., 31
Wollaston, Fred K., 203
women, 102; American, 133, 176; European,
    132; evacuation of, 176; Filipina, 133, 207;
    Spanish, 132, 133
Women's Relief Corps, 35, 237
Wood, Leonard, 31
Woodside, Robert G., 229
Wood, Tingley, 156
Workingmen's Party, 138

Young, Harry, 165

Zachary, Edward L., 87
Zandico, 175
Zollars, Charles O., 118